THE TOP GEAR STORY

MARTIN ROACH

D0170167

JB

JOHN BLAKE

Published by John Blake Publishing Ltd,
3 Bramber Court, 2 Bramber Road,
London W14 9PB, England

www.johnblakepublishing.co.uk

www.facebook.com/Johnblakepub facebook
twitter.com/johnblakepub twitter

First published in hardback in 2011.
This edition published in paperback in 2012.

ISBN: 978-1-85782-662-3

British Library Cataloguing-in-Publication Data:

A catalogue record for this book is available from the British Library.

Design by www.envydesign.co.uk

Printed and bound by CPI Group (UK) Ltd, Croydon, CR0 4YY

1 3 5 7 9 10 8 6 4 2

Papers used by John Blake Publishing are natural, recyclable products made
from wood grown in sustainable forests. The manufacturing processes conform
to the environmental regulations of the country of origin.

Every attempt has been made to contact the relevant copyright-holders,
but some were unobtainable. We would be grateful if the appropriate
people could contact us.

For my two little petrol-heads,
Super Sport and Little Turbo

Contents

Acknowledgements

The author would like to generously thank Jon Bentley, David Coulthard and Dr Kerry Spackman for their interviews. *Top Gear* has, of course, been the subject of huge media coverage and the following sources were extremely helpful in compiling this book: *The Sunday Times*, the *Guardian*, the *Independent*, the *Sun*, the *Daily Mirror*, the *Daily Mail*, the *Daily Telegraph*, the *Daily Express*, *The Man in the White Suit* by Ben Collins, *Flat Out, Flat Broke* by Perry McCarthy, *Top Gear* magazine. Also the brilliant fan site www.jeremyclarkson.co.uk, www.timesonline.co.uk, style.uk.msn.com, news.bbc.co.uk, www.petitiononline.com, www.hse.gov.uk, www.thefutoncritic.com, transmission.blogs.topgear.com, www.finalgear.com, www.c21media.net, web.archive.org/web, www.webcitation.org, news.scotsman.com, www.smh.com.au, www.theage.com.au, www.carsguide.com.au, jalopnik.com, www.vogue.co.uk, findarticles.com,

www.computerworld.com.au, www.newstatesman.com,
uk.askmen.com, www.imdb.com, www.brunel.ac.uk,
www.thesun.co.uk, homecinema.thedigitalfix.co.uk,
wikipedia.com
The official *Top Gear* website is at: www.topgear.com

Introduction

When I was a kid, my dad drove a chocolate-brown Hillman Hunter. It had shiny, faux-leather seats and no seatbelts in the front or rear. The music system was a cartridge player which took up most of the dashboard, yet we only had an album each by The Carpenters and Elkie Brooks to play on it. Us three kids would be crammed in the back and to this day, I don't know how we fitted everything in. We even drove to the south of France to go camping during two particularly ambitious summers – with a tent and two weeks' supplies for a family of five in the boot. I'm not actually sure that's physically possible, because now I'm a grown up, I seem to need a car the size of a small fuel tanker to get my small people around (which is still always full when we come back from Sainsbury's). But back then, the trusty (rusty) Hillman got us all in, suitcases precariously tied to a creaking roof rack, and off we went over the Channel. I think it took us about 79 days to get there the first time.

My dad used to fix cars on an evening after work to bring in extra money to feed his hungry hordes so my primary-school years were a time when cars were a piece of metal to get you from A to B or to generate cash for a new pair of shoes. They were a pragmatic assistant, a necessity and nothing more. For much of my early years, I had absolutely no idea there were car 'brands' and the caché of a so-called 'prestige' marque mattered not one jot because it didn't even register. Besides, even if I had pined for a classic badge, we simply couldn't have afforded one.

In compiling this book, I have tried to pinpoint exactly why it is that *Top Gear* is so massively popular. At the time of writing, somewhere in the region of 350 million people watch each episode. That's almost as many as *Baywatch*, yet Jeremy Clarkson, James May and Richard Hammond are certainly no Pamela Andersons. Of course there are several fairly obvious reasons: the brilliant presenters, the ludicrous stunts and adventures, the road-tests, the irreverent humour and bitingly funny scripts, all these things are core staples of a globally successful formula. But there's something more, something a little more nebulous: it's the fact that for some reason, to a sizeable chunk of the world's population, *cars matter*.

I remember vividly the very first moment when I suddenly realised this phenomenon. It was like a cloud of ignorance lifting from my eight-year-old eyes – I suddenly understood that certain cars were deemed 'better' than others. It happened when the music teacher at primary school bought a new car. I remember sitting in the maths class and one of the 'trendy' kids walked in and said, 'Guess what? Mr Hanley has only gone and bought a Saab 900 drop-top!' I didn't know what he was talking about. After some explanation, I realised he meant to say, 'Mr Hanley has only gone and bought a new car with a convertible roof.' But he hadn't just bought 'a car' – it was a Saab. And not just any old Saab, it was a 900 Series, no less … and convertible.

Suddenly, the penny dropped.

Ah, I get it …

A whole new world had just opened up for me.

Now, a good few road miles later, I sit here with that primary-school fascination for fast cars still burning brightly inside. When a supercar drives past me, I still emit the audible 'Oooohhhh' that the voice boxes of all genuine petrol-heads are equipped with. Or sometimes I opt for the sharp intake of breath – that works, too. When I recently saw a convertible white Bugatti Veyron in central London, I was quicker to stand next to it with my boys and get a photo than a stalker at a celebrity party.

I buy *Top Gear* magazine religiously and have a subscription to the kids' edition, *Top Gear Turbo* – in my son's name, of course – and yes, I 'help' him collect the trading cards. We once went to a toy store for a 'friendly' card-swapping morning with fellow collectors and I nearly had to be escorted from the shop because a dad jumped the queue for the Lambo Murcielago LP640 ('Rare'). I was outraged on my son's behalf, of course.

As I type this, I have a *Top Gear* battery-operated V8 engine pencil sharpener next to my keyboard; there's a Stig key fob hanging from the door to my office; on the back of my mobile phone is a *Top Gear* sticker, which says 'Only Supercars Allowed'; I have just had a shower with a Stig soap-on-a-rope and when I've finished for the day, I'll drink a coffee from my *Top Gear* mug. Then I'll read stories to my boys after first ticking off the latest trading cards we have just bought. Afterwards my eldest will go to sleep in a *Top Gear* duvet. I haven't quite sunk that low yet, but perhaps it's only time – they do make them in king size...

And that's what *Top Gear* so brilliantly taps into: it's some primal and at times totally illogical fascination with cars. I admit, when watching the show I do tend to drift – no pun intended – if the *Top Gear* team spend too long on a vehicle that takes longer than is decent to get to 60mph, but let's be honest, so do the presenters. That said, even when they are forced to focus on something that isn't supersonic, the way the programme reviews, tests and discusses all types of car is truly unique. However, it's the three presenters' own schoolboy passion for cars that is the biggest single draw for most *Top Gear* viewers. Sure, they have a massive knowledge of the machines they are testing and are all very accomplished drivers yet it's their child-like enthusiasm and playground camaraderie that is most infectious of all. Had Clarkson, Hammond and May been in my maths class that day at school, they would have been the first ones to jump up from their seats and run to the window to gaze adoringly at Mr Hanley's new Saab. Years later, they are effectively still doing exactly the same every Sunday night on our television screens.

I knew I had probably overdone the petrol-head life when my youngest, then aged two-and-a-half, saw his new pram and asked, 'Daddy, can we get black alloys?' I make no apology for this because I know that my little racing drivers understand, the presenters of *Top Gear* understand, the brilliant behind-the-scenes team at the show understand, and the millions of people all over the world who tune into the show every week also understand: *Top Gear* will be relevant and popular for as long as there are cars.

Martin Roach

CHAPTER 1

'Old' Top Gear

With the ubiquitous success of the current version of *Top Gear*, it's easy to forget that the show has a long and illustrious history. In fact, the first generation of *Top Gear* was broadcast for almost a quarter of a century, across 45 series and 515 episodes. The future television classic actually started off as a regional programme in 1977, but was deemed successful enough to be extended to a nationwide show the following year. Unconfirmed reports suggest the title may have been inspired by a John Peel radio programme of the same name and this first generation was broadcast from the old BBC studios in Pebble Mill, the then state-of-the-art complex in the Birmingham suburb of Edgbaston. The seven-storey site contained offices, television studios, radio studios, two canteens, a post office and a garden; among the projects that the studios were most famed for was the longest-running radio soap, *The Archers*, as well as the perennially popular *Pebble Mill at One* and *All Creatures Great and Small*.

1

It was from here that BBC2 decided to broadcast their flagship motoring show to the nation. Using The Allman Brothers' Band song 'Jessica' to open and with the closing credits usually sound-tracked by Elton John's 'Out Of The Blue' (from the *Blue Moves* album), the show launched with a stellar cast of highly respected presenters. Many of those faces came from highly cerebral journalistic backgrounds: one of the more established names was William Woollard, a former Oxbridge graduate who also served as a fighter pilot in the RAF. Among his other varied jobs before *Top Gear* were roles for oil corporations in Borneo and Oman and he even worked as a social scientist for various global companies. However, it is as a veteran of countless highly respected TV shows – both as a producer and presenter – that Woollard is best known, perhaps most obviously as a presenter of the seminal science programme, *Tomorrow's World*. This show was one of the BBC's longest-running programmes ever, notching up an impressive 38 years before its eventual demise in 2003. Woollard was a key factor in its success, appearing for 11 years on *Tomorrow's World*, winning numerous awards along the way, including several 'Top Science Presenter' gongs. He would also go on to present many series of *Horizon*.

So when Woollard came to *Top Gear* in 1981, he brought an enviable degree of gravitas and knowledge (a wisdom reinforced by the fact that he was a practising Buddhist). Perhaps more than any other presenter at the time, Woollard was best equipped to talk about technical car information in a way that made the material palatable to the common man, a skill he was renowned for and a facet that had been a key part of his success on *Tomorrow's World*.

At this stage, *Top Gear* typically had a central location for the links that ran through the programme, which would perhaps be a foreign motor show such as Turin or Paris, or maybe a rally stage, or an historic car collection. Each feature would then link back to (usually) William Woollard, who was steering the whole ship. The initial nature of the programme was also very journalistic, with factual and balanced reviews of everyday cars supplemented by road safety features all of which was presented in what was essentially quite a dry fashion, with little or no sign of the irreverent humour for which the series would later become so well known. Straightforward car reviews, motor shows, road safety issues, classic car competitions and a popular slot following rally formulae were the main fare (the show was even a sponsor of the 1987 and 1988 Formula 1 'Winter Series', the 1990 and 1991 Historic Rally Championships and the 1992 and 1993 British Rally Championships). It was a popular format: although initial ratings were modest – with the first batch of series attracting a few hundred thousand – the show was quickly launched on a steep, upward curve.

Woollard was not alone in bringing quality to the series. Other presenters included TV favourite Noel Edmonds, who was at the peak of his power in the 1970s and 1980s. His huge profile on BBC Radio 1 translated seamlessly to television, with massively successful shows such as *Multi-Coloured Swap Shop* and *Top of the Pops*. Edmonds would later go on to become one of the most powerful men in British TV, but it is his role as one of the original presenters of the first generation of *Top Gear* that is relevant here. His huge public profile ensured the show enjoyed high ratings and may have been responsible for drawing in viewers who might otherwise not have watched a car programme.

Another notable presenter was Chris Goffey, a motoring journalist who started out at the *Slough Evening Mail* and went on to enjoy a very fine journalistic background, writing for *Autocar* and *Motor Trader* (his son Danny would later become the drummer in Supergrass and subsequently appear on the charity show *Top Gear of the Pops* in 2007). It was Goffey's understated approach that most early *Top Gear* viewers would recognise as a direct contrast to the ever more ebullient presenting of the show's latter-day stars. Also in the ranks was Angela Rippon, the nation's favourite newsreader, she of the long legs made famous by *The Morecambe & Wise Show* of the late 1970s. Many of the presenters were graduates and it is noticeable how many different names and faces were tried and tested, with nearly 20 main presenters over the course of *Top Gear*'s first incarnation.

After the series had been running for a decade, a new face in the production team arrived and proved to be a major factor in the evolution of the show. Jon Bentley was an Oxford University graduate in Geography, who had initially taken a post-degree job working for Ford as a graduate trainee. He told the author how this eventually led him to working on *Top Gear*: 'I'd wanted to work in industry and had been passionate about cars from an early age. Frankly, [working at Ford] was a bit dull – I had to work out things like how many windscreen wipers were required a day in the Cologne plant. It was like all your worst nightmares about the car production line, where you're sitting there putting on the same bolt over and over again, but behind a desk. You end up looking at one tiny thing and never get to see the whole car.

'So I thought I should look for a more interesting job. One Monday, late in 1983, while scanning through the "Media" section of the *Guardian*, I saw an advert for a researcher's position on *Top Gear* so I applied for it.' Despite this, Bentley does not pretend that at the time he was a die-hard *Top Gear* viewer: 'I couldn't say I was a fan when I started working on it, because I hadn't really watched much of it – I was at the age when I didn't get round to watching telly much. Fortunately, when I was preparing for the interview, I discovered the Ford press office had copies of the programme on VHS. I didn't have a

VHS player but a friend did, so I was able to make a critique of three or four programmes before my interview. I also approached another friend of mine who was working on *Blue Peter* and spent a delightful Saturday afternoon attending a recording of that show by way of preparation.

'If anything, I think my boss counted my Oxbridge background against me but I came across as hugely interested in cars. I wrote things on my application form like the fact that I had several thousand car brochures – which was absolutely true. Back at university, for my rural geography dissertation I'd interviewed all the inhabitants of a village – the *Top Gear* producers liked that – and the combination of being able to mention sufficient eccentric statistics to demonstrate an interest in cars plus the fact that I'd done quite a few media related things (some journalism at college and an interest in photography) all added up, and they thought it was probably worth giving me a go.'

He remembers being thrown in at the deep end with a rather peculiar first assignment: 'It was *very* boring – the sort of thing that shouldn't really have been on the programme! I went up to Lancashire to investigate a company that had devised a tool for the home motorist to extract dents: you screwed a device into a hole in the wing and pulled out the dent. I don't think we should have done the item but I remember driving up the M6 in a rented dark green Sierra, thinking, "This is a wonderful way of earning a living", especially after having been chained to a desk at Ford.'

It seems strange in the media-saturated post-Millennial world that you could just apply for a job at such a prestigious programme with no previous television experience, but that is what happened to Bentley. 'It's never been that easy to define TV roles so at first it was a bit vague: when we visited a foreign motor show, I'd provide information for William Woollard on what to say, I'd look into stories and see if they stood up. I can remember having to drive round a director who didn't have a driving licence. There were very few researchers on the show back then, just me and someone else. It was a very small production team.'

He also remembers being struck by the approach of the existing presenting team: 'The existing presenters back [then] were very professional – people like William Woollard, Sue Baker, Frank Page and Chris Goffey (who was in my opinion the 1980s show's *enfant terrible*).'

However, despite the obvious respect Bentley had – and still has – for the veteran presenters, as a young buck taking his first steps into TV land, he was very rapidly and ambitiously projecting his own ideas onto the show's format. After six months his researcher's contract was renewed and he began to offer up more and more ideas for new features. Within a year of first starting, he would be directing his own pieces on the programme: 'I felt we needed a more opinionated, controversial and passionate view. As soon as I got established on the show, I started ringing up editors of car magazines to assess their potential presenting abilities. However, I found to my great disappointment that some of the best [magazine and newspaper] journalists weren't right for TV – they wrote wonderfully in print but weren't able to communicate their enthusiasm through speaking or in a way that would work on TV.'

While searching for new on-screen faces, Bentley was fast becoming a major player in the show's directing, even though he was first offered elements of that role when still only twenty-three years of age: 'I think it was my passion that won through – a lot of TV is still like that.' One of his first directing jobs perhaps reflects the (initially) more staid atmosphere on the programme: 'I did a piece about an elderly chap called Tom Swallow, who had written a motoring magazine in a German prisoner-of-war camp, called *The Flywheel*. He died recently and I recall hearing bits of my item on the Radio 4 obituary series, *Last Word*.'

Another item was inspired by Bentley's beloved car magazines: 'One of the great things about car magazines at the time – and you can still see it in *Evo* today – is the obsession with the corner on a deserted mountain road. I tried to replicate that in some of my first items by going up to the Yorkshire Dales, filming around Buttertubs Pass. There was a road test of the Fiat Uno Turbo and an item on the Naylor, which was a replica MGF made by a company in Bradford. The tests back then were more factual and less humorous, certainly.'

But it wasn't just the content of the scripts and reviews themselves that was vastly different to the current crop of *Top Gear*: the actual cars they reviewed were in huge contrast to the latter-day supercar focus of Clarkson and his crew (this monopoly of unaffordable supercars on the new generation of the series is the source of much criticism, which we will come back to later). Back in the 1980s, there was no such focus, far from it, as Bentley recalls: 'When I joined, we weren't supposed to road test supercars at all – it wasn't thought to be the sort of thing the BBC should do. I remember having to persuade my boss's boss that we should be allowed to do a road test of the Ferrari Testarossa versus the Lamborghini Countach as one of my first few items, and that it wasn't in some way a betrayal of BBC values to have cars in the show which almost all viewers couldn't afford. My argument was always that it was more elitist to suggest that everyone could afford to buy a new Austin Maestro (which nobody seemed to have any objection to us featuring) than it was to suggest that everyone didn't have the right to dream about owning a Ferrari.

'So I did get to direct the Testarossa versus the Countach at

Bruntingthorpe ... on 16mm film! We had Chris Goffey at the wheel, and it included some shots from the side of a VW Caravelle to get some good close-up tracking and a microphone under the bonnet for some cracking wild-track engine noise. [I was allowed to do this] providing I also shot a sort of apologetic intro, which would prepare viewers for the shock that we were testing cars that cost as much as a house.'

Another contrast to the post-2002 *Top Gear* is that the older series occasionally looked at two-wheeled vehicles. 'There was always no shortage of new cars,' recounts Bentley. 'However, I introduced a bit of bike culture with my early items as well – I can remember an eventful day shooting at a scooter rally in Scarborough – interest in scooters was going through one of its many revivals in the mid-1980s. Towards the end of the day, the scooter enthusiasts became quite lively and started throwing bricks at the camera car while we were doing tracking shots, albeit in a friendly sort of way! Fortunately no harm was done and the resulting positive piece was well reviewed by (of all newspapers) the *Daily Mail*.'

Another area of the motoring world that *Top Gear* featured very heavily back then, but plays virtually no part in the current format was rallying. William Woollard also presented *Rally Report*, the *Top Gear* spin-off focussing on the Lombard RAC Rally. Interest was reinforced by the presence of retired rally driver Tony Mason, who had been navigator to Roger Clark in winning the 1972 RAC Rally, as well as actually competing in the race himself in other years. One notable feature saw Mason join forces with Clark to test out a replica Ford Escort RS1600 rally car in a forest.

By the late-1980s – 1987 to be precise – Jon Bentley had graduated within the *Top Gear* ranks through the roles of researcher, assistant director and on to director. With the incumbent greater power and responsibility of this senior role, he felt able to instigate yet more changes: 'I found that when I moved on to directing items that focussed your mind much more, you were responsible for delivering so many minutes of television and it was up to you to make it happen. So, item ideas were never a problem but it was more difficult coming up with ideas for whole programmes. We were [still] a very small team, about six or seven people, excluding presenters. At that stage there was the executive producer Dennis Adams, a producer, an assistant producer, one or two researchers and two production assistants. It was a very low-budget programme – we had about ten shooting days for a half-hour show in the budget and about seven editing days plus some time for research and preparation. The team did grow a bit over the years but it remained quite a low-budget programme right through the 1990s.'

By now, *Top Gear* was winning substantial ratings, moving from the hundreds of thousands into 1.5 million and over the course of the 1980s and the start of the 1990s, on towards a peak of 5 million. This represented an audience share of 22 per cent, which for a BBC2 programme was superb; the show regularly appeared at or near the top of BBC2's most popular programme charts.

'From the start I tried to improve the show's journalism,' explains Jon Bentley. 'My aim in the 1980s was to try and make it more like *Car* magazine; that was a magazine I used to wait for eagerly and devour avidly every month. That publication was quite critical and controversial in its opinions on cars. Back then I think cars featured more in general conversation: people in pubs used to talk about whether the Sierra was better than the Cavalier – it was the most sophisticated product people used at the time. In some ways, technology has now taken the role that cars used to have. People now might have a heated debate about whether PCs are better than Macs, or whether Android's better than the iPhone. Back then it was about cars: a new Golf was an event.'

Bentley's rapid rise up the *Top Gear* career ladder continued and in 1987 (after a brief period working on attachment to the BBC's *Timewatch*), he became the motoring show's producer: 'I was joined by Ken Pollock, who was very keen on motorsport. Being producer didn't mean you stopped directing individual items but it did mean you were responsible for delivering the whole programme – still 30 minutes at that stage – and helping to manage any directors or other people who might be working on it.'

However, for the purposes of this book, Bentley's role as producer also came with one crucial new responsibility: he was able to introduce new presenters. Enter one Jeremy Clarkson ...

'I used to go on car launches occasionally,' recalls Bentley, 'either to shoot an item or, when the series was less active, to drive the new car and meet different people. On the Citroen AX launch (which I always remember as being in the New Forest, but may actually have been in Berkshire – well, it was in a forest, anyway!), I sat down at dinner and next to me was Jeremy Clarkson. He was a writer on *Performance Car* at the time, but I think he was on the launch because he used to syndicate local newspaper motoring columns and was writing a test of the new Citroën. We had a long conversation and he seemed exactly the sort of person I wanted as a presenter on *Top Gear* – funny, opinionated, passionate about cars but not in the least bit serious or po-faced. Perfect. I don't think I considered for a moment whether he [looked the part] or not.

'I'd become established as a producer [by then so] I felt in a strong position to back my hunch, arrange a screen test and convince my boss we should hire him. Of course these days if you feel like screen testing someone, you can just point your phone at them and record a video. Back then, in 1988, it was almost before the days of even VHS camcorders and you'd need a bit of investment in a crew with a sound recordist to go out and shoot a screen test, so I had to convince the powers-that-be to invest in a screen test day.'

A full day of screen testing was arranged at Shugborough in Staffordshire and Clarkson, along with an array of other potential presenters including several high-profile car magazine editors and writers, was invited along. 'I tested Jeremy [on that day] along with a few other people I thought might have potential. I asked people to bring along a car of their choice and talk about it for two minutes then I would supply a surprise car for them to talk about unprepared. I chose the 2CV because I thought it was universally known and the sort of car everyone would have an opinion on.

'Jeremy brought along a Range Rover and was very funny, streets ahead of the others. I hadn't read much of [his writing] but he just came over very well as a strong, lively personality. I kept that screen test tape for ages but one day when I went to look for it, I couldn't find it. A pity! I wish I still had it.'

Clarkson was one of the first new faces Bentley put forward and he was delighted when Jeremy was offered a job. The producer's gut instinct was quickly validated: 'We had a few meetings and I explained that the best way to write a TV script was to put the pictures on the left-hand side and the words on the right-hand side, make breaks for music or action, and think about how long each sequence should be. Jeremy just took to it immediately. I went out with him for the first couple of items but thereafter he became the sort of presenter who could almost be his own producer. You could put him with a director who was brilliant visually and very good at pace and music, and you knew you'd end up with six or seven minutes of great, memorable stuff. Always excellent!'

One of Clarkson's very first features was a test of a new Mercedes S-Class in the south of France, around 1991. 'I think the Merc S-Class was the first car test we did that had a bit of extra dramatic polish to it,' recalls Bentley. 'The director, Dennis Jarvis, cut a sequence of it driving round to Chris Isaak's "Wicked Game".'

And it wasn't just Clarkson who Bentley introduced to the show. Quentin Willson was a brilliant addition in 1991, a former used car salesman with an encyclopaedic knowledge of the motor trade. Willson actually founded a car dealership selling prestige and supercars such as Ferraris and Maseratis. His journalistic background boasted a deputy editorship of the second-hand car magazine, *Buying Cars*. Again, Bentley was a big fan: 'He was a car trader but also had an English degree, which may help explain his excellent way with words. I think he started running nightclubs in Leicester after university, and trading and writing about cars in his spare time. We needed a second-hand cars expert: I thought Quentin's writing was very good and as a car dealer, he fitted into the "poacher-turned-gamekeeper" role very well. I talked about him with Jeremy, who had met him and thought he had potential, too. So I arranged to meet Quentin in a pub in Ombersley and he seemed great for the job. His early items went down well – one on buying a second-hand XR3 and another on why you shouldn't buy a used Metro – slightly controversially in the case of the Metro, because of a perceived anti-Rover bias.'

Willson would appear on every *Top Gear* episode for a decade and was rightly seen as a stalwart of the show.

Contrary to widespread sources, Bentley confirms he did not introduce Tiff Needell to *Top Gear*: 'My colleague Ken Pollock introduced him. He saw an excellent driver, who could actually talk about his experiences at the wheel while driving. He was the first professional driver the show had, I think.'

He continues: 'However, I was very pleased to introduce Vicki Butler-Henderson. We needed to find another woman presenter and here was one who could drive on the racetrack. I saw her picture in *Max Power* magazine – I thought she'd be the younger male viewer's ideal fantasy girlfriend.' Butler-Henderson was a racing driver who brought a touch of class and a certain sex appeal to the show; she was from a racing family, with her grandfather, father and brother all involved in motorsport. She began racing karts when she was only twelve years old. In her twenties, she started writing about cars as well as still racing them to a very high level. After working at *Auto Express*, *What Car?* and *Performance Car*, she became launch editor at the new publication, *Max Power*, which is where Jon Bentley spotted her. His *Top Gear* colleague Jeremy Clarkson would later call VBH 'the personification of the Porsche 911 C4S'!

Bentley failed, however, to persuade the powers-that-be to recruit a certain James May, at the time a relatively unknown motoring writer who nonetheless already had many fans among the car magazine-reading public: 'I did a screen test with James on my drive with a Caterham in the early 1990s. He'd always been keen to work on the show. I thought he was great – funny and confident – but my bosses thought at the time that he was too similar to Jeremy, two relatively posh-sounding young blokes which is strange because when you put them together now, you see how different they are. He went on to join *Driven* [Channel 4's rival motoring show, launched in 1988], which started his presenting career.'

Notably, *Driven* had elements that differed to the old version of *Top Gear* but would prove very popular in later motoring shows:

the presenters – initially Mike Brewer, James May and Jason Barlow – interacted with each other on items, rather than alone and there was also a central location, in this case a truck on a race track, from where certain features were based. At the time of its launch, *Driven* quickly attracted a healthy ratings fan-base, perhaps the first sign that *Top Gear* would not have it all its own way.

Meanwhile, old *Top Gear* itself changed format in 1991. Instead of using the central location for key presenters to talk about upcoming features, it became a magazine-style programme (without a central location), namely just a series of totally independent items. By now, Woollard had retired from the show to pursue his own already highly successful television production company.

Even Jon Bentley himself briefly appeared in front of the camera in the latter half of the 1990s: 'I did around a dozen items. I think my boss and the producer who was then working for me, a chap called John Wilcox, thought I'd actually be quite good at it and should be given the chance to move from behind to in front of the camera. I really enjoyed doing it and I'm still proud of some of the items: I launched a car design competition, for example, and the person who won it went on to become a car designer. In the end, I didn't have time to develop this side of my career at that stage because there were so many other demands on my time.

'One of the last things I did as a presenter was an on-screen recruiting exercise, asking viewers to apply to be a researcher on *Top Gear*. The personnel department were a bit worried at first, but they approved it in the end – I don't think anyone had done this with a BBC programme before. I seem to remember several thousand people applied; it took a lot of going through but I looked at them all and it was very exciting. We spotted some good people out of it too, including Richard Porter who's currently the script editor on new *Top Gear* and the man behind car blog *Sniff Petrol*, as well as James Woodroffe who went on to be the executive producer of [Channel 5's motor show] *Fifth Gear*.

With such a glut of talent, *Top Gear* succeeded in shifting both public and motor trade perceptions: 'I think it had become a credible car programme [by now],' suggests Bentley. 'When I started on it, you had to apologise a bit when you mentioned it to car enthusiasts. Now it had become credible, interesting and enthusiastically viewed by car enthusiasts while at the same time being entertaining and accessible to general viewers.'

As Bentley's role changed within the programme's structure, so too did Jeremy Clarkson's profile. 'I recall buying my first Amstrad word processor,' remembers Jon, 'and thinking, "Right, now I've got a word processor, I need to think of some ideas for new programmes." One I eventually managed to sell to my boss was what became *Jeremy Clarkson's Motorworld*. It's an idea anybody could have had – quite generic, really – but it became a successful pair of series for us.'

This particular two-series show saw Clarkson travel the world looking at the car culture of various countries such as Monaco, India, Dubai, Japan and Detroit with each territory having its own show. There were 12 episodes across the two series and then a 'special' on the United Kingdom. Although the show was never a rival to *Top Gear*, it was important for two reasons. First, it highlighted just how capable Jeremy Clarkson was, and how his outspoken views and dynamic presenting style were perhaps already outgrowing the veteran motor show on which he first appeared on our screens. Second, Clarkson introduced a new face to the team behind-the-scenes on *Motorworld* – Andy Wilman, an old school-friend of his. Between 1994 and 2001, Wilman himself would actually present features in 35 shows of *Top Gear*.

Jon Bentley remained series producer of *Top Gear* until late 1996, when his boss Dennis Adams retired. He was then given responsibility for the whole motoring department at the BBC. During the next two years, his department produced 35 to 40 *Top Gear* programmes a year, a specialist show (*Top Gear Motorsport*), world rally coverage, a classic car series (*The Car's The Star*), *Jeremy Clarkson's Extreme Machines* and even a waterborne version of *Top Gear* called *Top Gear Waterworld*. The team also did a series of televisual car autobiographies, *Several Careful Owners*. By now, viewing figures for the main show were as high as 6 million.

In 1993, *Top Gear* was deemed successful enough to launch a spin-off magazine of the same name, which has largely been in publication ever since (and by the mid-2000s was the UK's biggest-selling car magazine). This hard-copy format allowed the production team to conduct surveys and certain features that might otherwise be restricted by the television licence fee's regulations – so, for example, the magazine was able to run an annual survey polling car owners' satisfaction with their wheels. Around this period, there was even a radio show spin-off too, although the format was naturally more limited in terms of talking about a car's aesthetics.

'I also introduced an extreme sports show called *Radical Highs*,' recalls Bentley. 'Someone approached me to work on *Top Gear* but I didn't think he was suitable. He did, however, have an interest in shooting extreme sports so I sent him round the world with his own camera shooting them. It was repeated for years!'

Meanwhile, *Top Gear* was coming under increasing budgetary pressures, despite having (initially) seen off many of the rival shows from other broadcasters in the 1990s. 'There was always a drive to cut budgets,' explains Bentley. 'One reason why we rarely had more than one presenter on the screen at a time was because two was thought to be an extravagance.'

In January 1999, Jeremy Clarkson left *Top Gear*, after 12 years on the show. Behind the scenes, events were concerning Jon Bentley, too: 'Towards the end of the 1990s, I became more and more embroiled in BBC management and more removed from the programme. As series producer I [had been able] to worry about the content, not the politics but [now] I had to play my role in a management team and that meant going down to London to attend meetings about the future of Radio 3 and attending long consultations about the fabric of Pebble Mill.

'At the start of 1999, Jeremy decided it was enough – he possibly saw his future at that stage more in general presenting. Meanwhile, Pebble Mill was having its own crisis so I decided to move on. I have been pretty good at spotting talent over the years, both in front of the camera and behind the scenes,' says Bentley, 'but Jeremy *himself* is the reason for his success, not me.'

Clarkson's vacant slot was taken by James May. Yet more changes were afoot, though: the programme had attracted increasing criticism for the content of many of its features. This new generation of faces had indeed coincided with the advent of *Top Gear* becoming far more light-hearted and humorous, something many fans credit Jon Bentley with starting. Interestingly, the car reviews were also liable to be much harsher than in the somewhat more liberal past. In response, motor trade and general press criticism began to rise too, with negative reviews of what was increasingly perceived as puerile schoolboy features that encouraged fast and dangerous driving and took an irresponsible approach to the environment and global pollution (sounds familiar?). *Top Gear*'s ratings started to slide ...

Then, to some people's surprise and to many critics' delight, in August 2001, the BBC issued an official announcement about the programme's future, saying it would be taken off air that autumn and the show had been put, 'On the blocks while we give it a full service and an overhaul.' Notably, the corresponding *Top Gear* magazine was not suspended and continued to sell heavily. The BBC also stated, '*Top Gear* has not been axed. It's been given a rest as we look at what format will suit car enthusiasts in the future.'

Was it all over?

CHAPTER 2

Jeremy Clarkson, Part I

One of Jeremy Charles Robert Clarkson's first jobs was as a travelling Paddington Bear salesman. It might seem a long way from there to becoming Britain's – and arguably the world's – best known motoring journalist, but in fact his first foray into the world of employment was because his parents, Eddie Grenville Clarkson and Shirley Gabrielle Ward, owned a business selling such bears near the family's Doncaster home (his mother was also a magistrate). According to some reports, their previous business was selling tea cosies. The bear line of work came about by accident, after they made two at home for presents for their own kids and people kept asking where they could buy them. With no small amount of ingenuity and boundless hard work later, the couple had a thriving business that was sufficiently profitable to send Jeremy to a private school.

He first attended the nearby fee-paying Hill House School and then moved on to Repton School in south Derbyshire (taking with him a vast collection of Dinky model cars). The school building at Repton itself is a colossal grand affair, a Hogwarts-esque country pile with a staggering history of academic achievement on the site of a former twelfth-century Augustinian Priory; the school itself dates back to the second half of the sixteenth century. One of the founding fathers of the halcyon Victorian era believed that 'healthy exertion of body and spirit together, which is found in the excitement, the emulation and the friendly strife of school games' was the way forward for his pupils. Clearly, he didn't have Jeremy Clarkson in mind.

So-called Old Reptonians include none other than writing legend Roald Dahl, who boarded there for four years (it was here that Cadbury's presented 'blind' confectionery tastings to pupils for market research purposes, an experience widely believed to have been Dahl's inspiration for *Charlie and the Chocolate Factory*). Other notables include novelist Christopher Isherwood, poet James Fenton, Olympian Harold Abrahams of *Chariots of Fire* fame, actor Basil Rathbone, no less than three Archbishops of Canterbury and Jeremy Clarkson, who is listed on their website as a 'journalist'.

In fact, Clarkson has gone on record saying he was bullied in school and that the 'fagging was brutal' but he has also pointed out that the baptism of fire applied to all new boys. One fellow pupil was a certain Andy Wilman and it was here at Repton that the two became firm friends and a future television partnership was born. It was their cheeky schoolboy humour, founded here at this fee-paying public school, that many years later would transform them into a household name and a TV production legend respectively. Talking in the *Guardian*, Wilman said that Clarkson at that age had, 'a massive gob, really bad music taste and massive hair – the full Leo Sayer.'

Clarkson's rebellious streak that has caused so many

controversies on the set of *Top Gear* was there from an early age: he is reported to have spent much time visiting the local girls' school as well as numerous drinking establishments around Burton upon Trent. He also enjoyed ribbing teachers and confronting those authority figures with whom he disagreed.

Despite this, the young Jeremy was academically excellent, gaining nine O-levels and easily graduating straight into the sixth form. Some reports suggest that until his voice broke, he even played the part of a pupil named Taplin in a BBC radio adaptation of Anthony Buckeridge's novels about a schoolboy called Jennings and his friend Darbyshire. The *Children's Hour* specials started in 1948 and were extremely popular for many years. They made much of the author's unique schoolboy language, such as 'fossilised fish hooks!' and 'crystallised cheesecakes!'

Unfortunately, just over two months before sitting his A-levels, Clarkson was expelled: his mother told *Auto Trader* that the school took a dim view of him 'drinking, smoking and generally making a nuisance' of himself. He was allowed back to take his exams but according to his mother, he didn't pass any (at the time he told her that it didn't matter as he was going to be a TV presenter). The current school website makes no mention of his expulsion.

Nonetheless, his public-school days were formative. With such an esteemed academic background – even allowing for his expulsion – it was not surprising that once unleashed into the outside world, Clarkson made rapid progress as an ambitious young man, despite having no A-levels. Clearly, there was aspiration in his genes – obviously his parents' own success proved that, but so too did the recently unearthed entrepreneurial ways of his more distant ancestors.

In a 2004 episode of the BBC's genealogical programme *Who Do You Think You Are?* Clarkson discovered that his great-great-

great-grandfather John Kilner had invented a famous rubber-sealed jar for preserved fruit which became an industry standard and was subsequently named after him. He started work in a glass factory and later set up his own glassworks with friends, which ultimately grew into a huge business. By the 1840s, he owned two colossal factories in south Yorkshire and was posthumously granted the only medal awarded to a British glassmaker at the Great International Exhibition held in London, in 1862.

There was a genuine family mystery discovered on the programme too. When John's son Caleb died, he left millions of pounds to his son George and a son-in-law in his will. However, further probate records show the two died with very little money. So, where had it all gone? One local legend suggested the son-in-law liked technology and in 1901, was said to have become one of the first people in south Yorkshire to buy a motorcar.

When asked to go on the historical show, Clarkson admits to thinking it was 'too boring to bother with'. However, on hearing all of his fascinating personal history, he says that he wanted to know what had happened to the money from this trademarked invention and secretly hoped the programme's experts might stumble across a piece of paper stating, 'Jeremy Clarkson is owed £48 billion'.

Fast forward to the 1970s and Clarkson's first job within the media was on the *Rotherham Advertiser*, but his fierce creative and linguistic streak quickly found the confines of local news media too claustrophobic. According to a later appearance on Radio 4's *Desert Island Discs*, it was 'in the middle of an assignment to a vegetable and produce show' that he handed in his notice. He would also work at the *Rochdale Observer* and later the Wolverhampton *Express & Star* but his sights were firmly set on something far bigger: television.

For now, he turned his back on journalism and went to work selling Paddington Bears in his father's business. Despite this, he realised he'd caught the reporting bug and it wasn't long before he returned to the journalistic arena. It was during those formative newspaper years that Clarkson had the idea to pen motoring columns and subsequently syndicate them to other local papers so in 1983 he moved to London and started his own business (with a partner) called the Motoring Press Agency (MPA). Nicholas Rufford, editor of *The Sunday Times*' *InGear* magazine, told the broadsheet that this intensive journalistic background explains Clarkson's meticulous approach to writing: 'He is an old-school journalist who learnt his craft the hard way. He delivers copy on time, word perfect, and can produce stories very quickly, even on a train. His headed notepaper says, "Jeremy Clarkson, journalist" – that's how he sees himself.'

The MPA led directly to Clarkson writing extensively for *Performance* magazine and his articles consistently proved both popular with the readers and elegantly written. As Jon Bentley has pointed out, it was while on a launch for the Citroen AX researching a piece for his MPA business that Jeremy Clarkson sat next to the-then *Top Gear* producer.

Officially, Clarkson first appeared on *Top Gear* on 27 October 1988 and was to feature on the original incarnation of the show for more than a decade.

CHAPTER 3

The Hamster and Captain Slow, Part I

In the week before Christmas 1969, on 19 December to be precise, Richard Hammond was born into a family steeped in automotive history. Both his grandparents worked in the West Midlands motorcar trade; his paternal grandfather, George Hammond, was a coachbuilder for Jensen, 'very much in the tradition of crafting cars.' George also taught Polish airmen to drive during the Second World War while his own father (and namesake) was a stoker on the railways. The previous two generations of Hammonds had been craftsmen, working as glassblowers in the famous Black Country factories in and around Dudley (they lived in Kingswinford, where coincidentally this author was born and bred; my own father worked in precision engineering, making tooling for car manufacturers).

Hammond's maternal grandmother, Kathleen Shaw, was employed in the Colmore Depot, a part of the Morris Motor Company. His great-grandfather on his mother's side was a jeweller but that was the exception, with most other relatives working in industry, mostly in tool-making or a number of brass foundries so the Hammond lineage is saturated with Midlands manufacture.

A young Richard Hammond first went to Sharmans Cross School in Solihull before attending the fee-paying independent Solihull School for Boys. Like Clarkson's Repton, this school dates back hundreds of years, in this case to 1560. Being a single-sex school, by his own admission the young Hammond was scared of girls. Although he had been 'great with girls' at primary, by the time he went to Solihull School for Boys this bravado had vanished and he would actually cross the street to avoid young females. Then, when he was a teenager, his mother Eileen and father Alan moved him and his two younger brothers – Andrew and Nicholas – to settle in the north Yorkshire cathedral city of Ripon.

His father ran a probate business in the market square and sent his sons to the mixed Ripon Grammar School. Hammond was brought up a Christian and even revealed that his parents met through the church (years later he was to present a documentary called *Richard Hammond's Search for the Holy Grail*). As he grew into his teens however, he grew disillusioned with religion, particularly when he became more aware of what he felt was the conflict it can cause in society. There is scant biographical information available about his school years and when he does talk of those formative days, it's usually in a jovial and rather nondescript fashion.

'I'll never forget standing outside a door,' he told the *Daily Mirror*, 'knowing that on the other side was not only a classroom full of strangers but also some of them were girls. I'd rather have walked into a room full of crocodiles! Then I discovered they were actually quite nice but I was hopeless at pursuing them.'

He had the usual schoolboy crushes although the biggest one obviously didn't make too much of an impression as he isn't sure of her name, possibly Sarah. But when she grabbed and kissed him at a school party, he was frightened away and 'went off her immediately'.

From 1987 to 1989, Hammond attended the Harrogate College of Art and Technology to study photography and television production, from where he eventually graduated with a National Diploma in Visual Communication. It was at college that he started to play bass guitar and joined in bands, as well as hanging out with his good friend Jonathan Baldwin (who would become a noted author and academic).

After graduation, he began working for several regional radio stations, including Radio Cleveland, Radio York, Radio Cumbria, Radio Leeds and Radio Lancashire. One of his shows was the oddly titled 'Lamb Bank' on BBC Radio Cumbria but by 1995, he had become restless and was looking for openings in TV work. The path to *Top Gear* began perhaps during this uncertain period when he landed a job with a PR company organising corporate events for the Ferrari Owners Club and Renault Sport, among others. Cars had always been on his radar: 'When I was five, I sat on my father's lap and asked him how many days it was before I could take my driving test.'

This PR work put him at the heart of the motorsport trade and with his effervescent personality and already-impressive radio broadcasting experience it was perhaps inevitable that TV producers picked up on his talents. Thus, in 1998, a team of satellite TV producers approached Hammond to present *Motor Week*, which he did for a year to great acclaim. At this point, the offers started to flood in, with work for various motor shows such as *4 Wheels*, *2 Wheels*, *Kits n' Cruisin'* and *Used Bike Heaven*. He even had a stint on The Money Channel's *Money Matters* and

Livetime for Granada Breeze. It was in 2001, however, that the call for an audition for a more famous motor show came into his agent's office and would soon change his life.

James May, the laconic driver christened 'Captain Slow' by his *Top Gear* presenters, shares his birthday with Cliff 'The Grinder' Thorburn, the snooker World Champion famous for being slow. Born in Bristol, on 16 January 1963, he has two sisters and a brother. His father was a steelworker, his mother a nurse. Early school years were at Caerleon Endowed Junior School in Newport, south Wales. As May hit his teens, the family moved north (just like Hammond's) and he then attended Oakwood Comprehensive School in Rotherham.

May has since said that although his family moved house quite often and 'all over Britain' when he was a child, he was very happy: 'we had food and shoes.' Like most boys of that age he wanted to be a fighter pilot although the statistical nerd was fighting to get out too, as he has revealed that he also fancied being a surgeon. He attributes his natural tendency for being thorough and meticulous to his dad and credits his mum for bringing him up to be 'nice'. May's father is also responsible for his love of cars: when he was three, he woke one morning to find a gleaming die-cast model of a beige Aston Martin DB4 on his pillow: 'a very exciting moment and the first spark.'

Perhaps not entirely surprisingly, May revealed to the *Sunday Mirror* that he was not really a lothario at school or in early adulthood: 'I was never a heartbreaker because I'm too soft but there have been enough girlfriends for me to know there's nothing odd.' As a grown man, he has said his idea of a dream night would be one with 'ladies and aeroplanes', so essentially not much has changed from teenage years!

Reflecting on life in a 2008 interview, May admitted that one of his regrets was not working harder at school: had he tried harder, he might have been able to pursue his dream job as a surgeon or pilot. To be fair, most fans would probably think he's still ended up with a pretty fine choice of employment, though.

However, there was little sign of the rebellious teenage ways of Clarkson, as among the knife-edge pastimes during these pubescent years, May was a choirboy as well as an accomplished pianist and flautist. Having said that, he told the *Independent* that, 'the moment that changed me forever' was 'punching a guy called Kenneth Ingram in the face after choir practice when I was nine. We had an argument over who would be head boy. It was a brutal arena, the village church choir.' As a teenager he used to earn pocket money by playing medieval banquets and even had to dress up as a minstrel on one occasion. May has always had a penchant for medieval history and music, so he enjoys visiting places like Wells Cathedral.

In fact, his musical prowess was sufficiently advanced for him to go on to study music at Lancaster University (years later when his *Top Gear* career was in full flight, he would be presented with an honorary Doctor of Letters degree from Lancaster). He loves classical music to this day and when he finally acquired an iPod in 2008, one of the first albums downloaded onto it was a Chopin piece (his favourite is that composer's 'Prelude No. 24 in D Minor for the Piano' and Couperin's 'Les Baricades Misterieuses' for the harpsichord – the instrument he originally wanted to study at university). It was while at Lancaster that he developed a more rebellious streak although when pressed, he actually clarified this by saying he 'was mildly rebellious, then ... I didn't set fire to anyone, I didn't murder anyone, but, you know, I did occasionally wear denim waistcoats and embroider my jeans ...'

After graduating, like many fellow students initially he had no focussed idea of what career to pursue, so he enrolled at an employment agency. The first job this temporary route secured him was working in the archive department of a women's hospital in west London and he also had a brief stint in the Civil Service. By the late 1980s, he migrated to working as a writer for *The Engineer*: the first leap from pen pushing to journalism was simply made by applying for an advertised job in the magazine. Soon he would also secure commissioned writing for *Autocar* magazine.

It is at the latter where the first signs of the cheeky schoolboy humour that would later equip him perfectly to work on *Top Gear* came into play. In 1992, he was given the task of compiling *Autocar*'s end-of-year 'Road Test Book' supplement. This was something he found deeply boring, perhaps exacerbated by what he himself has described as his 'innate laziness, deep down I am lazy.'

So, to spice up the tedium, he inserted a hidden message in the supplement by taking the initial letter of each spread of reviews so that when read in sequence, they formed a sentence. This crafty device is actually called an acrostic, a fact probably only James May would know. It took him two months to compile the supplement, including all the appropriate words to make up his secret message.

So what exactly did he say?

'So you think it's really good, yeah? You should try making the bloody thing up. It's a real pain in the arse!'

Later he said that he'd forgotten what he'd done because back then the lead time from editing and design to actually printing the magazine was well over two months. He told BBC Radio 2 how he eventually found out his employer's reaction: 'When I arrived at work that morning everybody was looking at their shoes and I was summoned to the managing director of the company's office. The thing had come out and nobody at work had spotted what I'd done because I'd made the words work around the pages so you never saw a whole word but all the readers had seen it and they'd written in, thinking they'd won a prize or a car, or something.'

He was subsequently sacked.

Still, a start in motoring journalism had been made. Unemployed briefly and with little money right before Christmas, he pitched numerous ideas to *Car* magazine and the publication was sufficiently impressed by his knowledge, experience and passion to offer him his own column. James May's writing is very fluid and understated in its humour (quite the opposite of Clarkson's brilliant and deceptively deft smash-and-grab prose) and he quickly acquired fans within automotive journalism and the wider reading public.

And this is how his path started to turn towards *Top Gear*; when Channel 4 launched the *Top Gear* rival, *Driven*, as we have seen he was approached and became one of the show's main three presenters. May impressed although the programme didn't, but nonetheless a stuttering move into television had been made.

As Jon Bentley has mentioned, the real leap came when Jeremy Clarkson decided to leave old *Top Gear*, which inadvertently provided the perfect opportunity for James to bring his many talents to the nation's foremost motoring show. At that point, by his own admission, he 'never imagined in a million years that it would turn into the phenomenon that it has. If I had, I would have thought twice about it, to be honest – I find being famous slightly embarrassing.'

Before that could happen, however, the old version of *Top Gear* itself was facing what threatened to be an almost terminal turn of events ...

CHAPTER 4

The 'New' Top Gear

When the BBC announced in the late summer of 2001 that *Top Gear* was being taken off-air for the aforementioned 'full service and an overhaul', many industry insiders predicted the programme was effectively in its death-throes. The announcement came some 23 years after the show had first been broadcast; given at the time of writing, the current more successful generation of *Top Gear* has only been on-air for eight years, that gives you some indication of just how successful and rare its predecessor's longevity was.

However, the turn of the Millennium was a very different place in TV-land from 1977. For one, the television landscape had changed immeasurably since the heady days of 6 million car enthusiasts tuning in. Magazine shows were a tired old format and recent additions to primetime schedules such as *Changing Rooms* and *Ground Force* proved hugely popular.

Second, despite various sources seemingly re-writing much of the old *Top Gear*'s history into a staid and unadventurous programme like some kind of benign and cosy old uncle, in its latter years the first generation of the show was a highly controversial programme. Jeremy Clarkson worked so well when he first appeared on our screens *because* he was outspoken, this is not something that evolved over time. This fact is reflected in the response from many quarters when the news filtered out that *Top Gear* might be facing a petrol-fumed end.

Although the BBC's statement simply said that every aspect of the format and show was under review, when directly asked about how terminal the decision was, they declined to rule out the series being abandoned for good. By 2001, ratings were well down on their lofty peak and the programme's style was increasingly criticised by industry insiders for being 'old fashioned'. Since Clarkson and Quentin Willson had left, ratings dropped further, struggling to get past between 2 and 3 million for most shows (although this was still substantial for a BBC2 programme and in fact had even turned back onto an upward curve of late).

Nonetheless, according to one motoring writer, Chris Gray of the *Independent*, '*Top Gear* has become a rotting old banger with less sex appeal than your granny.' Gray went on to vilify the programme, saying that 'Britain's most famously politically incorrect motoring show' was being pulled and bemoaned 'Clarkson's childish sexism and love of foreign stereotypes ... he turned laddishness into an art form and MPs condemned the obsession with speed and acceleration.'

Slightly oddly, two new motoring shows – including one with the name still involved (*Top Gear: Car Jack*) – were already scheduled for the following year. The *Car Jack* format was a review programme with most features done by the general public. The second show was to be called *Panic Mechanic* and boasted a bent for weird and wonderful design features as well as 'tough physical challenges', something more reminiscent of the latter-day success of *Pimp My Ride*. And so there were mixed signals.

The spectre of *Top Gear* wasn't finished yet, however. In 2002, a special was broadcast from the Birmingham Motor Show, presented by Northern Ireland's excellent Jason Barlow, who had presented alongside James May and Mike Brewer on *Driven* before moving to the BBC for the last two years of old *Top Gear*. Jason Barlow also went on to present the new BBC show, *Wrong Car, Right Car*, which ran for two series.

That said, the migration of presenting talent between rival TV stations was generally in the opposite direction: already several of old *Top Gear*'s presenters had transferred to Channel Five's new motoring show, *Fifth Gear* (initially written as *5th Gear*), including Vicki Butler-Henderson, Tiff Needell and Adrian Simpson. This was launched in 2002 with a host of famous faces and was at first a half-hour programme (until the longer formatted eighth series onwards) with a more factual bias. Sounds familiar? That's because according to the latter show's former producer Jon Bentley, any relation to the old *Top Gear* was not necessarily a coincidence.

Bentley had been approached to produce Five's new motoring show and given his vast experience and renowned passion for the subject was unrivalled in terms of what he could offer. He was one of several former *Top Gear* faces behind-the-scenes at the new programme: 'I'd kept in touch with some of the people who continued to work on *Top Gear* after I'd left. Late in 2001, I got a call from Richard Pearson and he said he'd left the BBC, joined North One Television and was setting up a new show called *Fifth Gear* for Channel Five. I thought this sounded great fun. I was series producer for the first few series.'

Bentley attended various meetings and the brief for the new show was made very clear: 'What they said was that they wanted old *Top Gear* … they wanted exactly the same, a very straight magazine show.' Five's decision, it transpired, might have been just the adrenaline shot that *Top Gear* needed.

Maybe the gusto with which Five launched *Fifth Gear* caused consternation in the back-rooms of the BBC? It's difficult to say, but what's clear is that with just one series of *Fifth Gear* completed, the BBC made another announcement. *Top Gear* was to be relaunched in a new format, with some new presenters and the full backing of Aunty Beeb.

While conspiracy theorists were enjoying the 'Will they/ won't they kill off *Top Gear?*' etc, two former faces from that programme had been quietly re-inventing the wheel. Some time during 2001, Andy Wilman, the former Repton school pal of Clarkson (as stated, himself a *Top Gear* presenter), had called up his friend and they'd met over a pub lunch to talk about the show and a possible relaunch. Wilman had tired of the old format and has since stated – in his famously brusque way – that it had become 'fucking old-fashioned'. Both he and Clarkson revelled in the opportunities to be outspoken, film outrageous features and generally make the show as much about entertainment as it was about cars.

And so they drew up a masterplan: the duo instantly became a potent creative force, drawing on their long friendship and substantial shared TV experience. As Jon Bentley says, 'Andy's a splendid chap, very hardworking indeed. They definitely have a very close relationship.' Over the coming weeks, this intensely creative partnership drew up a brand new template for any potential *Top Gear* relaunch.

First, it would be screened from a central location, in this instance an old aircraft hangar rather than the previous magazine style; another idea was to not shy away from supercars, in fact they wanted to gravitate towards them, so there was to be a news section that would quickly despatch important but 'boring' car news (with one-liners such as 'there's a new Nissan Micra out'); there would be an all-male presenting line-up; also a so-called 'Cool Wall' to post pictures of cars and rate their desirability (of more later); outlandish and indeed cutting-edge TV features were to be encouraged; they would always be outspoken and speak their minds about the cars they tested and there would be a smattering of celebrity guests. Wilman's defence of this bombastic and super-confident approach was simple: 'Do the Two Fat Ladies say, "And if you want to have a low-fat version of this recipe, you can use single cream"? They never do. They go, "Pile it on, heart attack now!"'

The BBC loved the re-invention and commissioned the first series of 'new' *Top Gear*, set to be broadcast on 20 October 2002. The plan was to have two series per year of between 8 and 10 episodes. In the new *Top Gear* office, an 'Ideas Board' for suggestions was put up and initially filled with suggestions for features from the production team; over time it has also hosted ideas from fans or members of the public. Each show would usually have four filmed features (although this would fluctuate, especially when more substantial challenges were screened). This meant the *Top Gear* team had to create and execute around 70 to 80 ideas per year: no mean feat, creatively or practically.

The *Top Gear* production set-up is unusual within the BBC. Wilman only works on the series and is invariably talked of as being very 'hands-on'. Famously direct, he has been described by one former co-worker as like 'a glum, but familiar uncle on a rare visit home'. *Top Gear*'s office itself is open-plan and the team say the production process itself is very 'organic'.

The show still used The Allman Brothers' Band theme tune of 'Jessica', albeit updated. There was one final change: whereas the old *Top Gear* logo used a cog for the letters 'O' and 'E' in its name, the new version only employed a cog behind the word 'Top'.

On that initial programme, the very first cars seen on-screen were a Ford Focus and a VW Golf; the team would be testing the Citroën Berlingo and Mazda 6 for the more mild-mannered viewer but they'd also be thrashing the beautiful Lamborghini Murcielago and the breath-taking supercar, the Pagani Zonda, as well as featuring the Ford GT40. There was Harry Enfield as a guest and a feature on how fast you have to drive to be too fast for a speed camera to nab you. Remember Jon Bentley having to battle to film the Ferrari Testarossa versus the Lamborghini Countach? Well, in the first series of new *Top Gear* alone, as well as the two aforementioned supercars, they also featured among others, the Noble M12 GTO, the Westfield XTR, an Aston Martin Vanquish, the Ferrari 575M Maranello, a Nissan Skyline R34 GT-R, the Bentley Image, the Honda NSX Type R, the Lotus Elise 111S, a Maserati Coupé, the Lotus Esprit and a TVR T350C! This was Andy Wilman and Jeremy Clarkson absolutely setting out their stall. Clarkson even introduced the new show as such prior to the opening credits of Episode 1, saying before the theme tune kicked in that it was 'a car programme', there'd be no cushions, no one would sing on the programme or get a recording contract, pointing out their test track was purpose-built and adding there'd be no bus lanes and no traffic jams.

Before moving on, it's vital to note one further addition to the show's personnel. In order to test the long list of supercars they were intent on featuring on the new *Top Gear*, the team had decided that they needed someone other than a presenter to trial the machines around the test track. So, in Episode 1, Clarkson explained this thinking and said they'd decided to look for a real racing driver because they have 'tiny little brains and worthless opinions'. Then, for the very first time ever, he introduced The Stig. At this stage, The Stig was wearing all black, à la Darth Vader.

For the first series, the presenting team was JC, Richard Hammond and Jason Dawe. Hammond's path to *Top Gear* had been a quirky one: contrary to Wilman's supposedly all-male line-up plan, unconfirmed TV legend has it that certain folk may have been considering whether to recruit a female presenter, but Richard Hammond was sent along too as he shared an agent with a woman that they were interested in.

Hammond was a long-time fan of the show and avidly watched old *Top Gear* as a kid. As we have seen, he had been making good progress on various cable TV channels but in mainstream terms, he was a relative unknown. At his audition, he made a good impression and was initially asked to make some short films for a possible *Top Gear* spin-off.

The *Guardian* quoted a 'former BBC executive' as saying, 'We interviewed lots of high-profile motoring journalists and half of them were scared shitless of Jeremy. The remarkable thing about Richard is he was naturally funny and he took the piss out of Clarkson, which Jeremy loved.' The *Top Gear* job was Hammond's. It was 2002 – a big year for Richard, as he also married his sweetheart, Mindy. Later, speaking to *Times Online*, Hammond made no secret of how excited he was to be on the series: 'Even when we were recording the first episode and Jeremy said, "Hello, and welcome to *Top Gear*", my immediate thought was, "Oh great, *Top Gear*'s back!" Then I suddenly realised, "Oh s***, I'm on it!"'

Alongside the show's patriarch Clarkson, Hammond's other co-presenter was Jason Dawe, a Cornish native who first started selling cars in 1986 when he worked at a local car dealership (including two separate brands crowning him 'Salesman of the Year') before graduating to become a sought-after motor industry trainer. After 16 years in the motor trade, he began working in journalism and picked up a reputation for championing consumers, helping them pick their way through the minefield that buying a car can prove to be. Dawe's participation in the new *Top Gear* therefore introduced a highly credible and investigative tone to the brash programme. His role quickly took the form of 'consumer's champion' with the more light-hearted features generally being presented by Clarkson and Hammond. However, at the start of the second series of the new generation, Dawe was replaced by James May.

Following the demise of the previous incarnation of *Top Gear*, May returned to his revered magazine columns. He was barely settled back in his journalist's chair before the new *Top Gear* producers called as they were looking for a replacement for Jason Dawe, who was to leave the programme after the end of series 1 in 2002. Despite earlier reservations about being too similar to Clarkson, May was the archetypal British gent: a more cerebral, stylish and pedestrian partner to the firebrands of Clarkson and Hammond. He has since proved the perfect foil for the other two's more exuberant personalities.

Speaking to the *Guardian* in 2008, a BBC executive recalled his audition for the new formatted show: 'James had a 14-year-old Bentley at the time. At the audition he said, "I've found out if you spend £50 at Tesco, you get £5 of free petrol. Now I can drive anywhere I like; the problem is my house is full of rotting food!" Everyone in the room laughed, Jeremy laughed. That landed him the job.'

With James May on board, the BBC now had the presenting line-up that would, over time, turn *Top Gear* into a programme watched by hundreds of millions of people around the world.

However, although different to its predecessor in many ways, the new format was not an immediate ratings hit; where the BBC played its trump card was in allowing the show to *grow*, giving Wilman and his production team the creative freedom and time to produce unusual features while allowing the presenting triumvirate of Hammond/Clarkson/May the opportunity to develop their characters on-screen.

The more caricatured elements of the three characters have only really developed over the span of several series and the show's ratings have subsequently gone up and up and up ... Wilman himself was quoted in the *Guardian* describing them thus: 'Jeremy is walk through a door rather than open it, Richard's a massively accident prone and cheeky chappie, and James is a pedantic nerd.' This was a formula that quickly proved highly successful: with the dream line-up, a healthy budget and the full backing of the BBC, new *Top Gear* set about becoming the most-watched and most successful motoring show of all-time.

CHAPTER 5

The Star in a Reasonably Priced Car

From the very first series of the new generation of *Top Gear*, a brilliant slot was introduced which has since become a TV institution, the so-called 'Star in a Reasonably Priced Car'. The premise was simple enough: each week, a famous face would take a cheap and cheerful car around the official *Top Gear* track, with their respective times posted on a lap time board. Initially introduced merely as a fun piece to feature some famous faces, it was also a clever way to segue in guest appearances without the celebrity just crassly plugging their new book or film.

The first-ever 'Star in a Reasonably Priced Car' was the comedian Harry Enfield. His appearance was pre-empted by Clarkson saying that normally when comedians make the big time, they go out and buy supercars yet Enfield had instead bought a Vauxhall Cavalier Convertible (which was hauled into the studio). He then swapped it for a Rover and this in turn was later exchanged for a Metro. At the time, Enfield was working the same circuit as comedians such as Rowan Atkinson (McLaren F1) and Steve Coogan (Ferrari 355). Inspired by such modest car taste, Clarkson announced the new weekly feature. He revealed that when searching for the 'Reasonably Priced Car', Hyundai had refused, so too had Daewoo and Nissan, but then Suzuki said, 'Have a Liana' – which was £9,999 on the road. Clarkson described this as the most beautiful car he had ever seen.

First of all, however, Clarkson, Hammond and Jason Dawe all crammed into the Liana to do a lap of the *Top Gear* track to test out the vehicle. They recorded a time of 1.50 seconds, even with three adults on board. For the celebrities themselves, on the day The Stig would show them the racing lines and coach them around the track before each of them was allowed several attempts at a lap time, although the fastest would be (genuinely) kept a secret until they were interviewed in the studio by Clarkson.

Enfield was not so quick: to this day he remains one of the slowest stars, with a lamentable time of 2.01. To his credit, as the opening 'star', he was the fastest guest celebrity on the leaderboard albeit for one week (behind The Stig and the presenters). However, with the very next episode in late October 2002, when supercar collector and accomplished racer Jay Kay of Jamiroquai fame came on the show, it quickly became apparent that for some celebrities this was not just a bit of fun. Kay has a well-documented fleet of supercars and was known to be a talented and naturally fast driver. First off, he chatted with Clarkson about how he felt his love of cars could be traced back to his famous mother's transient lifestyle (she was the brilliant jazz singer Karen Kay) and how he therefore spent much of his childhood on tour, travelling the UK with her. He then rattled off a dream list of cars that would make most men salivate – a Merc Pullman, Ferrari 550, a Lambo Miura SC and 360 Spider, an Aston Martin DB5, etc.

Then Jay Kay did his lap. Coming the week after Harry Enfield posted such a slow opening gambit, everyone expected Kay to handsomely beat that mark. And that's exactly what he did: his time of 1.48.3 was only two seconds behind The Stig and came complete with a fancy handbrake turn to finish! Delighted, he punched the air in triumph (notably, this was in front of a sparse studio audience, which in the early series were only placed in front of the presenters' chairs rather than the latter-day set-up of a 360-degree crowd). Seeing Jay Kay so excited was the moment when 'Star in a Reasonably Priced Car' became not just an entertaining TV slot, but a national sport.

In the second series, however, ultra-tall supermodel Jodie Kidd astonished everyone by taking three-tenths off Jay Kay's time, even though she could barely fit in the tiny Suzuki Liana. Perhaps viewers shouldn't have been surprised as she was in fact a veteran of the ultra-fast American Gumball Rally and even drove a Maserati Spyder at home. She compared driving fast on the lap to being on a horse, in that it gave her the same adrenaline rush. Later, The Stig revealed that in between corners, Kidd could be heard making 'Giddy up!' sounds.

The Stig told Clarkson with few notable exceptions, pretty much all the celebs he was coaching were highly competitive and keen to win (he also later revealed that in his opinion the most difficult celebrity was Tara Parker-Tomkinson as he felt she wasn't a very good listener). However, not all celebrities are so accomplished and much of the fun of this segment is when the celeb driver is utterly useless. The late great Richard Whiteley ambled in at a woefully slow 2.06 – in fact, both he and Terry Wogan were beaten by blind Bosnia war veteran Billy Baxter, accompanied by Clarkson directing him from the passenger seat.

But perhaps the most infamous early lap was by seasoned actor Michael Gambon towards the end of Series 1. A fan of the show from years back, despite his Shakespearian pedigree and English gentleman appearance he actually owns a Ferrari 348 (a famously difficult prancing horse to drive). He is a considered petrol-head, even taking his skills as far as flying planes and having an engineering workshop at home. Gambon said that he thoroughly enjoyed being trained by The Stig and revealed that the mystery racing driver talked in a French accent. When Gambon did his lap, he said that he didn't even know there was a camera in the car and the look on his face – like that of an angry taxi driver – suggested he wasn't fibbing.

He nearly came off the track several times but the most infamous moment came on the last turn before the finish line, when he lifted up onto two wheels, nearly rolling the car over altogether (Tom Cruise and Michael McIntyre would later do the same). Forever after, that part of the track has been named 'Gambon Corner' in his honour. His time of 1.55 was a wet lap, which left him rather lowly on the board. Interestingly, however, although his two-wheel antics on the corner became the stuff of *Top Gear* legend, The Stig later said Gambon had had the best appreciation of racing lines of anyone in the series thus far. However, Clarkson later referred to the part of the leaderboard with times of 1:51 or slower as the 'Thespian Zone', as there were so many classically trained actors posting such slow times down there.

Over time, the 'Star in a Reasonably Priced Car' feature has become a longer interview with the celebrity in question. Occasionally, however, the presenters make a diversion inspired by their guest. One such silly aside came with the foul-mouthed, but ultra-passionate chef Gordon Ramsay in Series 1, Episode 9. In the studio, Clarkson and Ramsay bemoaned women drivers and vegetarians before Jeremy announced that they had thought of a cunning plan to avoid having to eat dire motorway service station food (a pet hate of his). He'd worked out that if you taped certain cuts of meat to the engine itself and left them under the bonnet on your journey, they would cook as you drove along, thus avoiding the need to pay for vile service station food. He suggested they could even instruct the public on cooking times – for example, a rack of lamb might take two hours at 3000rpm.

You could see Ramsay's face drop as he then realised Clarkson had not only cooked food under the bonnets of three cars on the *Top Gear* test track, but also clearly wanted him to taste it. To Ramsay's credit, he tested the food with real enthusiasm and even critiqued it, albeit saying the lamb was 'Castrol-oily-greasy'. Perhaps he was in a good mood because his lap turned out to be the same as Clarkson's and second only to Jay Kay at the time. Stig fans note: the food was served by the mystery man, the first time he'd been in the studio.

Fellow celebrity chef Jamie Oliver later took his own VW Camper onto the track and The Stig belted it round the circuit while Oliver tried to prepare a salad in the back! Off-camera, The Stig then took Oliver round again in his own Maserati and succeeded in power sliding almost the entire circuit!

There have been three 'Reasonably Priced' cars featured since 2002. For the first seven series, a Suzuki Liana was used, which as Clarkson had revealed retailed for £9,999 precisely. Each car used is the standard road version with only the addition of necessary roll bars, safety seats and harnesses, for obvious reasons.

Apart from Gambon-esque acrobatics, the Liana also suffered a wheel falling off (when Lionel Richie and then Trevor Eve were driving), a dented boot, a broken suspension courtesy of Patrick Kielty, two destroyed clutches (David Soul) and countless mashed brake pads and tyres. For Soul's lap, the car was redecorated in *Starsky & Hutch* styling with a police flashing beacon and the infamous white stripe down the side. On more than one occasion, two Lianas were used and some interviews even comprised footage of both vehicles (although the actual lap times were from a single-car lap).

When the *Doctor Who* actor Christopher Eccleston came on the show, he was allowed to drive an automatic Liana as he did not have a manual licence. Worse still, when Johnny Vegas came along, he hadn't even passed his test at all and so he was given 'L' plates! According to the excellent fan-site, www.jeremyclarkson.co.uk, in its entire service the Liana covered 1,600 laps of the circuit and had its tyres and brakes changed 400 times.

The faithful Liana was replaced for the eighth series by a Chevrolet Lacetti, again retailing at around the £10,000 mark. With the lap time leaderboard now wiped clear and due to the intense competition this part of the show now attracted, the rules for celeb times were tightened, with only five practice laps allowed before a final timed lap was taken. The slowest-ever lap in this model was by Jimmy Carr, who had previously held second place in the Liana behind Ellen MacArthur, but in the Chevrolet he span off and crawled in at a snail-like 2 minutes 8.91 seconds. Billie Piper's lap was deemed 'incomplete' by The Stig, who said she had not completed all the corners: after Clarkson asked the *Top Gear* audience, however, they allowed her time to stand.

Then, at the start of Series 15, the Lacetti was replaced by a Kia cee'd (usually referred to by Clarkson as the 'Cee Apostrophe D'). Rather than simply explain that they had replaced the previous car, in true *Top Gear* fashion the team parked the Chevrolet Lacetti under a pair of 550-feet chimneys at a Northfleet cement works and blew up the monstrous columns while the entire carnage was filmed.

Contrary to the generalisation that is 'The Thespian Zone', the fastest star to date across all three Reasonably Priced Cars is the mega-moviestar Tom Cruise, who appeared in Series 15, Episode

5 during the summer of 2010. He lapped the circuit in the Cee Apostrophe D in 1.44.2, pipping his fellow guest – and co-star in the movie *Knight And Day* – Cameron Diaz by one second. Following Cruise's blistering success, there were many internet rumours saying the time had been fixed so as to pander to the Hollywood heartthrob's profile, an accusation strongly denied by the *Top Gear* producers. There is no evidence to suggest this: indeed, the lap was witnessed by many outside of the core backroom staff plus there are numerous stopwatches, cameras all synched up and even staff on certain parts of the track to ensure no one cuts a corner.

Andy Wilman pointed out that Cruise had turned up early and put more time into his practice than any previous guest; he went on to say that it saddened him that people might try and take the shine off such a fun moment before vehemently refuting any accusations of fixing. It is also worth bearing in mind that Cruise has a fleet of beautiful fast cars and is known to do many of his own stunts; on the day of the lap, he even took out a Bugatti Veyron and reached 190mph on the test track so this was clearly not your everyday celebrity tottering around a lap.

When Formula 1 stars come on the show to do a lap in the Reasonably Priced Car, they are given their own leaderboard, the assumption being it is unfair to list them next to celebrities and other non-professional racing drivers. Some observers have commented that the F1 drivers' times are not much faster than the various famous faces topping the 'Star in a Reasonably Priced Car' leaderboard, but don't be fooled. Neuroscientist Dr Kerry Spackman has worked in Formula 1 for years and explained to the author that this apparently small margin was very misleading: 'When Damon Hill and all these Formula 1 guys go round, it isn't that much quicker than the top [celebrity guests]. A normal car is just so jolly easy to drive; it's so forgiving even when it catches you by surprise. If the Reasonably Priced Car starts to slide out of control, a Formula 1 driver will have enough time to yawn, make a cup of tea and think, "Oh yeah, about now I'll give it a bit of a correction." But that's also why there's no real difference between a Formula 1 driver and the top guys in a Reasonably Priced Car because the car is so benign, so simple and so easy, there's not much you can really do [to be substantially faster]. Obviously *Top Gear* has had a number of celebrities turn up – there are a lot of petrol-heads out there, after all – and they all think they are pretty good but in actual fact, they have no concept, none whatsoever [of the skills of a racing driver].'

Spackman adeptly sums up the appeal of the Star in a Reasonably Priced Car segment: 'Jackie Stewart once said, "There's only two things you can't criticise a man for, one is his prowess in bed and the other is his driving." So many people I've come across fancy themselves as being pretty good at driving but even a very good driver like a saloon or touring car champion isn't up there with F1 drivers. The analogy I would use is that no one would ever say, "You know what? I think I'd take Nadal on in a game of tennis, I think I'd give him a good run for his money." If you've ever sat in a race car with a Formula 1 driver when he's driving in anger (I've sat in a car with a number of drivers), it's incredible. Yet every man fancies themselves as a bit of a good driver.'

The *Top Gear* test track was custom-designed for the show by engineers from Lotus. It is located at Dunsfold Aerodrome in Surrey, which was built in 1942 by the 2nd Battalion Royal Canadian Engineers and constantly used during the Second World War (thereafter it fell into disuse and like many British airfields, was turned into a race track). The track has been cleverly designed to include corners that punish oversteer, others that expose understeer; there are bumps and adverse cambers in difficult places, as well as straights demanding full-throttle power that would frighten anyone but the less-than-lunatic. When Richard Hammond first introduced the track in Episode 1 and talked the viewer through the corners, he claimed this was such a cunning leveller of a car's foibles that it made 0–60 and top speed times 'meaningless'. However, the 1.75 miles of circuit has played host to a party of the greatest supercars ever built and to date, the top of the leaderboard suggests power still rules the day. That said, when the fastest production car ever built – the Bugatti Veyron – first went round, it came only fourth, with Clarkson citing its excessive weight as the problem.

Some of the corners were already in situ, but others – such as Chicago and Hammerhead – have literally been painted onto the track to add extra challenges. According to *Top Gear*, they are repeatedly asked to host track days for fans and one can imagine the demand would be huge, but alas the track is essentially a figure-of-eight and so carnage would at some point prevail.

The track itself is a graveyard for failed celebrity laps but also an automotive Hollywood Walk of Fame, with several corners and names for parts of the track honouring former contestants and incidents. So we have 'Crooner Corner' named after The Stig's famed penchant for easy listening music. Then it's on to Willson, so-called for former *Top Gear* presenter Quentin Willson, the first part of the track where inferior cars start to struggle. Chicago is named not after the Mid-Western city in the USA but for the MOR band that's another Stig favourite; likewise Bacharach, as in Burt. Former producer and *Top Gear* legend Jon Bentley is celebrated with the infamous tyre wall, whose camera shakes if a car travels through fast enough. This is situated at the end of 'The Follow-Through', in itself the most extreme test of a driver's nerve on the track, with even supercars sometimes having to lift slightly to avoid oblivion. But perhaps most famous of all is Gambon – originally dubbed Carpenters after the classic genteel brother/sister duo from the 1970s. Oh, and Hammerhead is so-named because it's shaped like a hammerhead!

Of course, The Stig is the master around this track, but even he is sometimes beaten by the mental power of certain howling supercars. Most famously was a crash in the Koenigsegg, The Stig's biggest mash-up (of more later). There's a rumour that in late-2010, a computer console version of the *Top Gear* test track will be made available within the *Gran Turismo* game.

One other prominent feature of the new *Top Gear* format was the so-called 'Cool Wall'. This was one of many features introduced with the new format to get around a very pragmatic problem: it's so much more demanding to film a car review show in the post-Millennial era because *modern cars are so good*. The dark days of British Leyland that Clarkson has so controversially rebuked over the years are long gone, unionists no longer control the factories and as a rule, most cars coming onto the market have had billions of pounds in development spent on them. Very few modern cars go badly wrong; some even offer 'lifetime warranties', so confident are their manufacturers of the quality; others bought on the high street for relatively modest amounts are quicker than the rally cars of the 1970s.

So to some extent, *Top Gear* are frequently faced with the tricky problem that when a new car comes along to the marketplace, it is very well built, thoughtfully finished and altogether a soundly designed piece of engineering. This is a problem that the show's producer Andy Wilman directly alluded to in a book that he co-wrote with Richard Hammond, *What Not to Drive* (2006). So, apart from stunts and specials, the stars in cars and lengthy features, the show has had to come up with other ways of reviewing cars, the basic staple item on a programme such as this. For the majority of less-glamorous cars, one way of doing this is the so-called 'Cool Wall'.

Each week, photos of cars are held aloft and discussed/berated by the presenters, with occasional interjections from the studio audience, after which the threesome agree which side of the wall they can go on: 'Seriously Uncool', 'Uncool', 'Cool' and 'Sub-Zero'. Each presenter has different and highly subjective criteria for classifying a car's cool factor – for example, Clarkson uses the idea of whether the car would impress his celebrity crush, Kristin Scott Thomas (or more latterly, Fiona Bruce). Other times, he disagrees with Hammond and takes precedence by putting the photo out of reach of the diminutive star (when Clarkson slipped a disc, Hammond got his own back by placing a car photo at the bottom of the board). In Series 4, they also added the 'DB9 Super-Cool Fridge', having reviewed that car in a category of coolness all of its own (later adding another Aston, the Vantage). There has also been the 'Crock/Classic' Mini-Cool Wall for more vintage cars.

One definite rule-of-thumb is that any car owned by one of the presenters – regardless of how super-cool it had previously been – is automatically consigned to the 'Uncool' section. This seems harsh when it traps cars such as the Lamborghini Gallardo Spyder purchased by Jeremy after reviewing it in Series 8, Episode 7. Comparing the convertible Lambo with the new Ferrari 430, he damned the latter (unusual for Clarkson) as boring and serious, while revelling in the madness of the baby Lambo. He openly admitted to being in love with the Gallardo and admits – like love – that his feelings were not necessarily rational (he wasn't a fan of the hard-top Gallardo). So irrational in fact were his emotions that he promptly went and bought one, but in doing so consigned the beautiful supercar to eternity on the 'Uncool' end of the Cool Wall. (Note: the *Top Gear* team seem to like Lambo drop-tops, a style of car that had historically seen numerous supercars turn into badly handling death-traps; when Hammond went on the Paloma bull run, he happily compared the Lambo Murcielago to that adrenaline-fuelled experience.)

The 'Uncool' status bestowed on any presenter's car is perhaps more understandable for James's Fiat Panda, whose picture ended up several metres left of the board in an 'Uncool' anti-Aston section of its own. Usually, automatic 'Uncool' models include hybrids, diesels, most 4x4s, People Carriers and German cars. Worse still, the BMW 3 Series E90 was considered so ugly that it was not placed on the Wall at all.

Although many cars are consigned to oblivion due to entirely subjective reasoning, there are several hard and fast rules for avoiding the 'Uncool' part of the Wall: avoid buying celebrity cars; also those that are 'fashionable' such as Audi TTs or VW Beetles; supercars and sports-cars are not guaranteed shoo-ins; customising, accessorising or souping up an 'Uncool' car won't suddenly make it cool; the cost is irrelevant but the colour isn't; some cars are cool for boys but not for girls (and vice versa) and finally, it's not about an entire brand, it's each individual model.

After a fire on set in the summer of 2007, the 'Cool Wall' enjoyed a sabbatical before returning for Series 11 and is now long since established as a vital part of the show. As an aside, the *Top Gear* team also sell a *Cool Wall Activity Sticker Book* with its very own 'Cool Wall' poster, which you can put up and then attach various stickers of cars where you think they deserve to go. There is also a 'Cool Wall' app for the iPhone, where you can play along, too. I have both, naturally.

CHAPTER 6

Caravans

There's a conker tree at the end of my lane. My two little petrol-heads have just discovered the joy of collecting conkers and we are currently soaking the two largest in special vinegar-and-water solution prior to launching an all-conkering (apologies) assault on the English championships. It's a fabled and longstanding rite of passage for any self-respecting boy and his father. Of course, when you grow up, you still *want* to play conkers but society dictates it really wouldn't be decent for grown men to continue with such childish games ... unless of course you work on *Top Gear*.

With Series 1 flying the flag for testosterone-fuelled challenges and supercars, it was clear that the new version of *Top Gear* would not shy away from the more dramatic world of motoring. The on-screen chemistry between the three presenters was immediately apparent from May's first show in Series 2 and this is often best seen when they are basically fooling around. And what better to fool around with than a caravan?

The series has a hate-hate relationship with the little white traffic jam-makers. Over the years, Clarkson and chums have made no secret of their intense dislike for the homes-on-wheels (perhaps on a par only with cyclists). This has manifested itself into numerous hilarious stunts. The first time that the innocent 'van' was desecrated came in Series 2, Episode 1, when they burnt the show's debut caravan with the afterburner of a drag-racing jet car; however, the tense relationship really worsened in Series 2, Episode 6. For this show, the team tested the Mitsubishi Lancer Evolution VIII versus the Subaru Impreza WRX STI. After the clip had been shown, Clarkson revealed an out-take of himself in one of the cars, going berserk as the crew followed a caravan up ahead at a snail's pace. He went on to describe the hotel-on-wheels as 'the bane of our lives'. Clearly, something had to be done.

In response, the *Top Gear* team attempted to set a new land speed record for caravan towing. The current record stood at 128.8mph, so they sent new boy James May to a track to see if he could top that. Using a turbo-charged Mitsubishi Evo 7, which could generate more than 700bhp, a stunt driver called 'Lee' (notably not The Stig as would be the norm in later series) and an Abbey GT 214 caravan, they attempted – and failed – to beat the record time. A combination of cross winds, caravan kitchenette window blow-outs and ultimately, the Evo blowing a piston defeated them. Still, May had his revenge and dropped the caravan from a great height off a crane at the end of the show.

In Series 3 (otherwise largely dull when it came to fun features), the schoolboys/presenters took the caravan owner's car of choice – a Volvo 240 estate – and attempted to see how many caravans it could jump over, Evel Knievel style. They chose the car because it was 'the caravan's friend'. 'Every summer they ruin our roads,' declared Hammond, before going on to slaughter caravans as transport vermin. So, how many caravans could the Volvo jump? Not many, it transpired.

The vendetta was taken up a notch in Series 4 while playing darts with cars. Using a gas-powered cannon normally reserved for mad stunts in James Bond movies, Hammond and May perched themselves on the top of a quarry and proceeded to fire six old cars at a dartboard, way down below. After several disputed shots, they decided to clarify the bullseye with the placement of the ultimate target: a caravan. With telling poignancy, the very last car is a caravan-loving Volvo and Hammond triumphs by hitting the bullseye/caravan perfectly after which he announces: 'We are all winners because the caravan bought it!'

However, it was in Series 5 that *Top Gear* revealed their most vicious-ever caravan abuse when James May joined Hammond to play the aforementioned 'Caravan Conkers'. It was actually the much-maligned Health and Safety Executive (HSE) who inspired this challenge after they had declared in 2009 that children wanting to play the age-old game should wear safety goggles (Clarkson has gone on record as calling the HSE 'the PPD', which stands for 'The Programme Prevention Department').

Two enormous green cranes were provided by the same specialist team who had worked with the car-launching hydrogen cannon for the previous car darts sequence. Hammond and May then proceeded to engage in a three-round competition of conkers using a selection of six of Britain's finest fibreglass homes, such as the Musketeer, the Sprite and of course, the Ford Mondeo of the caravan world, the ubiquitous Monza. Before battle commenced, there was much talk of 3-er and 9-er conkers, with each presenter displaying a genuine glint that betrayed a childhood spent playing the actual game in the playground.

The caravans were painted a brownish-red to look like conkers but unfortunately the emulsion paint virtually washed off in the rain before filming began. Suspending the caravans high in the air and 50 feet apart, Round 1 went to Hammond's heavy Piper model, but May struck back with a surprise win for his Sprite Musketeer in Round 2 against the much-fancied Monza, only for Hammond to sneak a victory with a high-spec Abbey GT in Round 3, a caravan with hot and cold running water and a separate bathroom, no less, which must have given him the edge. It was all pointless, puerile and utterly great fun. May pretty much summed up the feeling of any 'bigger boy' watching this feature, when he said: 'It's better than working in a bank!'

Although this was perhaps their most violent demolition of the hated towing beast, undoubtedly the best *Top Gear* caravan jinx came in Series 14, when May went up in a caravan airship, racing Hammond on the ground in a Lamborghini. The very sight of the caravan strapped to the base of a Zeppelin-esque airship was perhaps one of the most bizarre of any episode of *Top Gear*, but things quickly started to go wrong. The original plan had been to land the odd-looking flying machine on a cricket pitch somewhere in Cambridgeshire (and ideally in the middle of a match for obvious dramatic effect) but strong winds rapidly blew the caravan airship off-course so it crash-landed in a farmer's field near the A428. Although the tabloids ran pieces about May's 'lucky escape', in fact no emergency services were needed, not least because the accident was at a recorded speed of 2mph. You walk at 4mph, so the 'crash' actually resembled falling over ... slowly. (Note: May once suffered a sprained wrist while 'travelling at speed' in a shopping trolley for *Top Gear Live* in 2006).

The humble caravan also found itself repeatedly battered as an indirect result of otherwise unrelated challenges, such as the time when the team were testing the resilience of a 911 Turbo and decided it would be a good idea to drop the German car from a great height onto a caravan. Later, the roles were flipped for a Toyota Hilux feature, when they dropped the caravan from a great height onto the pick-up – proving beyond doubt that despite their complaints about the 'van', if nothing else it is a highly versatile vehicle. Hammond has also tried to see how far a car towing a caravan can jump in response to the same stunt being done by the rival show, *Fifth Gear*.

Meanwhile, James May slept with the devil on his show, *Oz and James Drink to Britain*, in which he travelled the nation drinking with famed wine connoisseur Oz Clarke (surprisingly, you would expect May to be a nifty vino tippler, but he's actually a dedicated bitter man; he has also said: 'I've never quite trusted water, I don't think it's entirely healthy.'). May drove around the isles in a predictably British Rolls-Royce Corniche Cabriolet, but he risked the wrath of his *Top Gear* colleagues by spending good money on a 1978 Sprite Caravan for their sleeping quarters. Judas!

Of course the most obvious thing to do with a caravan is to go on holiday and that's exactly what the *Top Gear* team did in Episode 6, Series 8. They bought a lovely Elddis for £3,000 and attached it to a Kia, the Caravan Club's 'Towing Car of the Year' no less (Clarkson's own opinion of the brand is slightly less positive, dubbing it 'soulless'). The team set off for Dorset and before long there was a huge traffic jam behind them, with the three presenters cringing with embarrassment in the Kia. Hammond even declared: 'I can't bear the shame!' Clarkson made the point that while the Caravan Club claim their members will pull over and let traffic queues past periodically, he has never once seen this in 30 years of driving.

After the *Top Gear* dog ('TG') was sick in the car, they finally made it to the caravan site where they initially parked so badly that they wrecked a neighbouring tent, before Hammond went off for a cup of tea with the site's owner. At one point, Clarkson pulled out an AK-47 rifle, which he felt he might need for a weekend away with James May.

After a bad night's sleep, the next morning they went for a country walk with a grumpy Clarkson moaning about boredom; eventually they stopped to use their binoculars to spot interesting cars on a nearby A-road. On their return, Clarkson rustled up some food ... only to set fire to the caravan! After various abortive attempts to put out the blaze, the next-door tent also catches fire. Eventually they make a swift exit as fire crews and sirens blare out, as if to advertise their stupidity. So, an advert for the joys of caravanning this was not.

Notably, this particular feature did attract criticism in some quarters for being a little too scripted and forced; the team happily admit the 'accidental' caravan fire was staged for dramatic effect and that they paid the Emergency Services around £1,000 to attend the filming. Frankly, who cares? It was hilarious!

Later, when appearing on the comic TV show *Room 101* – where guests list certain items they hate – Clarkson sent a shower of things he detested into oblivion, including flies, *The Last Of The Summer Wine*, club-house snobbery at golf courses, vegetarians and ... caravans! (Comedian Sean Lock later put Clarkson himself in his own selection for oblivion.)

Of course kids in the post-Millennial world of stringent Health and Safety Regulations aren't always allowed to play conkers. The *Top Gear* presenters might possibly argue that the same ban should apply to adults driving caravans....

CHAPTER 7

'How Hard Can It Be?'

Top Gear's lavish production does not come cheap. According to some sources, a conservative estimate for a 'normal' show would be in excess of £100,000. However, executive producer Andy Wilman says they spend that 'on crisps'. If the figure is wildly short of the mark, it still looks like good value to the BBC, who sell the programme on to numerous countries where it is watched by 350 million people. When you rake in the licensing, merchandising sales and rights as well as peripheral earnings, it makes for a sizeable income stream against the original cost. Given that *The Simpsons* is rumoured to cost over $1 million per episode, that might just make *Top Gear* look like the TV bargain of the century.

It's easy to see where all the money gets spent. One enduring feature of the programme has been the various madcap challenges the *Top Gear* team set themselves. At first, these challenges were more often quite short clips and stunts – a bus jumping motorcycles, trying to run a car on poo or a nun driving a monster truck, for example. However, over time longer features started to creep in, often introduced by the presenters complaining about a certain problem within motoring, or perhaps a tricky issue facing car manufacturers preceded by the words, 'How hard can it be?' Although the phrase was not at first an official segment of the show, repeated use has turned it into a *Top Gear* perennial and one that is usually followed by a groan from the audience as everybody knows calamity is about to strike.

A personal favourite in this category is the so-called 'Toybota' challenge, in the third episode of Series 8. This was a frankly ridiculous, laughable yet brilliant challenge. Back in the studio, the trio had been lamenting the lack of a viable car that could also drive into and travel through water. Periodically, various zany British inventions promised to revolutionise this area of transport but let's face it, they never really caught on. Clarkson found this weird because we are, after all, an island nation and so *Top Gear* decided to do something about it.

The production team gave the three colleagues just two days to make their own amphibious cars, without actually telling them what the end challenge would be. Clarkson perhaps not surprisingly goes for the full power option, buying a Toyota Hilux truck – he named the good ship 'Toybota', a good choice of vehicle for sure. But then he wanted to strap two mega-powerful 500bhp outboard motors to the back of it. The expert brought in to save the presenter from imminent death watched aghast and had to explain to Clarkson that so much power was enough to empty most harbours and would make his Toyota un-sailable. Undeterred, Jeremy then proceeded to try out some sample boats and until the last second still insisted that they needed twin engines. He was also averse to making any form of hull, saying the whole point of the exercise was to make a car that could sail, rather than a boat that looked like a car.

Hammond was a little less ambitious in the power stakes and opted for a trusty/rusty VW Camper. He rolled up wearing motorbike leathers and quickly turned the traveller's van of choice into a houseboat. Then James May sailed in – literally – with his elegant Triumph Herald, complete with mast and sails. He seemed at ease with the prospect and was even said to be a 'sailor' although it later transpired that it was 31 years since he'd last set foot in a sailing boat! However, his effort did not get off to a good start when the car wouldn't even start. Cue much hilarity from his rivals.

While all this was going on, it's hard not to reflect again on the logistics of this entirely ludicrous piece of television. For a start, the presenters would need at least three separate film crews to capture the respective efforts of each design idea. Then there would be the mechanics of each car/boat, bringing in the expertise to transform them into amphibious sea-faring vessels (although Clarkson's 'expertise' seemed to consist of smashing the Hilux with a sledgehammer). And all the materials ... and fuel ... and insurance, and so on ... Imagine organising all of this. The end result is a brilliant feature, but one that only lasts a small segment of a one-hour TV show.

Amid a sarcastic comment from Clarkson that, 'It's the coldest March for 20 years because of global warming', the intrepid trio meet up at the calm, still waters of a rural lakeside. May's Herald was last to roll up and simply drove effortlessly into the water. Hammond, meanwhile, drove down a concrete ramp, broke the flywheel as he entered the water and rendered his vessel powerless before he'd even started. Eventually, he borrowed an outboard motor and they all set sail.

By this point a large crowd had gathered and to be fair, it

would make for a fairly odd sight! Ultimately, Hammond's car-boat capsized and he was forced to launch himself towards Clarkson's vessel for safety. However, that eventually capsized too after two miles and on the very last bend of the harbour, so it was left to May's more understated invention to 'triumph' (although even then he only managed to reverse halfway out of the water). Of course, it was all classic *Top Gear*.

Yet in the production office, there was a sense that with a little more time and thought, the amphibious car idea might have achieved more so two series later, the idea was revisited. This time the challenge was far more demanding: to actually drive to Dover and cross the English Channel to Calais – a preposterous notion, really.

This time the cars arrived looking much more sea-worthy. So, we have Jeremy's Nissan truck – christened the Nissank – with a stabilised outboard motor and endless amounts of internal welding to make it watertight. He even added some huge metal drums to aid buoyancy and was so confident of his vessel that he took a fishing rod with him for those quiet moments when he would be miles ahead in the race! Hammond turned up in a Volkswagen Transporter, albeit only in name, as it really looked far more like a tugboat; May's vessel was the Triumph, being almost exactly the same as before with a few minor additions that he explained, but no one else really understood.

It was clear that the production team knew this was a much more difficult challenge as all three presenters were now wearing life-vests. Indeed, Clarkson's pride came before a fall as they drove into the channel only to find the high winds and choppy waves too much within a matter of minutes. Clarkson and Hammond seemed genuinely frightened while May failed abysmally to even leave the harbour side. Day One of the shoot was eventually aborted and they decided to return the next morning when better, calmer weather was predicted. Hammond fared well initially but ultimately his car-boat sank; he and May were left drinking tea from a flask in the sea before clambering aboard Clarkson's admirably buoyant and working vessel.

With typical *Top Gear* gusto, they then announced that they were about to smash Richard Branson's one hour and forty minutes record for crossing the channel in an amphibious car, which of course they came nowhere near. However, after dodging mountainous ferries and tankers, they did eventually sight land and although they'd missed Calais, somehow they managed to scramble the odd car-boat onto dry land, much to the total bemusement of several hundred sunbathing French holiday-makers. They had landed in Sangatte, the highly controversial French town mostly famed in Britain for the illegal immigrants who used to stream across to the UK from this port. One is left to imagine how Jeremy Clarkson and his famously acid tongue explained to the watching Frenchmen what they were doing.

In the *Top Gear* studio perched on a sloping pedestal sits another battered old Toyota Hilux, the star of one of the show's most popular challenges ever: is the Toyota pick-up truck really indestructible? It was way back in Series 3, Episode 5 when the team first screened an Australian advert for the truck and pointed out that all the anti-American militia around the world seem to be filmed on BBC News driving those faithful old pick-ups, packed full of machine guns. So, in an attempt to find out just how strong the Toyota was, the trio bought a 13-year-old Hilux 2.4 litre Diesel for £1,000, with over 190,000 miles on the clock.

The team then put together a series of what can only be termed multiple attempts at grievous bodily harm on the unsuspecting truck. So we see them driving it down steep stony stairs, scraping it along walls, crashing into a (soon-to-be-notorious) chestnut tree, leaving it standing in the Severn

Estuary as the tide came in, dropping it from a crane, driving it through a wooden shed (the *Top Gear* production office, apparently), dropping a caravan onto its roof, smashing a demolition crane's wrecking ball into its rear and even setting fire to it. Amazingly, after all the abuse, it still worked!

The feature actually over-ran the episode because the truck refused to be killed. So, in the sixth part of the series, we witnessed the finale: they put the pick-up on top of a tower block, which was then demolished (how did it get there?) with Andy Wilman's '£100,000 just for crisps' budget. After the rubble and dust had settled, a mechanic came on site and without spare parts and only the aid of basic tools, he spent a brief few minutes under the bonnet. He reconnected the battery, put some diesel in it... Yes, it still worked! Clarkson called it 'automotive greatness'.

Aside from the brilliant television feature, it doesn't take a genius to work out the commercial effect of 350 million viewers around the world seeing this remarkable machine treated to such abuse only for it still to work. All hail the Toyota Hilux, one of *Top Gear*'s greatest-ever features!

Perhaps one of the series' most famous and brilliantly executed challenges was when the team decided to turn a Robin Reliant into a Space Shuttle (although they did not actually ask the ill-fated question, 'How hard can it be?', this stunt certainly falls into that category). I can't quite imagine the production meeting when the idea first came up but clearly no one dismissed it as absurd, so in Episode 4 of Series 9 (a very strong period for such mad features), we have the team working with space engineers to create the impossible: a three-wheel re-useable space rocket built from a car normally associated with Peckham's finest market traders. Perhaps only *Top Gear* could think of this and certainly, only *Top Gear* would actually go and do it! The show's production notes class this as 'easily *Top Gear*'s most ambitious film'.

Again, like the 'Toybota' feature, this is a stunning example of a clearly ludicrous idea being executed with considerable cost and precision. Despite the hilarious premise, they set about the challenge with no expense spared. The mechanical process started from a fairly simplistic base with Hammond saying they chose the Reliant because it was light, cheap and 'pointy'. The team called on the skills of The Rocketeers – the same team who helped them send a Mini down a ski-jump in an earlier challenge.

Very quickly, however, the project escalated and within a few seconds of screen time, we are shown an engineer's workshop containing a complex structure with a maze of high-quality welding and metal components carefully woven into its framework. Huge solid rocket fuel boosters towered above the Robin Reliant. Hammond and May were clearly stunned by the progress (Clarkson was absent, having declared this the most stupid idea ever and so he refused to get involved). For all the hilarity, this was not an actual gag – if successful, the Robin would become the largest non-commercial rocket *ever* to be launched in Europe.

Next up, they went to a high-tech wind tunnel where at first they just stood in it with the *Top Gear* dog (complete with goggles), but soon the boffins joined them to put a scale model of the Robin Reliant through its paces in order to check aerodynamic prowess. Needless to say, it was pretty useless and the bespectacled boffin-type offered no glimmer of optimism for its chances in space.

Pushing the boundaries still further, a scale model of the Robin was made and attached to a very expensive remote control plane, the idea being that once the rocket had flown in space, it would need guiding back to earth for its landing (even the usually daring Richard Hammond was not about to climb into this machine). So by now they had involved rocket engineers, remote control champion racers and tech-mad wind-tunnel geniuses.

The launch site was on a military base in Newcastle and once more the costs kept racking up: so we saw cranes, haulage trucks and endless personnel putting the Robin Reliant rocket in place. Despite the comic overview, the stunt was in fact highly dangerous, not least due to the presence of the volatile solid fuel mix of nitrous oxide and rubber – essentially laughing gas and old tyres. Worse still, the launch site was a military base renowned for having scores of unexploded bombs hidden underground.

Finally, the big moment came and Hammond and May were visibly exhilarated when the rocket launched into the sky. It was truly glorious and when the solid rocket fuel boosters detached on command, the engineers and presenters quite literally danced for joy. Their joy turned to despair as the second-phase rockets failed to detach and the overly heavy car-shuttle plummeted to earth, hitting the ground and exploding into a massive fireball. In the meteoric collision, nothing was left. The car was completely destroyed, but one badly burnt wing with a Union Jack sticker intact was recovered and now sits in the *Top Gear* office.

So, being critical, they didn't succeed in the challenge of making a re-useable space shuttle from a Robin Reliant. Apart from the fact that it's a pretty big ask, they did complete their challenge but for the final failure, though. So we are left with the teasing question: had the second-phase rockets detached on schedule, would the shuttle have landed safely and been a total success? We'll never know and it's pretty likely that BBC budgets will prevent them from ever trying again ...

The list of more daft *Top Gear* challenges reads like a surreal selection of crazy ideas that a bunch of young boys have dreamt up after perhaps having their first-ever pint of beer:

making a convertible People Carrier; grannies doing doughnuts and handbrake turns; can a rally pit team strip and rebuild a car faster than four women get ready for a night out?; can a stretch limo jump over a wedding party?; how many motorcycles can a double-decker bus jump over?; how many bouncy castles can an ice-cream van jump?; what's the best wig for driving in an open-top?; how easy is it to create a life-size remote controlled car?; can they beat the record for the most complete sideways rolls in a car ...

As Richard Hammond said when he was about to launch the Robin Reliant into space: 'If you're eight years old, you probably want to watch this ...'

CHAPTER 8

The Top Gear Specials: 'US Road Trip'

Of course, all this japery with blowing up caravans, encouraging nuns to skid, breaking numerous speed records and generally acting out endless schoolboy fantasies with cars makes for great TV, but where *Top Gear* really raise the bar is during their more substantial challenges. These are best exemplified by the small handful of so-called specials they have attempted. There have been four specials within actual series ('USA', 'Botswana', 'Vietnam' and 'Bolivia') plus two further stand-alone programmes ('*Top Gear* Winter Olympics' and 'The Polar Special').

In this writer's opinion, the best special of them all is the fabulous 'US Road Trip', first screened in Episode 3 of Series 9. The team hate fly/drive holidays and contest that the logistics of this type of trip and the myriad of problems encountered means that it's not a holiday at all, but a living hell. So, the premise was simple enough: is it possible to fly to America and buy a car more cheaply than you can hire one for a fortnight? Thereafter, can you travel through four US states and then sell the same car and get most of your money back? Equipped with just $1,000 each, they set about finding out ... and very nearly never made it back.

Clarkson's relationship – if there is one at all – with the USA is strained at best. He calls it 'the United States of Paranoia' and has been openly critical of Barack Obama, particularly in the aftermath of the President's acidic attacks on BP following the Gulf of Mexico oil spillage of 2010. Clarkson points out the absurdity of the fact that in the US, you need a permit for most things except buying firearms.

The plan was to create *Top Gear*'s very own road movie. As inspiration, the production crew used famous American flicks such as *Thelma & Louise* and *National Lampoon's Vacation*. Initially, the trip was meant to be merely a Cheap Car Challenge spread over two segments, but as the backroom staff researched and prepared the film, it became clear that they had enough scope to produce a lengthy and highly entertaining stand-alone programme. Surprisingly, it is also noted on their website as one of the most gruelling shoots ever, even taking into account the later 'Polar' and 'African' specials.

The team flew into the US and stayed at a very upmarket hotel before the trip began. On the first day, the trio was sent out to the rather salubrious areas of Miami to purchase a classic American car for their $1,000. With every dealership they tried, the options became more and more limited until eventually they were left with a handful of dishevelled-looking car lots in the openly dangerous parts of town. Dealerships such as 'We Aim To Please Motors' and 'Adolf's Cars' are all visited. At one point, Clarkson radios Hammond to tell him not to drive any further along a certain road as he will almost definitely get shot. Even the car dealers admit this, proudly showing Clarkson their rifles and handguns, explaining theft was a big problem and that a sniper's sight was entirely justifiable just in case the thief managed to start driving away. Clarkson was on brilliant form, seemingly unmoved by all this and even began to barter for the cars, by saying: 'How much murdering goes on here?'

However, the choice of car was limited and their final selection is hilarious: Clarkson bought a battered Chevrolet Camaro RS, principally because it's 'very popular with murderers'. It's a typical American muscle car, with a five-litre V8 engine, but this particular model also came with no air-conditioning, a broken rev counter, a radio with only one (gospel) station and just three previous murderers. He even found an old shirt hidden under the bodywork, which they presumed was from the last victim of the previous owner. When Clarkson took the Camaro back to the team's luxury hotel for the night, no one had forewarned the valet and he promptly asked the presenter to leave the premises.

On his first-ever trip to the USA and complete with cowboy hat and boots, Hammond rocked up in a Dodge Ram pick-up truck. James May was last – as usual – and arrived in an enormous 1989 Cadillac Sedan, which was so big that Hammond observed that it was a long walk simply to stroll around it. It had newspaper repairs to some of the bodywork and a broken number-plate saying 'Titanic'. May didn't care, he loved it. Meanwhile, Clarkson was already homesick: 'Florida is full of awful old people, fat people, nasty insects, people who offer you cheese and then shoot you!'

They all set off north out of Miami for a 90-mile trip along the highway to a race track. Funnily enough, the *Top Gear* team later revealed that one of the hardest parts of the show's production was finding a track in NASCAR-loving southern states that wasn't just an oval. This, according to Clarkson, is because having both right- and left-hand bends is too complicated for Americans. Eventually they located Moroso Motorsports Park, which was also infested with alligators.

Challenge One within the special was a timed lap around Moroso and for this, they introduced The Stig's American cousin, a very overweight racing driver wearing identical white racing overalls and helmet, said to be a CIA experiment gone wrong. He even emerged out of a classic white-trash trailer. The Camaro won in 1.09 minutes, easily ahead of May's lumbering Cadillac, which Hammond admitted had aged him just waiting to finish.

The second challenge asked the trio to accelerate to 50mph before slamming on their brakes to avoid plunging into an alligator-infested pond. They all managed to survive ... just! Then they were able to set off for stage three, an 800-mile road trip to New Orleans in the sweltering heat and humidity of the southern states. After running out of fuel and fixing a flat battery, they finally got started but by now Clarkson was extremely grumpy with the USA, warning the viewer that if they were thinking of going there, they should know that 'everybody's very fat, everybody's very stupid and everybody's very rude. It's not the holiday programme, it's the truth!' By this point the viewer was left eager for Clarkson & Co. to launch a no-holds-barred version of *Holiday*!

After a pit-stop to fit a barbecue to the back of his pick-up, an internal shower to Clarkson's Camaro and a clothes hanger (!) to May's Sedan, the team were informed that the only food they could eat that night was road-kill. Taking the names 'Brokeback', 'The Murderer' and 'The Captain', the trio then abort their attempts at CB radio, saying truckers only ever talk about the weather and prostitutes. Finally, they found their campsite for the night, only for Clarkson to disappear while May and

Hammond argued over who was going to 'peel' the only road-kill they'd found: a squirrel. So, where had Jezza gone?

What other show on TV would strap a cow to a car? Well, Alan Partridge once did, but he's not a real person. It's a fantastically surreal moment when Clarkson's Camaro appears over the horizon with a huge, bloated cow tied to its roof. The heifer in question had died of natural causes by the side of the road (although this didn't stop some *Top Gear* snipers complaining to the BBC about animal cruelty). In fact, it had died some days before being mounted to Clarkson's Camaro and once attached to the roof, the dead beast quickly began dripping bodily fluids all over the bodywork. For months after the film, the crew found their cameras, clothing and equipment smelling of dead cow.

While May slept, Clarkson and Hammond sabotaged his air-con and the night-vision footage of them sniggering as they ripped out his wiring is really no more than two naughty schoolboys up to no good on a field trip away from home. This particular clip perfectly sums up an undeniable part of the *Top Gear* appeal: it's a private joke shared by 350 million people, the equivalent of being invited in to the popular gang at school who play all the best pranks, but without having to take any of the risks. It's a voyeur's nirvana of practical jokes and dressing-room banter.

By now, all three presenters had become attached to their old bangers but the next challenge would not only deface the cars but also see one of *Top Gear*'s most genuinely sinister moments. The idea of 'baiting' rednecks was not a new one – originally there had been talk of driving a pink Smart Car as far as possible across Texas without being attacked. However, eventually the production crew issued the trio with a different challenge: each was allowed to paint provocative slogans on their rivals' cars. So, Hammond daubed Clarkson's car with the words 'Country &

Western is rubbish' and 'Nascar sucks' – given both are staples of Deep South life, this was a bad start. May's car was adorned with Clarkson's slogans 'Hillary For President' and it's worth bearing in mind that in the Republican-loving south Mrs Clinton is seen by many as the political Antichrist. Worst still – and as it turned out most dangerous of all – were the bright pink slogans that James May painted on Hammond's car: 'Man Love Rules' and 'I am Bi'. Given Hammond was sporting Aviator sunglasses, a cowboy hat plus boots and was constantly chewing gum – in other words, a southern cowboy stereotype – this choice of car graffiti turned out to be one provocation too far. Hammond had jokingly said the challenge was a 'once in a lifetime opportunity to get Jeremy killed' but he didn't know then how close he was to being frighteningly correct.

The convoy pulled up for petrol in a Bible-belt town called, bizarrely, Baghdad. Events soon took a nasty turn as they started to fill up. Suddenly the female station owner stormed out and started to shout at the trio, with one incensed comment caught on-camera being, 'Are you gay and looking to see how long it takes to get beat up in a Hick town?' The presenters were lost for words and clearly unnerved, even Clarkson, but it was about to get much worse: she disappeared to get 'the boys' and before long, a pick-up full of very large and scary-looking men skidded into the forecourt. Moments later, rocks began to crash down on the presenters' cars as well as those of the crew. Genuinely fearing for their safety, the *Top Gear* convoy sped off. The appalled southerners gave chase and the screen footage was even left blank for a few moments when the team realised they could be in big trouble. After a frantic stop to hastily wash off the offending graffiti and a frenzied race to the county border, as in an unexpected real-life horror movie such as *Jeepers Creepers*, both trio and crew eventually made it to safety.

Clarkson was left to rue the whole frightening episode: 'In certain parts of America, people have started to mate with vegetables!' On-camera, he admits that he's now so homesick that he pines for a homosexual British flight attendant to serve him tea and scones.

The brilliant piece of television came to a close with devastating poignancy: they arrived in New Orleans after all their tomfoolery and that redneck incident, only to suddenly be brought back down to earth by the horrific devastation caused to that city by Hurricane Katrina. The dynamic brilliantly brings home the human cost of this natural disaster. As the three drove round what looked like a war zone, their faces were genuinely pallid, open-mouthed and speechless at the blitzed landscape. Jeremy asks how America can sleep at night knowing New Orleans is still in such a mess one year after the hurricane struck. Suddenly, all thoughts of selling their cars and winning any challenge were gone; eventually they worked with a local mission to give the cars away to people whose lives had been wrecked by the storm.

Back in Blighty, Clarkson was still clearly exasperated and the following week's column in *The Times* made no attempt to hide his contempt for much of what he had just seen. Having kissed the ground when he landed back in Blighty, he proceeded to rail against the paranoia, the bureaucracy, the conservatism and litigation culture in what he called America's 'police state'.

When the team reunited in the studio to screen the trip, they revealed that in New Orleans an American lawyer had expressed her disappointment at the car they'd given away, saying it was different to what she'd thought had been offered, and apparently even threatening to sue for misrepresentation. James May was safe, though – he couldn't even give his Cadillac away! This masterful *Top Gear* special ends by rightfully being described as a 'proper *Boy's Own* adventure', before Clarkson concludes they have learnt two important lessons: yes, you can buy rather than rent and second, don't go to America. Genius!

CHAPTER 9

The Stig: Top Gear's Tame Racing Driver

As typified by the inclusion of Stig's American cousin in the superb 'US Road Trip' special, the brilliant presenting talents of the three main characters in *Top Gear* are substantially complemented by the show's 'tame racing driver', a cartoon character which had, in a very short space of time, become a central part of the programme's massive appeal.

At the time of writing, the real identity of The Stig has recently been the subject of a High Court dispute between the BBC and HarperCollins, publishers of the life story of a certain racing driver. *Top Gear* fans were shocked and excited in equal measure when it was announced that the man behind the famous white helmet had written his autobiography and was therefore about to reveal one of television's most closely guarded secrets but for now, let's rewind and trace the origins and history of one of modern TV's most famous images.

The Stig wasn't always so well known. For the debut

appearance on the first show of the new *Top Gear*, the character was a pragmatic and safe necessity. All three of *Top Gear*'s presenters are known to be very capable drivers indeed, far superior to the man on the street, but the quantity and speed of so many of the cars reviewed meant it made sense to have a 'professional' driver to really give the cars a lashing around the track.

So Andy Wilman and Jeremy Clarkson dreamt up the idea of employing a professional racing driver, who would remain anonymous at all times. There were a number of contenders who might fit the bill, but they eventually plumped for Perry McCarthy. Clarkson approached McCarthy at a party also attended by their mutual friend, Damon Hill. He explained that they wanted an anonymous racing driver for the show and that he would be called The Gimp – inspired by the silent masked figure in a particularly brutal scene from *Pulp Fiction*. Perry was interested, but not if they used that name, so Wilman and Clarkson flagged up a moniker they'd first heard used to describe new boys at Repton: The Stig was born.

Early Stig was a much less refined caricature at this point. Clarkson made his infamous gag about racing drivers having 'tiny little brains and worthless opinions' and also pointed out that they were usually very dull, something he termed 'Mansell Syndrome'. They didn't know The Stig's real name and didn't want to – all they wanted him to do was to go out on track and drive fast.

The Stig's first feature in the Zonda is then run and the all-black mystery driver clearly seen wearing green gloves rather than matching black ones. Also, the camera angles at this point are from the rear left passenger seats, rather than up close to The Stig from the front passenger seat, as became the norm in later series. The original angle actually showed more of the racetrack from The Stig's viewpoint and was in fact a very interesting approach. Back in the studio, the presenters apologised for the sounds of the Lounge that The Stig was playing, claiming he played this elevator music to calm himself down on track (maybe his dubious musical tastes were inspired by Clarkson, himself a huge Genesis fan; he'd even written sleeve notes to their box set, *Selling England by the Pound*). Notably, The Stig drove the Zonda so fast that Hammond then issued a challenge to any company who had a production car that they thought could beat its time.

Within a few episodes, The Stig's listening habits were universally abhorred and have since been the subject of much analysis over the years. Suffice to say, you wouldn't really want to have a long motorway journey with him, listening as he does to such music as Prog Rock, power ballads, jingles, Elton John, Abba, Chas & Dave, pan pipes, speeches, talking books, Morse Code and whale songs, to name but a few.

Each appearance by The Stig is pre-empted by a weird introduction and over the years these bizarre descriptions have taken on a life of their own; initially they did not happen with every appearance on screen and if they did, they would only be a brief one-liner such as 'His Holiness The Stig!' However, over time the introductions increasingly began to reveal odd snippets about this mysterious character, usually taking the form of 'Some say ...' followed by, 'All we know is he's called The Stig!'

Personal characteristics include having a left nipple shaped like the race track at the Nürburgring, his skin apparently has the same texture as a dolphin's, if you tune your radio to 88.4 you can hear his thoughts, after making love he bites the head off his partner, his earwax tastes of Turkish Delight, he's banned from Chichester, he isn't machine-washable, his tears are adhesive and if he caught fire then he would burn for 1,000 days.

As mentioned, the very first Stig was in fact the revered racing driver Perry McCarthy. Stepney-born McCarthy has a long and varied history of racing some of the fastest cars on the planet so he was perfectly equipped to be the show's test driver. A former Formula 1 driver for Andrea Moda, he also tested cars for Benetton, Arrows, Williams and BMW F1 before injury ended his career. Perry was once dubbed 'racing's unluckiest driver' but went on to build a hugely successful career in Le Mans. His reputation for being passionate about his chosen sport was confirmed when he once returned to a race circuit just nine days after his appendix had ruptured. He qualified for that race but was apparently withdrawn by his own team's doctors when they noticed his stitches had burst and his overalls were soaked in blood. During his career, he suffered some big crashes, including one at 170mph that his hero Ayrton Senna said he was lucky to have survived. McCarthy already knew Wilman and Clarkson and so when they approached him with the idea on that fateful night, he was delighted to be asked. At this stage, the secrecy was just 'a bit of fun' and he has since opined that no one could have ever imagined that the character would capture the public's imagination as it has.

McCarthy has since revealed that there had been plans to have him as a presenter on the show a few series in, not masked and hidden, but unfortunately this never transpired. He also quashed rumours that there were several Stigs in those early series, stating that it was always him apart from two occasions when other commitments prevented him from playing the role, at which point Julian Bailey – a former Formula 1 driver who raced for the Tyrrell and Lotus teams – stood in.

Perry enjoyed the cloak-and-dagger requirements of the job. Speaking to the *Mirror* in August 2010, he gave some fascinating insights into his role as The Stig: 'At first, it was great fun. I lost count of the times I'd be standing in a bar and

some guy would be going, "Of course, it's Michael Schumacher."
I never said anything.'

He has also said that he often played the role 24/7 when
working at the BBC. So, he would go in full costume into the BBC
canteen and even keep his visor in place when trying to drink
coffee through a straw or shovel sandwiches in through the small
opening. Perhaps best of all, as Gambon suggested, Perry often
spoke in a French accent – albeit faked – for extra mystery.

Almost straightaway, the 'Who is The Stig?' conundrum caught
the imagination of the viewing public and within a few episodes
of Series 1, websites and chat rooms speculated frantically about
his identity. The intrigue was sufficiently intense that in January
2003, the *Mirror* ran their own exposé claiming it was McCarthy
all along. Quoting a 'show insider' as a source, the newspaper
approached Perry about the story, but he simply said: 'I do know
who The Stig is, but I cannot comment any further.' Besides, the
talented driver himself was too busy at the time racing in Le
Mans to worry about speculation, a neat reminder that The Stig
is anything but a cartoon character and always a very real racer
with extreme driving talents.

However, the 'black' Stig lasted no longer than the first series.
After McCarthy revealed his identity in his excellent 2002 book,
Flat Out, Flat Broke, his contract was not renewed. By this time,
he had already started to tire of the rigours of the job, though:
'Burning round a track in a "Reasonably Priced Car" week after
week soon became a chore. I always gave it 100 per cent but I
was already getting tired of it.' After a priceless Jag was tested
and a complaint to the BBC followed, McCarthy became
disillusioned. Remember, at the time he was racing for Audi in
the Le Mans series and earning a hefty six-figure wage: 'I'd had
enough. And, I think, to be fair they'd had enough of me. I was
becoming tricky to handle. They didn't renew my contract and the

money was rubbish.' When interviewed on BBC *Breakfast News* in 2010, however, McCarthy was still visibly excited by the memories of playing the character. Referring to his caricature as 'Stiggy', he said it was a period of great fun.

Of course, the demise of the first Stig had to be reflected in the show itself. His departure was dressed up in a challenge for the opening programme of Series 3. After his final on-screen test driving the Porsche 996 GT3, Clarkson then announced that The Stig 'went off and joined the Navy'. The black Stig was seen being taken to *HMS Invincible* and asked to attempt to take a nitrous-oxide-modified Jaguar XJ-S to 100mph in the same 200 metres that it takes a jet fighter to achieve the same speed prior to taking off from the flight deck. In the previous series, the old Jag had beaten a fleet of supercars in a straight drag so he certainly had enough speed. The Stig even sat in with the fighter pilots for their briefing: this was explained as The Stig 'going *Top Gun*'.

On the aircraft carrier's flight deck, The Stig did indeed reach this speed but the carefully edited footage then showed him unable to stop and he careered off the end into the sea, off the coast of Portugal. All that was visible in the dark waters was a single black racing driver's glove. Back in the studio, Clarkson reported they had sent Navy divers down, but nothing had been found apart from the empty car.

Although the demise of the black Stig was as a direct result of McCarthy's departure, the filming of this aircraft carrier 'accident' hugely raised the profile of the character. Rather than 'killing him off', the ruse cleverly ramped up interest in the weird and wonderful figure. At the very start of the following week's episode, the new white Stig was introduced. Clarkson announced 'The Stig is dead!' and then played a montage of video clips of the Man in Black's finest moments. He then said: 'There's plenty more where he came from!' and went on to introduce the new Stig, standing on a backlit pedestal, this time cloaked all in white while sound-tracked by the theme song from *2001: A Space Odyssey*. The Stig's first test was in a new BMW M3 CSL.

As we have seen, at first The Stig's main purpose was posting lap times in the array of supercars and more normal vehicles that the show was reviewing. Over the years, however, that role has expanded greatly as his fame and notoriety ballooned exponentially. For the 'Star in a Reasonably Priced Car' feature, The Stig was always on hand at Dunsfold, in costume and in character, to train each week's celebrity. As his fame grew, The Stig started to make other personal appearances too. Away from *Top Gear*, he has also appeared in numerous Clarkson DVD titles such as *Supercar Showdown*.

By 2008, The Stig was a bona-fide celebrity in his own right and as such, collected *Top Gear*'s third award for 'Best Factual Programme' at the 2008 British National Television Awards. At the ceremony, he did not speak but instead handed an acceptance letter from the *Top Gear* team to host Griff Rhys Jones. After an apology for the presenters not being there, the letter stated:

> If you are reading this, please remember to give The Stig the award in his left hand because the right one is magnetic. Also, it's probably best to keep him away from the cast of *Coronation Street* since he seems to have got it in his head that Northerners are edible.
>
> Thanks again for the award.
> Jeremy, Richard and James.

(Note: This was not the first time that the actual presenters couldn't make an awards ceremony. Three years before The Stig filled in at the TV Awards, the show won an International Emmy in the 'Non-Scripted Entertainment Category'. Clarkson was unable to attend the glitzy bash in New York and the reason he gave was that he was too busy writing the next show's script. *Top Gear* has also been voted 'Best Programme of the Decade' by Channel 4, ahead of *Doctor Who* and *The Apprentice*, and has been nominated for numerous BAFTAs.)

Over the years, The Stig character has evolved into the focus of a massive slew of highly popular BBC merchandising activity. The 2009 *Where's Stig?* book, published by BBC Books, sold in excess of 250,000 copies. For Christmas 2010, you could buy a Stig advent calendar, a Stig keyring, desk diary, toiletry bag, pocket diary, wall calendar, jigsaws, flash drive keyring, tax disc holder, travel mug, mugs, bubble bath, a sonic toothbrush, T-shirts, stationery, duvets, lunch bags, school backpacks, floating pens, torches, alarm clocks, mousemats, posters, a soap-on-a-rope and even a Stig remote control helicopter and a children's outfit. I've been doing the *Where's Stig?* puzzlebook since Christmas 2009 – with my son, obviously – and I still haven't a clue.

As *Top Gear* literally expanded its horizons around the world with numerous overseas specials, then likewise The Stig had to broaden his universe beyond the confines of the BBC canteen and Dunsfold airport. With typical *Top Gear* verve, the fans were thus introduced to an extended Stig family tree, with numerous blood-relations. So, we have had the Stig's African cousin, who appeared in their 'Botswana' episode in Series 10. He was dark-skinned and wore only his racing boots and a loincloth – alongside, of course, his white helmet. His track test was conducted on a patch of wilderness passed off as a rally circuit. In 'America', we had The Stig's American Cousin with a suitably gargantuan belly forced into a rather unforgiving white race suit.

He was re-named 'The Big Stig' – not so much a broadened horizon as a bulging waistline.

There was also Rig Stig, who took the wheel of a brutally powerful racing truck, and true to *Top Gear* form, the stereotypes were in abundance with the whole right sleeve of his white suit being sunburnt. Just to even out the political scales, The Stig's Communist Cousin tipped up for Series 12's final episode wearing a suit in a fetching shade of Marxist red (later seen again in a DVD release for the 'Vietnam' special). His actual Russian clone on that country's version of the show was called Stigushka. Back in Blighty, Herr Stig was introduced in Series 15, with a nicely predictable German mullet sticking out from the back of his helmet and finally, Vegetarian Stig has helped the team test a hybrid car – and yes, he wore green and had solar panels on his helmet. Re-named Janet Stig Porter, he came to an untimely end after inhaling the apparently 'healthy' fumes of a technologically advanced hybrid car. A personal favourite is the Australian Stig for that country's own version of the show, who officially uses the same name but was unofficially christened 'Stiggo' by one of the presenters.

The Stig has become a phenomenon. Even his racing gear has led to some fans buying up identical garments, such as the Alpinestars GP Tech racing suit, or most stylishly of all, the White Simpson Diamondback motorcycle race helmet (originally, a Speedway RX helmet; a former *Top Gear* employee later put her leaving gift – a signed Stig helmet – up for auction, where it was expected to fetch £1,200). His boots were known to be a size ten and only a well-timed camera flash by an *Auto Trader* lensman could capture his eyes behind the visor, so we knew he was not a robot (although the eyes were rumoured to look like those of Damon Hill!). Or at least, he was only partially a robot, like a cyborg or similar.

Over the years, a number of people have been suspected of being The Stig. Numerous racing drivers such as Julian Bailey, Chris Goodwin, Damon Hill, Heikki Kovalainen, Tim Schrick and Russ Swift have been linked to the role by a gossip-hungry press but none of these theories were correct. Tiff Needell was also mentioned, but he has raced against The Stig at *Top Gear Live* roadshows on more than one occasion (and once tapped on The Stig's helmet to ask, 'Is that Perry in there?'). When Damon Hill appeared on the show to post a lap time, the media had been told it was Alan Titchmarsh as a decoy; this further fuelled speculation that former World Champion Hill was The Stig. Damon seemed genuinely awkward, causing further speculation, when asked by Jezza if he really was The Stig before ultimately denying it. When Jenson Button discussed with Clarkson the differing racing lines that F1 drivers took around the test track compared to The Stig, Button said, 'Well, obviously The Stig isn't a Formula 1 driver then,' to which Clarkson mysteriously replied, 'Might be.' When pressed, the BBC always maintained a stock answer, refusing to identify him and also ramping up the absurdity of the creature: 'We never comment on speculation as to who or what The Stig is.'

Although previously denied by Perry McCarthy, rumours persisted that The Stig was in fact more than one man, although again this was always played down by *Top Gear*. However, when The Stig does certain specialist tests, it is hard to imagine just one driver could fill the famous white boots. For example, 'The Winter Olympics' special saw The Stig take a full-size snowmobile down a near-vertical ski-jump ramp. Rumours suggest this may have been a famous Swedish snowmobile champion called Dan Lang. Likewise, when The Stig drove that huge racing truck, it was most likely this was also a specialist racer, not least because he proceeded to perform some incredibly deft and hugely difficult power slides in the massive machine.

Conjecture about The Stig's identity ceaselessly swarmed unabated all over websites. Then, in the summer of 2009, rumours started to leak out that the identity of the character might be revealed during the opening episode of Series 13, after he had first tested the startling Ferrari FXX track car. Millions tuned in to see the astonishing Italian hypercar – which costs £1.4 million and whose owners can only drive it on an approved track when Ferrari permit them to do so.

The FXX posted a brutally fast time of 1.10.7 minutes, which easily knocked the previous leader – the Gumpert Apollo – (1.17.1 minutes) off the top of the leaderboard, only for it to be disqualified for using slick tyres. However, such was the fascination with The Stig that the viewers and studio audience were not particularly interested in the scintillating lap time by one of the fastest cars ever built: this episode was all about The Stig.

The racing driver was then introduced to the studio audience and took his place in the studio car seats next to Clarkson. After some preamble, the crowd then began to chant 'Off! Off!' and eventually the mystery man lifted his helmet off to reveal ... Michael Schumacher.

Although Clarkson played along while Schumie seemed a little bewildered, no one actually believed that the seven-times Formula 1 World Champion was The Stig himself. Not least because Schumacher earns around $200 million every five years, which is certainly beyond even the BBC's oft-scrutinised celebrity pay budget. Speaking in the media, former Stig Perry McCarthy said, 'As if. Michael is worth more than a small country. And this is the BBC. Can you really see him wanting to drive a Vauxhall Astra round a track for £700 a week? That's all The Stig gets!'

To date, only one driver has ever beaten The Stig's time for a lap in the Reasonably Priced Car – 1:44.4 – and that is Rubens Barrichello. This came in July 2010 and a behind-the-scenes clip reveals just how much he enjoyed himself. He revealed that his goal had been to beat Nigel Mansell and the hardest part of driving such a basic car was finding the apex of each corner. Barrichello posted a Stig-beating time of 1:44.3. Clarkson had already noted that – unlike some F1 drivers – Rubens took exactly the same racing lines around the track as The Stig, something Lewis Hamilton also did. Notably, The Stig told Clarkson that although Hamilton's time of 1.44.7 minutes left him down the leaderboard, because it had been very wet on the day itself – usually attracting a four-second allowance – he regarded that performance as the most impressive. Notably, The Stig later revealed that of all the F1 drivers, only Mark Webber and Lewis Hamilton had let him show them the track's best lines.

Exemplifying the scientific and precise approach to the lap times on the test track, on the day of Rubens' record drive, Andy Wilman revealed that he had been wearing lucky underwear he'd had since 1995, originally for reassurance on aeroplane flights but now a totem for whenever the programme needed a good day at the office. So, a laser-like focus and exemplary driving skills, mixed with nerves of steel and reflexes of a ninja are not, after all, what's needed to beat The Stig – you just need lucky pants!

CHAPTER 10

Jeremy Clarkson, Part II

In British television terms, Jeremy Clarkson is without doubt one of the finest examples of the old adage, 'you either love him or hate him'. Indeed, when Channel 4 broadcast a list of the *100 Worst Britons We Love To Hate*, Clarkson came in at a respectable No. 66: and that's what Jeremy Clarkson thrives on. Seriously, I think if there came a day when everybody agreed with him, he'd quit.

Nonetheless, as *Top Gear*'s success increased throughout the 2000s, Clarkson's personal profile rocketed and he is now one of the most famous household names in Britain. For many, Clarkson has become the unofficial voice of Middle England, especially Middle English men. We live in the age of the New Man: this is a man who exfoliates and moisturises, who cries at rom-coms, who understands that his wife may need a hand with the children and he's not averse to reading chick lit. But a metrosexual Clarkson is not: he likes – among many things – fast cars, fags, beer and speaking his mind. In a sense this is typical of a large chunk of *Top Gear* viewers and where Clarkson has won so many fans is because *he is unashamed* in his ways. Indeed, he's proud of them and if he senses the slightest whiff of political correctness, he'll attack it with venom.

The logical manifestation of Clarkson's 'apolitical-political' appeal was the 2008 'Jeremy Clarkson For Prime Minister' campaign, which unsurprisingly attracted rafts of column inches in newspapers and internet coverage. A petition was started on the No. 10 website forum by a group calling themselves simply 'The UK Public', with the original submission made by a mysterious man, known only as 'Joseph Dark'. Its mission statement was as follows: 'This petition calls on the UK Public, in a display of national pride and solidarity, to show through electoral strength and direct political action, its disgust and displeasure in the politicians and government of today, and the lack of tangible opposition. Only by the election of Jeremy Clarkson, a man whose integrity and straight talking has earned the public's respect, to the position of Prime Minister of the United Kingdom of Great Britain, can the Great British Public once more regain its trust in its leaders, and be raised back to its position of authority in the International Community!' The hyperbole accelerates as the copy goes on to say: 'Clarkson is as close to a god [as] any mere mortal can get. His straightforward no-nonsense attitude would make our country great once more.'

Jeremy Clarkson actually shares his birthday – 11 April – with a previous British Prime Minister, George Canning, although his predecessor is somewhat older, having come to power in 1770. However, tenuous as this ancient political precursor was, within a few weeks nearly 40 Facebook groups were calling for JC to become PM. The petition was a perfect opportunity for critics and fans alike to regale or lambast the *Top Gear* presenter. His

Sunday Times and *Times Online* columns were plundered by numerous magazines and websites for examples of what his manifesto might actually contain, although even a scant perusal would make it clear this would be a thicker publication than an Argos catalogue. Short of ideas, he is not.

The original petition quickly gained over 50,000 signatories and for a week or two, the on-line campaign was the talk of most offices and factories around Britain. At one point, there were in excess of 264,000 signatories in total across all forums. A rival petition *not* to make him PM, meanwhile, had attracted only 87 names. Eventually, Clarkson spoke out and said he would make a poor prime minister as he was always contradicting himself; even the office of No. 10 got involved with a very firm tongue-in-British-cheek response. On a YouTube video posted on the official Downing Street site, a 55-second clip showed the famous black door of No. 10 opening, sound-tracked by typically elegant classical music, before the camera swept up an historical staircase lined with pictures of previous leaders. Then a photo of Clarkson looking statesmanlike is focussed on and a caption states that officials 'have thought long and hard' about the petition and the fans of Jezza have made 'a compelling case'. However, it quickly dismisses the notion, saying, 'On second thoughts ... maybe not', before No. 10's email address zooms off the screen to the sound of a racing car engine.

Notably, Richard Hammond and James May did not appear to have signed the petition. Clarkson no doubt found great humour in a similar internet campaign regarding Hammond – not quite so politically motivated, albeit perhaps far more popular: the petition wanted to make Hammond the new Dr Who!

So, let's humour the notion for a moment and project what it would actually be like if Jeremy Clarkson *was* Prime Minister. Of course, there are elements of his personality that might cause a few ruffles in the House of Commons. Quite how the Speaker of the House of Commons would react to statements such as that Americans 'barely have the brains to walk on their back legs' and people should avoid Norfolk unless they like 'orgies and the ritual slaying of farmyard animals' is open to conjecture. Besides, he was already not very popular in the House: an early-day motion tabled by two Liberal Democrat MPs – Norman Baker and Tom Brake – pushed for him to be summoned to the House to explain 'a curious and misguided attitude to the real and major threat posed by climate change'.

Let's face it, Clarkson is not one for holding his tongue on matters that he thinks important. The *Daily Mail* observed, 'some of his views would make Genghis Khan blush,' while the *Mirror* called him 'a dazzling hero of political incorrectness.' Clarkson joined in the 'JC for PM' fun some more with a light-hearted sample of his manifesto in the *Sun*. His opening gambit was to reverse all the new laws passed by PM Tony Blair and his deputy, Gordon Brown, since New Labour came into power in 1997, with particular highlights being 'the bloody environment', 'the hunting ban', the 'endless tax demands on motorists ...' He closed by saying he was off for lunch and then a holiday – which is, after all, what a lot of people think politicians do anyway.

There were few dissenters, it seemed. One who did voice his concern was Clarkson's good friend, the writer AA Gill, who perhaps knows the man far better than most and therefore has a right to comment: 'It couldn't get any wronger than having Jeremy in charge,' he said in *The Times*. 'I would have problems sending my child to a nursery school that had Jeremy on the Board of Governors. I say this with love and respect, but I just don't want him ever to have a switch that's attached to anything.' He went on to deride Clarkson's denial of global-warming as

'Canute-like', but conceded that his friend's much-admired wife Francie would make a brilliant First Lady.

There was perhaps a genuinely political motivation behind the light-hearted nature of this mammoth petition, however; for years the eccentric political satirist Screaming Lord Sutch and his Monster Raving Loony Party had come to represent people who were so disillusioned with British politics that they needed an exaggerated protest vote, the chance to tick 'None of the Above' while still registering their voice. Screaming Lord Sutch was involved in politics across four decades but tragically, the great British character committed suicide in 1999, a year after losing his mother. Some therefore suggested that JC had effectively taken up his baton; given that Clarkson had no hand in the petition, perhaps it would be more accurate to say the British public themselves were looking for someone to fill the void.

Critics would, of course, point out the irony of calling Clarkson a 'Man of the People' since he is a former public schoolboy and the fees at Repton are currently in the region of nearly £10,000 a term, a figure completely beyond the means of most working-class men, who watch him with great admiration. However, perhaps the reason why Jeremy maintains such an appeal is that although he does have some of the (albeit generalised) trappings of the public-school lifestyle – he supports hunting, he enjoys cigars, etc. – he is otherwise very much a typical, outspoken British male. He doesn't play polo or tick many of the stereotypical boxes of the middle classes. With class divisions crumbling in an increasingly fragmented British class society, Jeremy Clarkson's fans don't question his roots – in fact, many probably don't even know or care.

Clarkson is certainly no fool – he knows that his comments irritate as often as they entertain, but he enjoys being the *bête noir*. When a survey of young Londoners revealed that 16 per cent of 16–24-year-olds would like to see Clarkson as their city's Mayor (the same figure backed *The Apprentice* star and noted entrepreneur Sir Alan Sugar), Jezza responded with a column in the *Sunday Times* explaining what he would do, if he did take the top job in the capital. This also gave an insight into what might have happened, had the 'Clarkson For Prime Minister' petition succeeded. Having initially thought he would be mad to give up driving Ferraris for a living to earn far less and be criticised every day of his life (no change there then), he pondered about certain parts of the mayoral job that he would like: 'As far as I can tell, the job of running the capital is no harder than being a lift attendant.' So we have Clarkson's official-unofficial Mayoral manifesto suggesting he'd get rid of all bus lanes, sell the Mayoral eco-car and buy a Range Rover, go to The Ivy for lunch most days, take in a West End show, reintroduce fox-hunting in Islington and Hackney, increase the congestion charge to £50 a day so that only smart and expensive motors could be seen in London and finally replace Marc Quinn's statue of a woman with no arms and legs in Trafalgar Square with a full-size bronze model of a Spitfire. Oh, and pass a law banning people from entering the London Marathon in diving suits or chicken outfits.

If Clarkson does have a dominant overarching political position, it's his belief that government should not interfere with people's lives: he once famously said those in power should 'build park benches and that is it'. He was a virulent critic of the New Labour 'Nanny State', particularly the proliferation of bans, including hunting and smoking prohibition (on National No Smoking Day he deliberately smokes as often as circumstances allow); the Congestion Charge and other attacks on motorists are all similarly despised. Not surprisingly, he has little time for ramblers and endured a lengthy legal wrangle over a right-of-way dispute on his Isle of Man second home. He is probably not the greatest fan of the European Union and given the urban myths about bans on bananas that are too bendy, etc., it would be no big surprise.

As an aside, Andy Wilman concurs with this stance about the 'Nanny State'. He has even suggested there is a sociological reason for *Top Gear*'s popularity, in that since New Labour came to power in 1997, they had proceeded to preside over a Nanny State that was constantly placing limits and restrictions on people's lives – health and safety, car legislation, anti-smoking legislation, etc. – and he believed there was therefore an undercurrent of 'people who get nagged to fuck' who found *Top Gear*'s irreverent middle-fingered salute to authority a refreshing way to spend Sunday evenings.

Clarkson has, of course, had his own dealings with prime ministers, notably former PM Gordon Brown. While on a tour of Australia in 2009 to promote *Top Gear Live* (an extravaganza of fast cars and stunts, now a globe-trotting arena spectacle), Jeremy was speaking at a press conference when he called the then-PM a 'one-eyed Scottish idiot', an observation that naturally caused immediate uproar. The comment came during a discussion about the global financial crisis and Clarkson was actually complementing the Australian Prime Minister Kevin Rudd on facing up to the extent of the damage. His actual words were as follows: 'It's the first time I've ever seen a world leader [Rudd] admit we really are in deep shit ... He genuinely looked terrified. Poor man, he's actually seen the books. We have this one-eyed Scottish idiot who keeps telling us everything's fine and he's saved the world and we know he's lying, but he's smooth at telling us.'

Even Clarkson himself seemed to know he'd possibly overdone it this time, because at the actual moment in the press conference he turned to Richard Hammond and said, 'I said that

THE TOP GEAR STORY

out loud, didn't I?' although he then laughed it off. The press conference was filled with the usual 'Clarkson-isms' such as calling *Top Gear* studio fans 'apes' (he's also dubbed them 'oafs') and saying if the show's motorcycle stunt riders were killed, 'it's not the end of the world' because they are French. But it was his views on Gordon Brown that journalists fixated on and the incident soon threatened to cost Clarkson his job.

In fact, Brown lost an eye in a schoolboy rugby accident and Clarkson's comment was seen to be in poor taste by many politicians and people in the media, as well as the Royal National Institute for the Blind and other disability groups. Soon he faced an almighty barrage of criticism over his remarks. Various Scottish politicians urged the BBC to take Clarkson off air. The Rt. Hon. Lord George Foulkes, a former Scottish Labour MP, said: 'If the BBC banned Jonathan Ross for what he said [the message Ross, along with comedian Russell Brand, left on actor Andrew Sachs' telephone answering-machine] and they have taken Carol Thatcher off air for something she said in private ['golliwog'], then something should be done about Clarkson. He has insulted Gordon Brown three times over – accusing him of being a liar, having a go at him for having a physical handicap and for his nationality. It is an absolute outrage of the worst kind.'

The RNIB's chief executive Lesley-Anne Alexander said, 'Clarkson's description of the Prime Minister is offensive. Any suggestion that equates disability with incompetence is totally unacceptable.' Fairly soon it became apparent that Jeremy had completely overstepped the mark and he issued the following apology: 'In the heat of the moment I made a remark about the Prime Minister's personal appearance for which, upon reflection, I apologise.' However, he later watered down the apology somewhat in his weekly newspaper column, clarifying that he was only sorry for making the remarks about Brown's eye and his nationality, 'But the idiot bit – there is no chance I'll apologise for that.' Downing Street would not be drawn into the furore and simply declined to comment, arguing that, 'Mr Clarkson is entitled to his own interpretation of the economic circumstances.' However, Peter 'Mandy' Mandelson was a little more acerbic: 'I've got absolutely no repeatable views to express on Mr Jeremy Clarkson.'

Coincidentally, when Clarkson appeared on *Who Do You Think You Are?* in 2004, he'd been so disappointed at the apparent provinciality of his ancestors – who seemed to have always lived within a few miles of each other and rarely travelled – that he declared: 'I'm the product of 200 years of interbreeding, I'm surprised I haven't got one eye!'

Despite the clamour for his scalp, the BBC refused to sack the presenter and simply stated that he had apologised and no further action would be taken because of this. They were then accused of hypocrisy since Carol Thatcher had been axed from her role on *The One Show* for one particular off-air comment.

Then in the summer of 2009, Clarkson's venom for Brown was circulated once more as he was allegedly overheard to make an off-air remark in which he described the PM as 'a silly cunt'. There were media reports at the time of a disagreement with a top BBC executive but the Corporation denied that he had been chastised.

Clarkson's outspoken ways occasionally backfire. In October 2007, a serious breach of data occurred when two computer discs owned by HM Revenue and Customs containing the personal details of those families claiming child benefit in the United Kingdom went missing. In all the ensuing frenzy lambasting the loss of data and the sense of panic about what harm could be done, should the information fall into the wrong hands, Clarkson announced that it was an over-reaction typical of the over-suffocating Data Protection Act of 1998: 'All you'll be able to do with them is put money into my account, not take it out. Honestly, I've never known such a palaver about nothing.' And to prove it, he published his bank details in the *Sun*, as well as information about how to find out his home address. Shortly afterwards, it transpired that a third party had set up a £500-a-month direct debit from his account to Diabetes UK; also that this person's identity was protected by the very same act that Clarkson had been railing against.

In his following week's *Sunday Times* column Clarkson admitted that he had been wrong. Fraud expert Andreas Baumhof of online fraud protection company Trust Defender commented at the time: 'He probably thought, "What can you do with this personal information?" and he got screwed straightaway because they can do a lot of things with this. He was pretty open and published all this information in the article, but a lot of people give out a lot of information on things like social networking sites that on their own is not very valuable but when you combine all these details with other information, they can become really valuable.'

At a motor show appearance on stage with Formula 1's David Coulthard, another of Clarkson's comments came back to bite him. In an exclusive interview for this book, Coulthard said: 'I was speaking alongside Jeremy, and only a few days before in his column he'd said some fairly unkind things about me, I think one of them was that I reminded him of an alien! As he was talking to the crowd, I interrupted him and said, "What I really want to talk to you about, Jeremy, is why you said I look like an alien!" I got my own back, but he took it in great spirit and it was all good fun.'

Coulthard would later get the ultimate revenge in Series 14 of *Top Gear* when he appeared in a feature on F1 art. As well as an exhibition of motorsport paintings judged by the series trio, there were various other exhibits of car-related sculpture and art, including pieces the presenters had to make themselves, with varying degrees of success/abject failure (James May's metal sculpture actually set on fire). They were also challenged to run the PR for the art show to achieve a record number through the gallery's doors, which after much stumbling and ramshackle attempts at advertising, they eventually succeeded in doing.

Clarkson also tried to create some art using a Red Bull Formula 1 car, one example of which was to spray-paint it ultra-violet, then send it round a track so that the wind blew the fluid all over the aerodynamic curves, after which they could create a luminous piece of art from the result. Another idea called upon Coulthard to sit in his racing car while the exhaust pipes were filled with paintballs. Then, with Jeremy standing behind the car, DC pressed the throttle and out flew various paint pellets at high speed. Unfortunately for Clarkson, the canvas he was holding in front of his wedding tackle proved too fragile to stop the speeding bullets of paint. 'It was great,' recalls Coulthard, 'because I got to do what all the car manufacturers and press offices would love to do, which is to shoot Jeremy Clarkson in the testicles!'

If Clarkson were to run the country, he might want to get someone else to look after the Foreign Office (international relations are probably not his strong point). Ask the staff from a Hyundai UK stand at a motor show, who claimed he'd said they were 'eating a dog'. In 2007, headlines such as Clarkson Offends Malaysia followed a piece that declared one of that country's cars to be the worst in the world. Clarkson called the Perodua Kelisa 'unimaginative junk, with no soul, no flair and no passion' and set about it with a sledgehammer, then hung it from a crane and blew it up. Writing on *Times Online*, Clarkson went on to say, 'The inside is tackier than Anthea Turner's wedding and you don't want to think what would happen if it bumped into a lamppost. Also, its name sounds like a disease.'

Jeremy usually refers to inhabitants of France as 'Frenchists' (May has also said he finds France 'intensely irritating') and any review of an Italian/German/French car is inevitably peppered with descriptions revolving around the more colourful – and comic – national stereotypes. Thus Clarkson regards most German cars as too serious, lacking humour, Italian cars are fiery and unpredictable but have soul, Scandinavian cars are very precise, American cars too muscle-bound and loud ... and so on. This is perhaps not surprising since the presenter has conjectured some machines have souls and cites the loss of Concorde as an example. (Note: he was actually a passenger on board the last-ever British Airways Concorde flight in October 2003.)

When Clarkson was reporting on the Tokyo Motor Show in 2005, he made comments about foreigners that typify both his sense of humour and also the rabid reaction these remarks often provoke. He was sitting with Richard Hammond as the latter suggested that to emphasise the new Mini estate was 'quintessentially British', they should have supplied it with teabags and teaspoons. To which Clarkson added his penny's worth, saying they should make a car that's quintessentially German ... giving it 'trafficators that go like this [he imitated a Nazi salute] ... a SatNav that only goes to Poland ... und ein fan belt that lasts a thousand years!' (This comment took place in the studio and was part of an ad hoc improvised chat about the motor show rather than some scripted gag.)

That very night, the BBC received numerous complaints about those particular comments, including one that said Clarkson's words were 'poisonous rubbish' and 'a racist slur'. Initially the head of editorial complaints did not uphold this particular one but the disgruntled viewer then took it further. The BBC Board of Governors is responsible for overseeing the running of the Beeb and also ensures that the Corporation serves the public interest, given it is licence fee funded. They are also responsible for monitoring the effectiveness of complaints handled by the BBC. Their case notes are incredibly formal (as they need to be) but reads rather incongruously when you see the actual off-the-cuff exchange between Clarkson and May, thousands of miles away from Broadcasting House then hauled up, written out and analysed verbatim. Still, there is a formal process to follow.

There are many parameters against which the Board of Governors have to quantify a complaint, but perhaps the key issue here – as in the majority of the complaints against *Top Gear* – is whether the BBC demonstrates 'a clear editorial purpose' in the offensive comments or actions while also taking into account the potential age of the audience, its composition and expectations.

Ultimately, the Committee decided the audience would have understood the jokes 'as an established element of [Clarkson's] television persona' and that Clarkson 'often uses the most exaggerated stereotypes to support or defend his opinions and would not have taken his comments seriously.' The complaint was therefore not upheld.

It is many, many years since the show had been a dry magazine review programme and a viewer would have to live in a cave not to know that Clarkson and Co. were often outspoken. Even as far back as 2002, the presenter had filmed a five-part series called *Jeremy Clarkson Meets The Neighbours*, in which he travelled around Europe in a Jaguar E-Type meeting various nationalities and usually coming home with a reinforced view of his own personal stereotype. While there is no doubt that some of the team's comments might be offensive to some, it does beg the question: why are these viewers watching *Top Gear* in the first place?

Regardless of the light-hearted nature of the PM petition and Clarkson's frequent comical observations about our overseas friends, through his role on *Top Gear* and his hugely popular column in *The Times*, Jezza is, reluctantly or not, a political figure. On one occasion, this proved very much the case when he was confronted by a gang of 'hoodies'.

In the December of 2007, Clarkson left the quietude of his blissfully sleepy English home in Chipping Norton to take his daughter and her friends for a birthday party in Milton Keynes' snow dome, Xscape. By his own admission, his local paper considers it has something of a scoop if a kitten goes missing, but the urban landscape of Milton Keynes is altogether a different place.

Clarkson had snuck outside like the naughty schoolboy he still is to have a crafty cigarette when he noticed a small gang of 'youths' approaching him. Writing in his *Times* column, he revealed that at first he assumed they were just *Top Gear* fans but the atmosphere quickly changed to something rather more sinister when they asked if he had any personal security guards with him. He suddenly realised events might not be so innocent and politely asked them to leave him alone. But they didn't: as he started to walk away, they followed him.

It's worth bearing in mind here that what strikes you most of all when you see Jeremy Clarkson in the flesh is just how tall he is. He has an abundance of confidence and is famously brash and outspoken but at the same time, having such a large stature (he's just one inch below legally being declared a giant!) must boost his self-belief, should this ever be challenged or waiver. Yet all this seemed not to matter one iota to these youths.

Obviously unsettled, Clarkson decided to grab the ringleader by his hoodie and lifted him off the ground, telling him it would be best if he left. But he didn't leave; nor did his mates. At this point, Jeremy admitted that he was finding it hard to tell if the kid was 18 or 8 years of age – and if anywhere near the latter, then the countless photos that the hoodies were taking on their mobile phones might prove damning in the papers the next day. He put the youth down and after being sworn at and having various gestures thrown his way, the gang retreated back to wherever they'd come from. However, a 14-year-old girl later contacted Thames Valley Police to inform them that a man had been abusive to her friend.

Thames Valley looked into the unpleasant incident and even interviewed Clarkson as part of their procedures. Ultimately, they stated that not only did he do nothing wrong, if anything he was the victim. Police also spoke to witnesses at the centre who told them that the group of youths had been warned away by security staff earlier that day. A police spokesman said: 'Mobile phone images were viewed as well as CCTV footage and it became apparent that, if any offence had occurred, it was the man who was the victim. There is no evidence that a crime took place and therefore there will be no police action.' Meanwhile, Clarkson said he did not wish to make a complaint.

The situation outside the snow dome in Milton Keynes must have been threatening because Jeremy is not easily frightened. After all, he's been in fighter jets, supercars and endless automotive bumps and scrapes. Even when he describes something on-screen as 'terrifying', there's the sense that he doesn't really think so. In a fans' Q&A in 2005, he was asked what would truly scare him and his response was indeed chilling: 'Being left with a baby with a full nappy to change.'

For a Series 3 feature on boy racers 'cruisin'', he went along to the legendary Ace Café, just off the North Circular in northwest London to spend an evening of testosterone and burning rubber with the leading racers *du jour*. Originally a Mecca for old-school

Café racers on classic motorbikes, who used to pelt up and down the main road trying to achieve the magic 100mph (hence the nickname for some of them, 'Ton Up Boys'), the venue has since evolved and now attracts a variety of car and bike clubs, who put on monthly nights as well as annual events. In this case, it was a so-called 'Maxin' Relaxin'' night and the general demographic predominantly young, urban lads (Asians, West Indians and whites in equal measure). And there was a point to the location: Citroën had given away free insurance to many seventeen-year-olds as part of an incentive package and with premiums for teenagers rising into thousands of pounds year on year, this proved a canny sales tactic, creating a virtual car subculture overnight.

The car park was rammed with drivers showing off their beautifully customised and cherished vehicles. For many this might be an intimidating atmosphere, but Clarkson seemed genuinely in his element and far from uncomfortable, he actually enjoyed poking a little fun at their language and was clearly endeared by the jubilant atmosphere. When one of the kids told him, 'It's about flexin', man!', Clarkson merrily ridiculed him but in return the Citroën owners were laughing and jibing him back – it was all genuinely good fun.

In the week following the Milton Keynes incident, writing in his *Sunday Times* column, Clarkson used the altercation to make a powerful point: that in his opinion, Britain's suburban towns and cities are awash with similar feral youth. Clearly he had been riled and lambasted those parents who claim trouble-makers are 'good boys', saying if a young lad gets stabbed or shot, 'If he was such a frigging angel, what was he doing on a derelict building site at four in the morning, you halfwits? He didn't deserve to die, for sure, but you do, for having the parenting skills of a Welsh dresser.'

He went on to berate the restrictions placed on teachers who are unable to discipline disruptive kids for fear of being arrested for assault. The rest of the article was classic Clarkson: vocal, colourful language, throwing out insults and statements like shotgun fire and even referring to an 'Albanian nonce' in prison at one point. So, how did he sum up his solution to the shockingly indicative incident from his Milton Keynes' trip? In his opinion, all the troublemakers should be rounded up in one class, their teacher given immunity from prosecution ... 'and a sub-machine gun'.

CHAPTER 11

Top Gear Haters

So, where do you want to start?

If Jeremy Clarkson became Prime Minister, plenty of people would be horrified. And it's not just Clarkson they detest – it's *Top Gear* too. Let's start by taking it right back to old *Top Gear* and most notably, Jeremy's review of the new Vauxhall Vectra, possibly the first real sign that his opinions on cars might be causing major ruffles within the motor industry. Of course, he'd said negative things about cars before: the slight rancour that a negative review of the new Metro generated within the industry was an early sign that the motor trade would not always be so reciprocal in their relationship with *Top Gear*.

There are numerous examples prior to Clarkson even joining the show of car reviews causing controversy. For example, after Noel Edmonds described the Fiat Strada as 'not very good', the manufacturer threatened legal action against the BBC unless Edmonds retracted his statement and issued an apology. As a general rule of thumb, though, most motor manufacturers had a healthy relationship with old *Top Gear*. 'Healthy, but independent,' as former *Top Gear* producer Jon Bentley puts it. '[Car manufacturers] were always pretty good, actually – they rarely complained.'

However, by far the biggest rumpus caused by a review on the old generation of *Top Gear* came after a piece by Jeremy Clarkson on the 1995 launch of the new Vauxhall Vectra. Among various negative comments, he said: 'I know it's the replacement for the Cavalier, I know. But I'm telling you, it's just a box on wheels.' Clarkson described the Vectra, especially the chassis, as one of the worst cars he'd ever reviewed. At one point, he stood next to the car and drummed his fingers on the roof without saying anything. The manufacturer was appalled, claiming his review had been 'totally unbalanced'.

'Jeremy was very critical about the car,' remembers Bentley, 'but in a more entertaining way than he had been before. When Jeremy had been highly critical of the Mk V Escort in 1991, he did it in a more straight, factual way and we didn't get any criticism from the manufacturer although maybe Ford's attitude to criticism was slightly different [to Vauxhall's]. And besides, [Jeremy's] message would have been the same even if he had delivered the criticism in a more conventional manner.

'This time, however, we faced what amounted to an orchestrated campaign of letter writing, largely from Vauxhall dealers. We had to draft in extra staff to handle the thousands of letters. But Jeremy's opinions on the Vectra were ultimately proven correct by the test of time. The car was rather lazily engineered and not very good – it didn't handle well and was unreliable.'

British Leyland and latterly Rover have come under the glare too. Clarkson has made no secret of his dislike for many Rover models and this was rooted deep in the company's earlier genesis as Leyland. Over the years, he has scoffed at Leyland's designers for living in a town that housed the Bullring; he described the factory as no more suitable for producing a car than a stable and warned not to get him started on the unions, who at one point began over 300 industrial disputes in six months. He also said he'd been told by fellow journalist Richard Littlejohn that in the difficult 1970s, the latter had visited many homes of Rover paint-shop workers only to find their lounges decorated in TR7 yellow or their bedrooms painted in Allegro beige. And what was the Government subsidy (i.e. the sum paid by the taxpayer) for all this at British Leyland? According to Clarkson, some £3.5 billion.

Reviewing the litany of takeovers, failed designs, poor sales, strikes, government bail-outs and other assorted manufacturing disasters, Clarkson once said: 'Never in the field of human endeavour has so much been done, so badly, by so many.' He has also written that since he was a kid, he thought of the British car industry as 'a fountain of woe, waste and doom' populated by militant unionists in donkey jackets and Birmingham accents, standing around smoking braziers. It's hard to see how someone who attracts several million viewers every Sunday on prime-time TV won't make a huge impact with observations such as these.

Although both these comments came after the final death throes of Rover, they were preceded by many similar such statements. It was only Clarkson's opinion of course, but his words are always high profile. If you want to place an advertisement in *The Times* taking up as much space as his column, it would set you back thousands of pounds. That sort of publicity hits home.

Indeed, workers at Rover were so annoyed that during the dying days of the Longbridge Rover plant, they actually hung an

'Anti-Clarkson Campaign' banner on the building. Given this was once the biggest car factory in the world and Rover was the last remaining British-owned-and-built car manufacturer, Jeremy's criticisms proved particularly unpopular. Many went so far as to directly blame him for the company's eventual demise. Walking a mile in their shoes, it must have felt harsh hearing his words on TV or reading them in a broadsheet: after all, their jobs, their incomes and their homes were at risk. But it wasn't meant to be a personal attack and Clarkson was always extremely careful to criticise the management and unions rather than go for the workers: it's easy to see how his words would have been wounding, though.

Richard Hammond clearly understood the serious side of the car industry: as already noted, his grandparents had worked in Birmingham car-making factories. Speaking later about the demise of Rover, he summed up the personal impact of the company going out of business: 'When the Rover P5 was built, it was fashionable and it was a luxury but the world has moved on and I don't think the brand did. What it comes down to is someone going home and saying, "My job's gone."'

When the manufacturer finally imploded, Clarkson said he sympathised with the workforce of 6,500 but could not get 'emotional' about the company itself. In fact, he admitted that his first thought on hearing the news was 'good' because Britain could now get on with something that it was good at instead. Writing in his *Sunday Times* column, he said Rover was far from a national institution and seemed unrepentant about his criticism of the company, again particularly the management. As for the Rover owners themselves, whose cars were now effectively without a warranty, he declared it was their 'fault for buying a stupid car' and for 'buying British' on principal in the face of widespread industry advice to do otherwise. But his sharpest venom was reserved for the management: 'This is, of course, the plague that besets all British inventions. It's always allowed to fester by idiotic management.' No respect for the dead here.

But this was not just a personal vendetta: Clarkson rightly pointed out he was simply a motoring journalist – albeit perhaps the most famous one we've ever seen – but nonetheless when he specifically criticised a car, he was merely stating his opinion (and very often basic facts). It's important to remember that although Clarkson is a super-famous celebrity, part of his job is still to review cars and so it follows, he countered: was he supposed to review a bad car and say it was a good one just because it was British? Also, it's only fair to point out that he doesn't hold back from berating foreign cars if he doesn't like them. He needs to be objective, rather than sentimental (remember the headed notepaper: 'Jeremy Clarkson, Journalist'?)

In response to the criticism, in Episode 7, Series 10, *Top Gear* ran a feature that set out to prove Leyland had actually made some good cars after all. It was hard to watch the piece and not notice a very large tongue in the cheek of each presenter, not least due to the nature of the challenges they set. Each one spent around £1,000 on a Leyland classic: Clarkson rolled up in a stylish Rover SD1, favourite of many 1970s TV cops; Hammond came in a once-trendy Dolomite Sprint, complete with alloys and wooden inlay; then James May came in third in his legendary Austin Princess from 1978 – famous, he said, for being the first production car to have 'obscured windscreen wipers.'

The three 'vintage' cars were driven to an automotive test track, where the trio used them to undergo some of the most bizarre *Top Gear* tests ever. Thus we had a case of parking on a steep hill and using the handbrake – simple enough for all except Hammond's Sprint, which immediately careered down the hill and even smashed into a sign warning of steep ascents. Then there was a skidpan test, a timed lap against a Japanese Datsun (widely seen as a symbol of the reliability from the Far East, which some argue killed the British car industry), there was also a 'power' lap and then a trip along a cobbled test track with a colander of raw eggs above the presenters' heads. And finally, they did a lap around the *Top Gear* test track with the car completely filled with water. For this entirely pointless exercise, the presenters wore snorkels and wet suits: Hammond did half a lap, May completed two (despite his car being berated as an 'Austin Colander') and Clarkson never made it to the first corner because the rear door of his Rover fell off. And the winner was ... James May's mustard-yellow Princess!

In their defence, *Top Gear* also ran an extremely poignant feature – albeit again with a fair few smirks – on the demise of the British car industry in Series 15, Episode 6. Having already reviewed the stunning new Ferrari 458 Italia, the team then used a budget of £5,000 each to buy three British roadsters: the Jensen-Healey, a TVR S2 and a Lotus Elan. The presenters said they wanted to prove to the show's producers that home-bred sports-cars were not horrible and unreliable – and that hot hatches such as the Peugeot 205GTi did not signal the end of the British roadster.

They reported to the Lotus factory in Norfolk and were handed their challenges. The Jensen that Clarkson pulled up in was designed by a father-and-son team and designed by the same man who worked on the Aston Martin Lagonda; May's TVR and Hammond's Lotus Elan were then previewed with an increasing sense of comedy. May's TVR's carpet was pulled back to reveal some graffiti of a naked lady and the factory worker's signature, 'Nobby'. Hammond pointed out that at least the Elan's engine was Japanese and therefore reliable.

As they drove round the track, they talked about their cars and the comedy increased. Hammond pointed out that the Elan was released around the same time as the Mazda MX5, but in his eyes was more elite and desirable than its Japanese counterpart, partly because it didn't sell in such 'massive, vulgar numbers' as the Far Eastern rival. Meanwhile, May claimed the delay between pressing the throttle and subsequently getting any power in his TVR was an innovative safety feature to make sure the driver definitely wanted to accelerate.

The trio was then sent to Blackpool's former TVR factory via the former Jensen building in the West Midlands – but not before 'blowing up' The Stig when he turned on the ignition in a German-made Astra, apparently a 'known fault'. On the journey, the script turned more serious as Clarkson pointed out that in 1913, there were 140 car manufacturers in Britain but by now it had all gone 'so wrong, so fast.'

Hammond, meanwhile, noted that because parts of his Lotus were falling off, he was lighter and therefore more fuel-efficient – again, a deliberate piece of British engineering; as indeed was a 'safety feature' gap in the window that allowed in rain and fresh air to alert the driver if he was becoming drowsy. Hammond's number plate was an anagram of 'Liar', May's was an anagram of 'Gosh' and we were left to work out what Jeremy's number plate might spell out: CTU 131N.

Reaching the 'beautiful' city of Birmingham, Hammond reminded viewers that his grandfather had made Jensens. Things turned poignant as they walked around the derelict Jensen factory, wondering what the designers and engineers behind the marques (and indeed, former British manufacturing in general) might feel if they were to witness such widespread industrial abandonment.

After dragging a Citroën under a lorry (with The Stig 'on board'), Clarkson then drove his TVR directly underneath the same vehicle only to emerge unscathed – further proof, they claimed, that the UK roadsters were safest. Next, they took the cars through a carwash and unsurprisingly, Hammond was completely drenched in his Lotus. A trip to a garden centre and on to Blackpool wearing various strange hats confirmed that by now the piece had descended into farce. Yet, even after all the hilarity, they walked around the disused TVR factory and suddenly the humour vanished: discarded car moulds and rusting bonnets littered a deserted factory: so many memories, now all gone. The trio later admitted that they hated this part of the feature and said it was genuinely horrible to film it.

For anyone in doubt as to whether the feature was objective or not, it's worth bearing in mind two of Clarkson's comments along the way: it never rains in the UK and you never see roadworks on a British motorway.

Although *Top Gear* inevitably attracts criticism from motor manufacturers (after all, it is a car review show), most of the haters speak out as a direct result of peripheral topics and comments discussed on the programme. The most obvious opponent is perhaps the lobby of environmentalists who despair at *Top Gear*'s attitude to global warming and other related ecological issues. When Jeremy makes such comments as 'I care more about the colour of the gear-knob on my Mercedes SLK than the amount of carbon dioxide it produces,' he must surely expect a reaction.

And in September 2008, that's precisely what he got when a green protester attacked him with a pie after the TV host had attended Oxford Brookes University to collect an honorary degree. The award was for his long-standing support of engineering: in the BBC series *Great Britons*, he nominated Victorian engineering genius Isambard Kingdom Brunel to compete with others such as Winston Churchill, Oliver Cromwell, Charles Darwin, Admiral Lord Nelson, Sir Isaac Newton and Shakespeare. Five years earlier, Jezza had already received an honorary degree from Brunel University for a similar premise.

Back at Oxford Brookes in 2008, Clarkson even joked beforehand that he expected flour and eggs to be hurled when he arrived, enough to turn him into a 'giant human pancake'. And he was nearly right. The incident started when he was in a marquee, while outside waited an environmental campaigner (or an 'eco-mentalist' as the presenter sometimes calls them) called Rebecca Lush. When he came out, she ran after him and threw a banana meringue in his face – organic and homemade, naturally. Later she declared that due to his lofty status, getting a direct hit on the face was 'like playing basketball!'

Clarkson's response was surprising and very self-effacing: 'Great shot!' he said, before pointing out to waiting newspaper photographers that the meringue itself was a tad too sweet for his liking. He later implied that a few of the paps in attendance were aware of what was about to happen and had even goaded him to come out from under the safety of the marquee. 'I have to say that,' he continued, 'at the PR level, it was a fantastic result for the environmentalists. One-nil to them!'

But Lush was not alone in her distaste for Clarkson's environmental views. Around 3,000 people had signed a petition in the weeks prior to his appearance at Oxford Brookes, asking for the honour to be withdrawn. Transport 2000 even went so far as to ridicule the entire ceremony, saying the decision to honour Clarkson was as if Scotland Yard had paid tribute to the work of Inspector Clouseau. Among the signatories were workers from the nearby Cowley BMW factory reputed to be unhappy with Clarkson's infamous criticism of MG Rover workers.

Lush herself was passionate in her campaigns and had even

gone to jail for four months in 1993 for her part in an early road building protest on Twyford Down. A self-proclaimed eco-activist, in the inevitable glare of publicity after the meringue-hurling incident, she was quick to publicise her cause: 'It's about the survival of our species, it's about people, and transport is the fastest-growing contributor to climate change.' Rebecca had previous form with pies, too – she'd thrown one in the face of an American envoy during environmental talks at The Hague and another at the then-transport secretary, Alistair Darling; she'd also chained herself to diggers and stood in front of bulldozers. Here was a woman of conviction and her tactics of direct action seemed to work. (Note: Lush's three erstwhile *Top Gear* enemies would later chain themselves to buses at Hammersmith Bus Station in response to Greenpeace's lengthy campaign against 4x4s).

But she was not alone, not by a long chalk: the list of incidents on *Top Gear* to enrage environmentalists is a long one. When Clarkson tested a Land Rover Discovery on the side of the Scottish mountain Ben Tongue in Series 5, there was uproar amid allegations that he had desecrated precious virgin peat bogs. The piece had simple enough ambitions: review the new Land Rover and decide if it was a genuine off-roader. He began by saying the Land Rover Discovery used to be the car you'd buy if you couldn't afford a Range Rover (he'd used this damning broadside before, in a devastating blow to Porsche Boxster owners worldwide, saying they only bought the German soft-top because they couldn't afford a 911). Clarkson claimed this was effectively broadcasting to the whole world the fact that their lives hadn't quite worked out the way they wanted them to!

Forgetting the environmental rights and wrongs and the eco-campaigners' impending fury for a moment, the actual appraisal of the Disco was a devastatingly simple piece of Clarkson car-reviewing brilliance – a reminder, if you will, of his longstanding roots in motoring journalism right back to *Performance Car* days when his writing and extensive knowledge got him noticed in the first place. He discusses the rear folding seats that enable seven people to board the Disco but then he picks up a small child and points out a stunningly obvious flaw: if you are holding a child in one hand, it's impossible to put the seat down with putting the child down (and onto a potentially dangerous road or car park) first. 'Someone wasn't thinking,' tut-tuts Clarkson. His simple observation must have been devastating for Land Rover designers – harsh, but fair.

Journalistic brilliance is not what this piece will be remembered for, however. As a remix of Kate Bush's 'Running Up That Hill' soundtracks the ascent up a mountain that Clarkson reveals has never been driven up before, you can almost hear the blood pressure of numerous eco-campaigners rising thunderously. He even utters the words 'peat bog' and that's where it all went wrong. Environmentalists were furious at the potential damage they said he might have caused to the landscape, pointing out the fragile eco-systems that survive in such peat bogs and how the emissions and tyre marks could cause irreparable damage. Dave Morris, director of the Scottish Ramblers Association, remarked: 'We found Clarkson's stunt highly irresponsible. Driving to the top of a mountain over open ground is inevitably going to cause damage to the countryside. And when viewers see a man like Clarkson doing this it encourages them to try to do similar things. It is wrong for the BBC to promote such hare-brained and reckless behaviour.'

And it wasn't only the eco-campaigners who were riled by Clarkson: after the shoot, he jumped into a helicopter to head down south for an urgent meeting but mistakenly took the keys to the Land Rover with him. He had to make a hasty about-turn and hover over the car before dropping the keys down to a frustrated and tired production crew waiting below!

It wasn't the first time that the show had run into problems with environmentalists either. In 2004, the BBC paid £250 in compensation and issued an unreserved apology to a Somerset Parish Council when Clarkson deliberately rammed a Toyota Hilux pick-up truck into a 30-year-old Horse Chestnut tree in an infamous feature. His response was: 'The Parish Council is funded by central government, which is funded by me so it's my tree!'

The presenter has implied that many 'green campaigners' are actually former trade unionists or CND protestors whose causes have dissipated and so they need something else to focus on. And quite often on the show, ecological concerns are dismissed almost as an aside: for example, when introducing a feature on life-size remote control cars in Series 7, Richard Hammond points out that the *Top Gear* office gets lots of letters from boffins, usually about 'something dreary like global warming.'

Often Clarkson's newspaper columns are the source of much of the ire directed towards him, rather than his comments on *Top Gear*. In 2005, he told the *Independent*: 'Of course there is no doubt that the world is warming up, but let's just stop and think for a moment what the consequences might be ... Switzerland loses its skiing resorts, the beach in Miami is washed away, North Carolina gets knocked over by a hurricane – anything bothering you yet? It isn't even worthy of a shrug.'

Top Gear is also unlikely to be on the Christmas card list of road safety campaigners. It's perhaps inevitable the show will never going to appeal to such people, especially those who may have lost loved ones on Britain's road network. Although the first generation of the show featured a large number of safety films, the new programme was slammed by campaigners and it's not hard to see why. Take the very first episode of new *Top Gear* when a feature was broadcast in which the team attempted to discover if a car could travel fast enough not to register on a speed camera.

The premise was this: a speed camera takes two photos in rapid succession and compares the distance travelled between the two images to calculate an exact speed. However, *Top Gear* conjectured if the car was travelling sufficiently fast enough, it would have passed the camera lens range for the second photo, therefore no second snap could be taken and no comparative calculation made. In other words, it would be travelling too fast to land a speeding ticket.

The production team are no fools and so the presenters continually stated the feature was 'in the name of scientific endeavour'. Really, this was disingenuous and always spoken with a slight wry smile. The first car to be tested by the all-black Stig was a Honda Civic Type R doing 129mph but it failed abysmally and was clocked. Next up was a Mercedes CL55 AMG, which reached a mighty 148mph but was still done for speeding. The third and final car was the insanely fast (and beautiful) TVR Tuscan S, which raced to 170mph past the camera. Back in the studio, the team revealed that the TVR was nowhere to be seen on the second photo and therefore it had indeed been going too fast to get a speeding ticket.

Quite how the stunt resonated with swathes of boy racers across the country who might see this as a challenge is unknown. Suffice to say, safety campaigners were appalled and it was not the last time they would lock horns with the show.

Although he has talked of driving extremely fast on public roads at various times, at the time of writing it is believed Jeremy Clarkson has a clean driving licence despite writing on *Timesonline.co.uk* that, 'on a recent drive across Europe [in a

Bugatti Veyron] I desperately wanted to reach the top speed but I ran out of road when the needle hit 240mph.' This is selective, though – Jeremy has been a keen advocate of a restricted 20mph speed limit outside schools, for example.

James May insists *Top Gear* are responsible for the road tests themselves: '*Top Gear* never does anything reckless on a road,' he told the *Daily Mail*. 'When we go on a track, we go mad, set things on fire and Jeremy crashes, but that's what tracks are for. Apart from anything else, none of us can afford to break the speed limit – our careers would be instantly ruined. Remarkably, Jeremy is quite a courteous driver, even though he's very rude in every other respect.'

The *Top Gear* crew have done other 'road safety' features, too. One investigated that age-old concern about how close you can drive to the rear engine of Boeing 747 without being obliterated by the jet stream – something Clarkson dubbed 'a public service film.' These 400-ton monsters of the air have 58,000lb of thrust on each engine and can reach 575mph, yet the man on the street still doesn't know just how close he can drive without getting killed to death, as Clarkson would say. Well, trusty old *Top Gear* did the test and the answer wasn't pleasant: a 1.5-ton Ford Mondeo was blasted 50 feet and ripped to shreds, while for those intrepid hippy-esque *Top Gear* viewers (now *there's* a minority), a 2CV was launched 100 feet along the tarmac and completely destroyed.

A more obvious and very real safety issue broached by the *Top Gear* crew was the terrible number of deaths on level crossings every year. In Series 9, they teamed up with Network Rail. The initial premise seemed serious, with Clarkson stating that elderly drivers are three times more likely to crash than their grandkids, pointing out how many had driven the wrong way down motorways or even into the sea (sadly, *sans* May's sailing boat-car). Pretty quickly, the sombre tone is somewhat undermined by the flaky statistics he offers, such as the number of people involved in such incidents: 'many people are injured every year.'

They then place a *Top Gear* perennial, the Renault Espace, on a railway track and hurtle a train right into it (it wasn't the first time the car had been mangled by the *Top Gear* team – a previous episode saw them attempt to make their own convertible People Carriers, a feat 'achieved' with the use of grinders, cutters and various other somewhat brutal tools!) The slow-motion carnage at the level crossing is genuinely shocking and instant death would have been unavoidable for the driver. It's replayed several times, with each slower version more appalling to watch. A very clear advert was painted on the side of the train stating 'Level crossings – don't run the risk' and when it was replayed in slow-motion, the message was loud and clear.

What is clever about the piece is that although Clarkson is unable to resist making gags about health and safety (and even ends by saying the real message is 'Always wear a high visibility jacket'), in fact the viewer comes away from the feature determined never to run a level crossing. Even with this safety piece, complaints followed the screening as the previous week in Cumbria, there had been a train crash with one fatality.

Still, certain groups are not for turning. In 2005, Transport 2000's spokesman Steve Hounsham issued the following statement: '[*Top Gear*] glamorises speed and fails to make the connection with danger on the roads. Through the use of Jeremy Clarkson as presenter, with his distinctive image, it is in danger of encouraging a 'yobbish' attitude on the road ... Everyone is talking about how to reduce car use, cut climate change emissions and make the roads safer, but, to quote in perhaps its own language, *Top Gear* effectively sticks up its fingers to this ...

If we must have Jeremy Clarkson on the television, let's give him something useful to do, such as trying out public transport or road-testing new bicycles. Perhaps he would like to drive a bus; he'd find it just as much fun as a Ferrari.'

And it's not just road safety campaigners who fall out with *Top Gear*, so do road users. Take that hardy British favourite, the White Van Man. The team are famously hard on this particular species of British driver and regularly poke fun at him. On one occasion, they bought a van for £1,000 (ostensibly a 'Cheap Car/Van Challenge') and then had to come up with, and paint their own company name on the side before attempting a series of challenges. The tests included a straight 'van drag' race although rather more dragging than racing was going on, as all the vans were so slow (indeed, the *Top Gear* cameraman was so used to faster cars launching from the start that he swept the camera down the track before the vans even left the line!).

Next up was a cargo drop, with each presenter ordered to load their vans with the usual removal men's gear such as lamps, mattresses, paintings, chairs and ... an illegal immigrant each! The first time I watched this feature, I laughed aloud before thinking, 'Thank God they haven't said what country the immigrants come from, they might just get away with it!' ... only for it to be revealed moments later, with spectacular lack of political correctness, that they were Albanian. And it got worse: May was struggling to get his goods loaded and so he gave an immigrant some cash to help. While Clarkson bemoaned manual labour, one of the immigrants just ran off. Undeterred, the three pals then used a laser measuring device to see who could get in their white van and do the closest bumper hogging before attempting – and largely failing – to complete their own door repair.

Quite how the whole sequence was supposed to appease the white van men who took exception to *Top Gear*'s repeatedly derogatory remarks is unclear. At least on occasion they have 'celebrated' the white van such as the time when they tried to lap the Nürburgring racetrack in a stripped-down model in under 10 minutes to celebrate the 40th anniversary of the Transit.

Then there's the lorry drivers: during one feature in the opening episode of Series 12, Clarkson commented that being a truck driver was a really hard job: 'You've got to change gear, change gear, change gear, check mirror ... murder a prostitute. Change gear, change gear, murder ... that's a lot of effort in a day!' Given only two years earlier, five prostitutes had been murdered in Ipswich, the comment was bound to cause trouble. The BBC said it was merely a 'comic rebuttal' of a common misconception about lorry drivers and even Eddie Stobart, the name behind the nation's most famous haulage firm, said it needed to be taken with a pinch of salt.

Clarkson played it down again, saying people shouldn't worry about what a 'balding and irrelevant middle-aged man might have said.' Poking fun at his detractors, on the very next *Top Gear* he said he had an apology to make about something that had been in all the papers, only to proceed to say sorry for forgetting to put the 911's lap time on the board the previous week! Later, broadcasting watchdog Ofcom said they would not launch an investigation despite over 500 complaints.

And it's not just lorry drivers who take offence at the show's choice of words. The phrase 'politically incorrect' was virtually invented for *Top Gear*. As already noted, it's a fact that Clarkson and Co. have riled numerous 'foreign guests' with their comments about Polish SatNavs, dog-eating car executives and illegal immigrants but there's always more work/offending to be done. In a summer 2009 episode, the presenters were testing saloon cars and summed up which model would suit which type of person. Obviously such broad-brush strokes used to describe a car are bound to generalise but for some viewers, their comments went a step too far. While pointing out that one particular saloon was for businessmen, they also placed a pie and a key on the bonnet of an Audi. Back in the studio, James May then denigrated Richard Hammond as a 'steak and kidney pie lock unlocker' and then Clarkson waded in, suggesting the car was more suitable for those whose business was selling pegs and heather. (Incidentally, over the years they had used the word before, calling a hammer 'the tool of a pikey' and have variously used the term to insult each other.)

Several viewers complained but the media's reaction was even more terse. Jodie Matthews of the *Guardian* was not impressed and eloquently explained why: 'A typical example of the blokey, exclusive, bullying humour that has made the show so popular? ... Isn't this a good thing? The answer to these questions is a firm no. This old-fashioned racism is not funny and has serious political effects. Its apparent acceptability is a damning indictment of how slowly we as a culture are moving in terms of changing attitudes towards Gypsies and travellers.' She goes on to lambast the in-joke as a snide way of sidestepping the censors and suggests such verbiage is directly linked to 'a strategy of racist discourse since at least the 19th century. It was effectively employed by George Smith of Coalville in his anti-Gypsy campaigns of the 1870s, and even by those who sought to romanticise Gypsies in the late 1800s,' therefore 'reinforcing ethnic and cultural stereotypes.'

For Matthews, *Top Gear* choosing to make remarks such as these is 'unoriginal and boring; we have heard it all before, for centuries.' Similar criticism followed what some viewers saw as the inappropriate use of the word 'gay' or other comments that risk offending the gay community such as use of the rhyming slang 'ginger beer' or remarks about being 'bummed'.

Not all of Clarkson's enemies or critics are campaigners, though. One of his most high-profile spats was with Piers Morgan, the acid tongued former *Sun* columnist, who dominated much of Fleet Street as the *Mirror*'s editor before a faked military photo scandal cost him his job. Thereafter, he turned his hand to becoming one of the world's most famous TV personalities on shows such as *America's Got Talent* as well as his own chat shows.

Jeremy Clarkson was one of three people that Morgan says he has had a long-standing dislike for (the other two being David Yelland and Ian Hislop). So, why was there such acrimony between the two? Well, Morgan had published pictures of Clarkson with his female producer in a car. Clarkson was livid and, as a happily married man, incensed by the invasion into his privacy and the implied insinuation. The resentment festered for three years and then at a Press Awards ceremony in 2004, Clarkson actually hit Morgan. Thereafter the former Fleet Street man suggested to *The Times* that Clarkson believed that because 'he's a *Sun* and *Sunday Times* journalist, therefore he's immune to the normal coverage of a TV star who might give fancy interviews about his solid marriage.' He went on to say, 'I actually didn't care that much about the Clarkson stuff until he began behaving ridiculously, smacking me round the head. He's perfectly entitled to smack me around the head, but the idea that smacking editors will help your PR is rather short-sighted.'

Of course, not all criticism of *Top Gear* is aimed at their outspoken views or mad stunts. Sometimes it's just direct slating of the show itself. One such regular criticism focuses on an alleged repetition/overuse of sequences: for example, the frequency of military hardware. In the last show of Series 1, *Top Gear* ran a feature that saw a TVR versus a Harrier jump jet; back in the 1960s the Harrier was first tested at Dunsfold airfield, no less. But we have also famously seen Clarkson avoid the bullets of the Irish Guards in an SLK55 AMG. This latter scene was at the Eastmere 'village', a replica of a German hamlet that had originally been built post-war to allow Cold War British soldiers to practise fighting the Russians. Of course the Health & Safety bods wouldn't allow live bullets to be used – not even against their nemesis Clarkson – so he wore a special jacket, which picked up the laser 'bullets' that the soldiers fired.

We've also seen a Lotus Exige tracked by an Apache gunship, which was very exciting, proving the Norfolk-built sports-car remains the best handling car in the world by avoiding the helicopter's laser missile lock altogether (there was a fake missile lock and destruction of the Exige at the end of the piece). Yet we've similarly seen tanks chasing Range Rovers, also with a fake missile hit at the end of the piece. Too much similarity is an accusation also raised over numerous games of car football, caravan bashing, excessive supercar coverage and so on.

Other critics say even some of the language is repetitive. Clarkson has used the word 'savage' to describe several cars' acceleration: the Enzo, Nissan GT-R and the Ariel Atom being three examples.

Other critics complain about the resources used and some of the statistics for producing *Top Gear* are indeed mind-boggling. In 2009, the Ministry of Defence attracted a fairly heavy battering of criticism when it was revealed that they had spent 141 days on *Top Gear* stunts – this at a time when there was frequent demands for troops in combat to be supplied with more armour and other life-protecting equipment. The *Top Gear* stunts included using specialist military equipment worth billions of pounds. Information was made public following a canny claim by the Press Association, who were then able to reveal that among the MoD 'appearances' were: the Apache helicopter trying to get that missile lock on the Exige, a parachutist from the Red Devils display team racing Richard Hammond in a Porsche Cayenne, *HMS Ark Royal* being used in a film about the Rolls-Royce Phantom, an RAF Typhoon racing a Bugatti Veyron at RAF Coningsby airfield, a beach assault with the Royal Marines while driving a Ford Fiesta, including Lynx helicopters and amphibious landing craft and a game of 'British bulldog' against high-tech armoured vehicles.

The MoD usually supplied this hardware free of charge and argued this was brilliant publicity for a generation who might be considering a role in the armed forces. They further responded to the criticism by pointing out that a 30-second advertisement for the MoD would cost at least £50,000 and that all filming took place during scheduled training hours: 'Showcasing our people and equipment on popular television programmes is an excellent way to raise public awareness about the work of the armed forces and to encourage support for our troops.'

However, the real problem for the *Top Gear* producers is this: how do you keep coming up with ideas to fill an entire hour's worth of TV every Sunday? To date, there have been 15 series of the new generation of the programme, covering 123 one-hour episodes. That's a lot of TV. Then there are the specials, spin-offs and charity episodes. The crew might spend many days on location filming a piece (and an inconsiderable amount of cash in the process) only for that feature to use up perhaps ten minutes of screen time. There are – unavoidably – a finite number of ways to review cars, talk about them and show them off. Likewise, there are only so many words you can use to describe speed, acceleration, power, handling and so on.

Although it's understandable that critics raise such complaints, it seems extremely unforgiving and harsh when directed towards a production set-up that is widely regarded as one of the finest in modern television. And that brings me back to being a *Top Gear* fan: the show's critics may sometimes be right but I still love seeing the gang do this stuff.

In turn, the *Top Gear* team is usually pretty thick-skinned about any abuse. Indeed, Clarkson is not about to concede to all the *Top Gear* haters. He has variously defended his words and the show's actions, but as we have seen, when he feels he has overstepped the mark then he will apologise. In the face of growing dissent over his brusque approach to so many subjects, Clarkson sounded weary when writing in *Top Gear* magazine that the criticisms of him were as much indicative of an ever-growing and insidious culture of positive discrimination, which he felt was beginning to suffocate TV and media creativity in general. He suggested in their liberal haste to balance out too many white heterosexual male presenters, TV bosses were obsessed with having 'black Muslim lesbians' on TV shows and continued: 'Chalk and cheese, they reckon, works but here we have *Top Gear* setting new records after six years using cheese and cheese. It confuses them.'

The article was in the wake of the BBC having to combat the flames of a 'racism' row in 2009 surrounding the highly popular *Strictly Come Dancing*, when Anton Du Beke referred off-screen to his dance partner Laila Rouass as a 'Paki'. Du Beke immediately apologised, but then the show's presenter Bruce Forsyth said the country needed to get a sense of humour, which further angered some people. Brucie himself then issued a statement to clarify his words, saying, 'Racially offensive language is never either funny or acceptable.' And just as the BBC was attempting to draw a line under the controversy, Clarkson penned his far-from-innocuous thoughts in *Top Gear* magazine. As is often the way, however, his words were selectively quoted: yes, he'd said that but he also defended women drivers and asked why there were none in Formula 1. By way of proving that women are brilliant drivers, he finished the column saying the worst driver in the world was *Top Gear*'s own studio director.

Clarkson's producer, his old school friend Andy Wilman, is even less forgiving. He admits that he finds it hard to take the BBC seriously when his team are hauled in over yet another complaint and has also gone on record saying that he 'can't be arsed with Ofcom'.

On one occasion in 2009, it momentarily seemed as if the *Top Gear* haters might have finally secured their victory after all. Shortly after the Gordon Brown 'one-eyed Scottish idiot' incident and the later c-word furore, *Top Gear* ran a compelling feature on the new V12 Aston Martin Vantage (Series 13, Episode 7), with the usual insightful and entertaining comments about a car that the show had historically been extremely positive about. At the end of the piece, however, Clarkson was filmed driving the beautiful car through classic British country roads but he suddenly turned melancholy, mulling in quiet tones about how that type of car was under increasing pressure from noise, safety and environmental campaigners. Perhaps in any other series, this might have been taken at face value but given recent problems, his closing comment that this 'feels like an ending' was imbued with massive symbolism. There was no last-minute gag, no tongue-in-cheek side remark or cheeky look to camera: only what appeared to be genuine sadness.

That same night the internet was swamped with rumours on Twitter, in chat rooms and forums – was *Top Gear* over? Was Clarkson tipping us off this was it, that the game was up? Was that shot of the Aston cruising over the green hills the last-ever clip of *Top Gear*?

Well, no. The BBC denied this was the end and said a programme as popular as *Top Gear* would not come to a close without the public being duly notified more formally in advance. Clarkson swiftly backed up his employers, saying in his *Sun* column that the show would return for a new series unless he got 'struck by a giant meteorite or spontaneously combusts'. In fact, they had already started to film new episodes and so, in an indignant verbal volley bound to infuriate all *Top Gear*'s many critics, Clarkson went on to insist: 'Fire up the Vantage!'

Some of the *Top Gear* old guard. *Clockwise from top left*: Quentin Willson, Tiff Needell, Vicki Butler-Henderson and Kate Humble.

Above: The original 'black Stig', Perry McCarthy (*left*)　© *Getty Images*

Below: New *Top Gear* – Jeremy Clarkson, James May and Richard Hammond filming at Dunsfold Aerodrome.

Above left: the second Stig in his legendary white suit. The Stig character has been instrumental in the success of 'new' *Top Gear*.

Above right and below: The globally successful *Top Gear* has bagged a whole host of awards, not least a prestigious Emmy.

Clarkson and Hammond taking part in one of *Top Gear*'s famous challenges – constructing stretch limousines from ordinary cars to transport celebrities to the 2007 Brit Awards.

More of the *Top Gear* crew's hilarious antics – including attempting to sail the Channel in boats made from cars (above). Clarkson, May, Hammond and The Stig have also staged crazy events to promote *Top Gear Live*, such as crossing Tower Bridge in a tank and parking a Maserati GT on a pedestrianised street in Dublin.

Above: *Top Gear* has come in for criticism from safety groups, particularly after Richard Hammond's horrific high-speed crash in 2006. James May then courted controversy by taking to the skies in 2009 in a caravan suspended from an airship.

Below: The best job in the world at the best TV show in the world – another day in the office for The Stig.

Some of the fastest and most expensive cars in the world have been round the *Top Gear* track – including the Bugatti Veyron (*above*) and the Koenigsegg CCXR (*below*).

Above left and right and *below left*: The *Top Gear* dream team – Jeremy Clarkson, Richard Hammond and James May.

Below right: Ben Collins, the man controversially unmasked as The Stig in 2010.

CHAPTER 12

Cheap Car Challenges

An enduring and favourite *Top Gear* feature is the so-called 'Cheap Car Challenge'. Clearly this part of the programme is not used to review new cars, but usually serves as a way to prove (or disprove) a point about the motoring/transport world or sometimes just to have a ludicrous day out. Budgets range from under £1,000 to as much as £10,000 when they were buying 1970s' supercars (a Maserati Merak, a Ferrari 308 GT4 and a Lamborghini Urraco). The team has also spent £5,000 finding a track day car that's useable on normal roads and among many others, tried a 'How much lorry do you get for £5,000?' They also filmed a cheap Porsche challenge and then a follow-up: the 'Cheap Coupés that aren't Porsches' test.

So, for the category of challenges that are filmed to prove a point, we see them buying a car for £100 to prove it's cheaper to drive old bangers to Manchester than catch a train (which cost about £180). Clarkson's Volvo 760 GLE won, principally because he only paid £1 for it! It was picked up as a former trade-in at a local dealership close to his Chipping Norton home. He'd been concerned that purchasing the car himself would leave him accused of using his profile to get a cheap head-start, so he actually sent his wife in to buy it.

The *Top Gear* team has also driven around the M25 in a petrol and diesel version of the same car to examine fuel efficiency, attempted to get from London to Edinburgh and back in an Audi on one tank of diesel and subjected a Renault Scenic and Ford C-Max to one year's worth of wear in a night to test its hardiness. To prove roadworks take too long to complete, they undertook a week's worth of repairs near Bedford, Warwickshire and tried to complete the job in one day. With sustenance provided by roadside berries and later fish and chips, the team and their gang actually finished the task on time.

Some of the challenges are mainly for comedy value, albeit with an undercurrent of seriousness, such as the 'Can you buy an Alfa Romeo for £1,000 or less without it completely ruining your life all the time?' For other challenges, however, the team is just having fun, there's no serious side to a piece whatsoever and it really is all about the entertainment. For example, how about the time they tried to make their own police cars for £1,500? Equipping their chosen steeds with various frankly ridiculous contraptions, such as a homemade stinger, a paint-spraying theft prevention device and wheel spikes, among other tasks they had to attend and clear up a traffic accident and then best of all, chase a criminal – in this case a white-suited tame racing driver called Ronnie Stigs – around a track and apprehend him.

The only slivers of possible seriousness were the digs reserved for the Health and Safety Executive, making the point that before a police team can deploy the so-called 'boxing in' technique, in theory they have to meet 13 separate criteria – all in the heat of a high-speed car chase. This piece was interspersed with a policeman telling the camera in dry detail about the methodology of chasing stolen vehicles, no doubt fulfilling the advertorial appeal of the feature to the Force. As ever, Clarkson scoffed at the protracted way of stopping criminals and the bureaucracy involved: in his opinion, you should be able to ram the car thief off the road or pull up alongside the vehicle and blow his head off. Now there's one for the Police Complaints Authority!

The cheap car premise has, of course, also been used for some of the show's best long-form features. It's at the heart of the previously mentioned 'US Road Trip' but also two further *Top Gear* specials, namely the treks through Vietnam and Bolivia. In the former, they travel 1,000 miles from Ho Chi Minh City north to near Hanoi, unusually this time mainly on motorbikes. The same distance is travelled through Bolivia in South America, a journey party to some hilarious scenes trying to get their three chosen vehicles on a raft, repairing a fuel cap with a tampon and waterproofing an engine with a lubricated condom. Sounds daft, but this particular special was a big ratings winner for the BBC.

The same restricted budgets were the impetus for the team's excursion through Botswana for one of the programme's other specials. With *Top Gear*'s ever-expanding horizons, it was perhaps inevitable that they headed over to Africa. They were sent packing with just £1,500 each, under instruction to buy a strictly two-wheel drive, non-off-road vehicle with which to drive across the entire country, from the eastern border of Zimbabwe to the western border of Namibia, a distance of around 1,000 miles. The rules also stated that if one of the three cars broke down beyond reasonable repair, as a punishment the journey would have to be completed in a VW Beetle because they all dislike that particular German car so much.

Clarkson chose a fetching 1981 Lancia Beta Coupé, which

proved a disastrous choice and was constantly breaking down. Richard Hammond opted for a 40bhp Opel Kadett from 1963 (we are told it's the same age as Jezza but in better nick) and James May bought a 1984 Mercedes-Benz 230E. The first challenge was to prove to people who live in Surrey that you don't need a 4x4 if you live up a lane that occasionally gets leaves on the road. The cars quickly started to go wrong, with the Lancia's rally heritage counting for nothing and May finding he had the knob from a five-gear Merc glued to what he now discovered was a four-gear car. Driving through dense bush and wooded plains, the cars nonetheless somehow made it to camp, albeit with Hammond's broken alternator meaning he had to light up the path with a hand-torch.

While the 'wooden spoon' of the old VW Beetle followed them like some automotive Grim Reaper, the trio started the most obviously dangerous part of the journey: to cross the Okavango Delta game reserve, which is teeming with wild animals. By this point, Clarkson and May had already stripped their cars of much of the bodywork, so they had to stop off at a shanty town first to have hasty repairs done, using tarpaulin and bits of old wood. While May wasn't looking, Clarkson hid a cow's head in his boot in the hope that it would attract lions but this backfired when they tried to move the animal's head to May's tent, only to discover they'd put it in Hammond's sleeping quarters by mistake.

After sinking in a stagnant pond, Hammond's car was completely flooded but he declined the offer of simply shooting the floor to let the water out. By now he had become sentimentally attached to his classic car and the other two presenters fell about laughing when he revealed that he'd named the Opel 'Oliver'. The last laugh was with Oliver, though: after a night of extensive repairs from the flood damage, the car was raring to go, leaving Clarkson, 'speechless for first time in 47 years.' Afterwards they had to cross the salt flats of the Makgadikgadi Pan, which left Clarkson and May's stripped-out cars (and eyes) filled with dust (and yes, the decision to drive over those fragile salt flats caused uproar among environmentalists; fears of an influx of boy racers flying to Botswana to copy the salt flats' race proved unfounded, however).

All three made it to the Namibian border, but who was the winner? None of them, it transpired, because only the dreaded VW Beetle trailing behind had actually made the entire journey without modification! It's unlikely the £4,500 spent on the vehicles for this particular Cheap Car Challenge was even a fraction of the show's final budget, though.

CHAPTER 13

The Bugatti Veyron

When cars are sent to *Top Gear* for testing, it's usually left for the manufacturer to insure the vehicle and take any subsequent damage on the chin. This is often a new set of tyres or a burnt-out clutch or brake disc and with cheaper cars, writing them off is not necessarily a problem. As former producer Jon Bentley recalls, the car makers are normally fairly laid-back – after all, they are potentially getting a very high-profile advertisement (provided the review is positive, of course): 'The manufacturers would loan the car for about a week. In the early days, I used to worry about tyre wear. I can recall doing an item on the principles of car handling with Tiff Needell and at the end, I looked at the tyres on this BMW 535 after we'd finished filming and I was like, "Arrgghh! These tyres are in a terrible state!" I rang them up and was told not to worry about it.'

This philosophical approach is not applied to every make of car, however. The most obvious example is the world's fastest production car, the Bugatti Veyron. In this case, the manufacturer (actually Volkswagen) was perhaps understandably rumoured to be initially reluctant to hand over the Veyron, which sells for around the £1 million mark. This is not uncommon with such supercars. Some years earlier, the landmark hypercar that Ferrari released under their owner's name – the F60, aka the Enzo – was considered by its maker to be inappropriate to give to *Top Gear* at all. The show's producers repeatedly tried to secure a test car but the team at Maranello refused to be moved; they even asked Jay Kay but perhaps understandably, he wasn't about to hand over his pride and joy!

It was a full two years before they eventually succeeded with typical *Top Gear* guile and craft. Nick Mason, drummer with rock legends Pink Floyd, had bought an Enzo and he agreed to 'lend' the car to the show for testing provided they plug his new book. Of course, any programme on the BBC is not allowed to advertise so in order to comply with the licence fee, Clarkson said they would do no such thing and instead came up with a cunning plan.

He then proceeded to reside over a feature where the greatest Ferrari ever built was described as being comparable only to Nick Mason's new book. Both he and Mason –'author and part-time drummer' – held copies of the new publication while they chatted and Clarkson even waved a copy in front of Mason's face as he talked. The 'plug' even came complete with a Tesco 'Every Little Helps'-style till ring! It was very funny and somehow *Top Gear* managed to get away with it.

Perhaps it wasn't entirely without precedent when a few years later, it was whispered that Bugatti were similarly reluctant with their stunning Veyron. As a quick historical aside, the re-launch of the Bugatti marque in such a phenomenal way seemed a surprise to many, but actually the company had been there before. In 1992, the brand had launched the EB110 SS and its history and spec reads like the Veyron of some 13 years later. Back then, Bugatti's new owner Romano Artiolo wanted to build the most technically advanced supercar ever – just as his VW counterparts did with the Veyron. Again, like the Veyron, they created brand new techniques, including the first-ever use of a carbon-fibre monocoque chassis, originally developed on French space rockets. The early 1990s' design even had a speed-sensitive rear wing for high speed, just like the Veyron. And the price was £281,000 – in today's money about £500,000 (some way short of the Veyron's hefty price tag). The acceleration was 0–60 in 3.2 seconds, compared to the Veyron's 2.5 seconds. And yes, they also called the extreme model 'Super Sport', too.

Fast forward to 2005 and Bugatti once more shocked the world with their new car. The Veyron is widely regarded as the greatest production car ever built. For sheer car pornography, however, the Bugatti is the 'Linda Lovelace' of the road. The mind-boggling statistics are worth dwelling on momentarily, not least to explain why the three battle-hardened presenters were so keen to get their hands on one and why they genuinely salivate every time they sit in the legend. The car possesses an apocalyptical 1001bhp, which hurls it to 60mph in 2.5 seconds, on to 100 in 4.5 seconds and ultimately onwards to a top speed of 253mph. By then it's chewing up the road at nearly 400 feet a second. Its monumental engine is basically two massive four-litre V8s strapped together with four turbos and all gelled together by slithers of VW engineering genius. To cool the colossal engine at its heart, the beast has 10 radiators that can suck in 10,000 gallons of air every minute when at full tilt. Bugatti even found that when they fitted slimmer door mirrors to try and get less drag, the nose of the car started to lift as the mirrors had been creating such downforce at that staggering top speed. The Bugatti's moveable rear air brake generates as much braking force as a basic VW Polo; the indicator costs £4,500, the tyres will set you back about £18,000 and only last for approximately 3,500 miles – if you drive carefully. A service is in the region of £12,000.

And yes, it's true: the car does cost £5 million to make and then it's sold for around the £1 million mark – a huge financial loss for the Volkswagen group, who own the marque, but a stunning piece of engineering brilliance that has quite simply redefined the very meaning of 'supercar'. Given the constant pressure on fuel economy, the environment and safety, the Veyron may possibly never be surpassed.

So, imagine *Top Gear*'s frustration when Bugatti wouldn't allow them to test a Veyron around their test track. Over the years, plenty of gleaming supercar metal or carbon fibre has been battered there so if it did exist, then perhaps Bugatti's initial reluctance could be forgiven. Fortunately, when they finally agreed to give the car up, boy, did *Top Gear* do them proud! Perhaps for no other car has the programme gone to such extreme lengths to film the most stunning features, time after time.

It would be a full two years after the car's initial launch when they finally got their hands on one for the *Top Gear* test track, but its first appearance on the show was in a brilliant race that occurred in Series 7, Episode 5, aired on 11 December 2005 (the year of the launch). The challenge was simple: what's the fastest way to get a truffle sniffed out of the ground by a sniffer dog in Italy all the way back to London? Clarkson had to drive across Europe in the Bugatti from Alba in northern Italy and race May and Hammond in a Cessna 182 private light aircraft, with the finishing line being a restaurant at the top of the NatWest Tower in London.

Over the years, there have been many 'improbable races' but this feature still ranks as one of Clarkson's greatest-ever performances. In this author's opinion, it is also *Top Gear*'s best-ever race; they've run some fabulous races over the years, pitting the Nissan GT-R against a bullet train in Japan, a Mercedes Benz SLR McLaren against a passenger ferry, a Ferrari Daytona against a powerboat, as well as a variety of cars against a plethora of opponents including pigeons, skateboarders, parachutists, rock climbers, snowmobiles, greyhounds, kayaks, rollerbladers, a 'tall man' and of course, a snooker player but the Veyron versus a plane was the finest *Top Gear* race by some margin.

Clarkson has driven hundreds, probably thousands of cars in his time and even when it's a particularly purist Porsche or an especially bad family saloon, he seems able to muster some enthusiasm. However, the beauty of this debut Veyron feature is that he didn't have to pretend about anything – he was in sheer heaven. From the moment he pressed the beautifully polished 'Start' button on Bugatti's monster, he was in his element. The first words out of his mouth were, simply, 'This is fast!' Unadulterated joy was clearly visible on his face and audible in his words and as such, made for classic telly. Among the gems he came out with were his summing-up of the landmark car as, 'a triumph for lunacy over commonsense, a triumph for man over nature and a triumph for Volkswagen over absolutely every other carmaker in the world!' My own particular favourite was when he tried to capture just how ferocious and breath-taking the car's acceleration was: 'You can't just put your foot down in this thing whenever the mood takes you … you've got to think, is there another car within a mile of me?'

Meanwhile, Hammond and May stumbled about doing lengthy pre-flight checks on the Cessna. In October 2006, James had obtained a light aircraft pilot's licence having trained at White Waltham Airfield. Here at the airport he was filmed at ease and enjoying himself, while Hammond was frustrated and impatient to get airborne. This episode as good as any portrays their hilarious 'double act', the perfect foil for Clarkson's 'bad guy' image – a motoring Laurel and Hardy, if you will.

After leaving Italy, Clarkson headed into 'car hating' Switzerland and was so confident about victory that he stopped off for tea – although the feature notably doesn't mention the number of petrol stops he would have had to make (using Bugatti's own statistics, the car's petrol consumption is between eight and thirteen miles per gallon, falling to three miles per gallon at higher speeds). He also takes up time phoning for an insurance quote, only to find that the 'happy' man on the other end of the line thought the Bugatti was a Rover! Because the car didn't come with a Bluetooth device – standard even in most cheap cars these days – Clarkson had to wear one of those annoying ear-pieces to make this call. For the purposes of this book, the author successfully obtained a quote for a Bugatti and if you drive like a nun and have never had a speeding ticket of any description, it would set you back just over £25,000 a year!

The comedy was ramped up as Hammond berated the ramshackle plane while May then admitted he had had to land because he was not qualified to fly in the dark. James himself has owned two planes: a Luscombe 8A Silvaire (now sold) and an American Champion 8KCAB Super Decathlon, allegedly with the registration number G-OCOK, a crafty reference to his catchphrase (such as it is) on the show of 'Oh, cock!'

After revealing May's night-time flying curfew, a frantic rush to the Eurostar and eventually a Routemaster 'dash' across London ensued, only for the duo to discover that Clarkson had already arrived at the restaurant at the top of the NatWest Tower with enough time to spare to order a pint and his pasta ... with truffles, of course.

Then Clarkson summed up what he calls 'the best car ever made' in what is probably his greatest-ever impassioned speech with the words: 'It's a hollow victory, because I've got to go for the rest of my life knowing that I'll never own that car; I'll never experience that power again.' Mind you, Jeremy's now so successful and famous that maybe one day that will change. So, was James May suitably impressed by all this hyperbole? No, he was asleep ...

As an aside, this trip is a great example of how seamlessly edited *Top Gear* can be. When you step back from the exciting race, you have to ask how they get the shots of the car speeding along picturesque roads, or in this case the footage of May flying his 'toaster with wings', as it was called. The simple answer is that after the presenters have completed their actual race, the film crew go back and painstakingly shoot footage to embellish the programme's aesthetics. Clarkson has gone on record to state that the programme's races are never fixed and cited one example of a cameraman having to urinate in a bottle because there was no opportunity to slow down and relieve himself properly. In this case, the Bugatti was deemed so powerful that they actually sent The Stig to safely complete the extra footage.

As we have seen, in a later article for *The Sunday Times*, Clarkson intimated he'd actually tried to take the Veyron to its top speed of 253mph, but had run out of road at 240mph. Given the only roads in Europe where those speeds are legal are on the Autobahn in Germany, we can only presume that's where he took a detour to try out the full force of Bugatti's masterpiece.

The next time we see the team playing with the Veyron is when *Top Gear* wanted to test out its claimed top speed of 253mph. So who was chosen for this task? Why, the man christened Captain Slow, of course: James May. Actually, he did have 'previous'. In fact, James has travelled faster than any of the other presenters, reaching 1,320mph in a RAF Eurofighter Typhoon for his programme, *James May's 20th Century*. He's even been to the edge of space, travelling in a Lockheed U-2 spy plane to a height of 70,000 feet, which also makes him one of the highest humans in history, other than actual spacemen.

So in Series 9, Episode 2, May found out if the Veyron did exactly what it said on the tin and achieved that ridiculous speed of 253mph. This makes James May one of the fastest drivers in history, even including professional racers. Bugatti are rumoured to have a little book of those who they can confirm have achieved such a speed.

James had, in fact, topped 200mph several times before in numerous supercars on the show but this was far more bizarre: 'What I found weird about it, and this will seem absurd, is that 253mph feels a lot faster than 200mph,' he revealed in the *Daily Mail*, 'At 250, it suddenly gets to the point where things are happening faster than you can process the information.' Yet he became so accustomed to the staggering top speed that he found when he'd slowed right down to 70mph that it felt so pedestrian that he almost opened the door and got out, while waiting for it to roll to a halt. He maintains the Veyron's engineering is so perfect that reaching such a speed was in fact relatively easy.

May is making light of his achievement, however. Speaking exclusively for this book, the eminent neuroscientist and motorsport expert Dr Kerry Spackman explained why driving at such prodigious speeds is deceptively difficult: 'It's not just the sheer speed, it's the visual richness coming by. So if you're in a jumbo jet going 500mph, and you're looking out of the window at this great big fluffy cloud in the distance going by, it's no big deal because it's not visually rich, the clouds are big and they go past at a distance. However, when you're close to the ground and certain things are going by at a very high speed, your brain gets overloaded. What tends to happen then is you get tunnel vision where everything outside a certain area isn't processed: you can see it but your brain just decides there's just too much going on out there; all it can really focus on is what's immediately in front of it in a small area. So you can see everything but you can't do anything with that vision, the brain says it's all too complicated to deal with.

'What James May achieved was tremendous. If you think about it, the human brain evolved over millions of years to deal with a top speed of about 30kmph if you're lucky on a horse, or less if you are running. If you tune something for the normal environment it operates in, it works very well. Even up to about 50kmph, we are pretty aware of everything around us; however, as you get faster and faster, you start to attend to less and less.

'Imagine a TV screen playing back some footage, a single frame at a time. At slow speed you can tell each individual frame apart and as you speed the frames up, all that happens is they begin to flicker faster and faster. But you still see them as separate frames. Then all of a sudden your brain is overwhelmed and can't keep up, and then suddenly everything merges into a smooth movie. That's a television picture. This is an analogy with what's happening [to May in the Veyron] – at some point, the brain simply can't cope with everything so instead of trying to resolve all the detail, your brain starts to take shortcuts. Like the TV frame suddenly switching to a movie, it's a non-linear process. So, 300km/h isn't just three times 100 km/h; there's a real transition where it suddenly gets hard. Professional racing drivers have of course had years of practice to train the brain [in] how to cope with this but an amateur like James can quickly get overwhelmed. So when he was doing this extraordinary speed, he was getting bombarded with visual richness and the complexities of the task, trying to control the car and suddenly it can become overwhelming – it was remarkable.'

And what other TV show would race a fighter jet against a car? For a brilliant Series 10 Veyron feature, *Top Gear* didn't pick any old fighter jet either, but instead the revolutionary Eurofighter Typhoon, one of the most technologically advanced aircraft ever built. They had included fighter jets before, such as when they used the Harrier Jump Jet to analogise the new TVR 350c (the point being both were excellent updates of previous models), but this Typhoon piece was altogether different. The race – at RAF Coningsby airfield – was understandably one of *Top Gear*'s most complex shoots, with a reported 60-plus personnel on site for the day. Once again, the Veyron was getting the star treatment from *Top Gear*.

Another heart-pounding moment for Bugatti and *Top Gear* fans came in Series 12, when May drove the Veyron against Hammond's all-time favourite supercar, the stunning Pagani Zonda F. But the best head-to-head of all came in the following series, when the crew flew to Abu Dhabi to perform a straight drag race between the Veyron and the legendary McLaren F1. The sight of the Veyron streaming up a one-mile Abu Dhabi road alongside the McLaren is possibly one of – if not *the* – favourite clip in the entire history of *Top Gear*. It wasn't a fair fight, of course: remember, the Veyron is far more powerful in terms of bhp than even a F1 car (its top speed of 400kph is beyond the usual F1 top rate of 360kph).

On the day of the drag race, Hammond raced the Veyron while The Stig took the wheel of the F1. The McLaren F1 actually beat the Veyron off the line and held its own to around the 125mph mark, but then the colossal Veyron engine kicked in and left its rival for dust. Hammond said the slower start was due to leaving the Veyron's launch control switched off, which he only did to make it 'more interesting'.

One final mind-blowing statistic: if you set up a drag race in a McLaren F1 and a Veyron, you can let the F1 get to 120mph before the Veyron even starts and it will still reach 200mph first; in fact, if the Veyron starts at exactly the same time as the F1, it will get to 200mph and then nearly back to a standstill before the McLaren has yet to hit 200.

But the purpose of the Abu Dhabi drag race wasn't just to burn up prodigious amounts of fuel and tyre rubber: the show cleverly highlighted the contrasting design ethos in each car. The F1 has long been heralded as the ultimate purist's car, a stripped-back, no-frills racing experience on the road; the Veyron by contrast, has comfortable leather seats, a CD player, air-conditioning, all the mod-cons. The fact that The Stig was given the F1 is itself an indication of its racing purity (and therefore the skill needed to drive it), compared to the 'everyday use-ability' of the Veyron.

For this viewer at least, it wasn't about the actual race or the rights and wrongs of the designers' respective approaches, as much the sight of the two automotive legends on the same strip of tarmac. Just the thought of the two greatest cars ever built on the same piece of road was exhilarating. Having been lucky enough to travel in an F1 but not a Veyron, I have a soft spot for the former and was slightly saddened to find it so brutally despatched, but it almost wasn't about the winner: this was just such a beautifully filmed and subtle piece of TV.

In Series 15, *Top Gear* went to the very limits of the Veyron's capabilities once more when they tested the souped-up Super Sport version to see if its claimed top speed of 258mph (257.91, to be precise) was accurate. So, which red-blooded, death-defying, psychotic daredevil would Bugatti allow to take this beast on the road and film the speed record attempt? Why, Captain Slow again, of course. According to reports, the only reason why he was made to test this brutal hypercar was because Clarkson had hurt his neck driving a lorry through a brick wall and Hammond claimed to be unavailable as he was 'selling fish at Morrisons' (namely filming adverts for that supermarket, for which he is ridiculed mercilessly by his colleagues). May certainly lucked out with the testing of such a car and eventually reached a top speed of 259.11mph. After he climbed out, the Bugatti test driver got in and promptly took the Super Sport to 267.86 mph across the required two runs, confirming its status as the world's fastest production car (faster even than Bugatti had suspected).

At the time of writing, the Super Sport stands proud at the top of the *Top Gear* lap times with a stunning record of 1.16.8 minutes (nearly a full two seconds faster than its 'slow' sister car, the standard Veyron). Even the Gumpert Apollo, basically a racing car just about made road legal and safe, can't live with that – but for how long?

The Bugatti's apparent invincibility is regarded as so complete that it seemed to many no coincidence that in early 2010, Ferrari's chief executive Amedeo Felisa declared his company were no longer interested in such extravagant speeds: 'Top speed is not important to us anymore.'

Yet the Bugatti will not have it all its own way. Initially all contenders trembled, but then along came the American-built Shelby SSC Ultimate Aero. Made by a company whose founder invented a revolutionary scanning system for breast cancer, the Shelby can reach 256mph. Then the Bugatti hit back with the ludicrously bullet-like Super Sport and in October 2010, the new SSC was unveiled, boasting 1350bhp in a car only a third as heavy as a Veyron. It can wheel-spin in fourth gear above 100mph. Apparently.

So, where will all this speed freaking lead us? At the time of writing, several manufacturers are developing and building cars that may well top the Veyron Super Sport. One such model, the Transtar Dagger GT, comes with an estimated top speed of 314mph. If it ever materialises, there can be only one TV show to review it ...

CHAPTER 14

Richard Hammond, Part II

*T*here's a *Top Gear* sketch where Richard Hammond is seen casually walking around his 'estate' – the grounds of his £2 million mock castle in Herefordshire – talking about how driving fast cars for a living, mucking about with his mates and having a beautiful wife and kids is a dream life. He knows this very well, nothing is taken for granted. Speaking to the *Guardian*, he once said: 'My work spaces are the studio, the Cool Wall, the bunker and the track outside. Oh, and anything with a steering wheel. I have sat in a car driving in the hills of St Tropez and I've thought, "Another day in the office."' Generally, and contradictory to the oft-quoted British attitude to success, Hammond finds most *Top Gear* fans are supportive of him doing so well: 'If people are jealous of me, they are very generous. They come up and smile and say, "You've got the best job in the world."'

Hammond's wife Amanda is known to her friends as Mindy and the Hammond clan live near Weston under Penyard, Ross-on-Wye (they also own a plush apartment in central London). Mindy loves cars too, something which Hammond says is very fortunate for him! He appears to be a fond advocate of the country life and frequently involves himself in the local community: according to some reports, when he was announced as president of the 31st Herefordshire Country Fair – normally a sleepy, modestly rural event – over 15,000 people turned up on the day hoping to catch a glimpse of the star. So, Hammond is a petrol-head incarnate but he's also a country bumpkin, having a coterie of creatures that includes three horses, three dogs (a Bull Mastiff crossed with a Great Dane, a Border Collie and a Poodle called Pablo), two cats, a rabbit, ducks, chickens, goats and sheep. 'I think it is immensely beneficial to be around animals,' he told *www.timesonline.co.uk*, 'physically, mentally and spiritually. I watch the way that my two-year-old interacts with the dog and it is a wonderful thing.' However, he is not a fan of all animals – as revealed in the *Top Gear* 'Bolivia' special, he apparently has a phobia of insects.

When he does venture to the city, Hammond is known to cycle around London on a hybrid bike (Clarkson is famously not a fan, dubbing them among other things 'ethnic peace bicycles'). Of course, Richard is often spotted by passers-by, who invariably heckle him in good humour: 'When people see me out on it, they always call out, "Where's your Ferrari?" Of course I haven't got one, I work for the BBC.'

But his private garage has graduated somewhat from his first car – a 1976 Toyota Corolla Liftback, a slightly odd-looking, very early hatchback on which he painted a Shelby racing stripe before ultimately writing it off in a crash with a Volvo. Quite in contrast to his small frame – which has seen him christened 'The Hamster' – Hammond is a big fan of American muscle cars and over the years, has presented passionate and informative *Top Gear* pieces on that genre of car. In his own garage, he has had a

Dodge Charger, a Ford Mustang and a Dodge Challenger, as well as the quintessentially British Morgan Aeromax and the classic vintage icon, the Jaguar F-Type, as well as a Land Rover Defender. He loves monster trucks and is also an avid motorbike fan, for which Clarkson and May constantly lambast him; he has owned many Porsches over the years, that being his favourite marque.

As a quick aside, one of Hammond's most fun pieces (and one where you can tangibly see in his delighted schoolboy-ish eyes that he can't quite believe what a fantastic job he has), came in Series 4, when the team invited the aforementioned nun onto the show to drive a monster truck. This bizarre spectacle followed on from some grannies doing doughnuts in Series 1, but that clearly wasn't dangerous enough. Enter stage left Sister Wendy, who we are told prays five times a day and devotes her entire life to God; she was confronted by the monster truck Blown Thunder, complete with its behemoth dragster engine and 1700bhp, which was capable of jetting the near-five ton vehicle to 60mph in four seconds. Sister Wendy proved quite adept and commendably vaulted the old bangers, whispering an endearing 'Oh, my sweet Lord!' as she did so.

Back at Castle Hammond, Richard also loves to keep fit. In July 2007, when much of Britain was underwater due to the country's most severe flooding in living memory, he was on a late-night charge back to his Herefordshire mansion to be home for his daughter's birthday the next day. However, the weather was so calamitous that he gave up driving his 911 after more than 13 hours stuck in stranded traffic, even though he was still some 16 miles from home. So, at 3am he parked up his Porker and ran all the way back, arriving exhausted but in time for his little girl's birthday at 5.30am. He has run marathons and even needs occasional osteopathy to ease aching joints as he runs so much. A fit hamster indeed!

He admits he likes to look after himself. One of many running gags on *Top Gear* (apart from the relentless barrage about his height) centres round Hammond's alleged use of teeth-whitening kits. For example, after he'd tested a Marcos in Series 7, the footage returned to the studio only for Clarkson to pull such a kit out of the rear seat; likewise, in a 2009 episode the presenters phoned around for car insurance, giving their ages as seventeen, and a teeth whitening kit was seen on Hammond's desk (later, in a one-off interview with Sir Stirling Moss, he is filmed having false eyelashes applied).

Perhaps the most laughable but endearing jokes at his expense came while testing the Bowler Wildcat in Series 2. This machine was (very) loosely based around the Land Rover, but that's like saying a superbike is 'loosely' related to a pushbike: the £50,000 beast was capable of a 0–60 time of 4.8 seconds (that's a tenth quicker than an Aston Martin DB7), it boasted a whopping five-litre V8 engine and could drive at high speed across mountain ranges normally populated only by goats and glaciers. Hammond had an absolute blast and later said it was the most fun he'd ever had in a car, but the best part was during the test itself when in an unguarded moment of pure adrenaline he shouted, 'I am a driving god!' Of course, May and Clarkson were in hysterics back at the studio and re-played the tape for extra embarrassment. (Interestingly, all that off-road power translated to a very average Stig lap time of only 1.39.4, perhaps slowed down by the rendition of 'Stand By Your Man' on the stereo.)

Hammond is often cited as the 'kids' favourite' from *Top Gear* and this is backed up by his ventures into children's TV. The first notable foray was as presenter of Sky One's *Brainiac: Science Abuse*, which he did for four series. He also presented *School's Out*, an adult quiz show for the BBC, where celebrities are tested on questions they should remember from school, a similar premise to the hugely successful *Are You Smarter Than A 10 Year Old?* He has since begun to branch out into non-motoring documentary-length features, such as *Should I Worry About ...?*, *The Gunpowder Plot: Exploding The Legend* and *Richard Hammond's Invisible Worlds*. In September 2008, he presented the first episode of *Richard Hammond's Engineering Connections* on the National Geographic Channel, examining famous inventions such as the Airbus A38 and Wembley Stadium. His most slapstick venture is clearly BBC1's *Total Wipeout*, where contestants are sent around an assault course of obstacles, mud and water hazards – which is actually filmed in Argentina, although Hammond does all his presenting from a studio in London.

His most popular children's show is *Richard Hammond's Blast Lab* for the BBC. Set in a fictitious underground laboratory, apparently beneath Hammond's stately home, he was joined by such colourful characters as Ninja Nan. Taking a lead from his *Top Gear* 'day job', Hammond has quite frequently blown up caravans in the name of science for kids.

On *Blast Lab*, there's an 'intelligent' Opel Kadett that comes onto the show and answers kids' questions by flashing its lights, depending on whether the response is correct or not. This is, in fact, the very same car that Hammond found during the *Top Gear* 'Epic Road Trip' to Botswana – he loved the vehicle so much that he shipped it back to the UK, where it was restored by a team from *Practical Classics* magazine. On *Blast Lab*, the car is seen with the number plate OLI V3R.

Hammond has also presented several one-off specials, such as the annual Crufts awards; perhaps most bizarrely, he has twice presented the British Parking Awards at the Dorchester Hotel, which includes a variety of categories including 'Parking Team of the Year' and 'Best New Car Park' – I am not making this up!

No doubt, this must have provided Clarkson and May with much mirth. Presumably he didn't win an award at The Dorchester: on the BBC2 quiz show, *Petrol-heads*, Hammond was tricked into pranging his classic Ferrari while attempting to parallel-park blindfolded.

Richard regularly contributes numerous newspaper columns to the *Mirror* and is a regular (and always extremely popular) guest on high-profile chat shows; he has also written several best-selling books. A sure sign of The Hamster's exploding personal celebrity came with ITV's February 2006 launch of *Richard Hammond's 5 O'Clock Show* with his co-star, Mel Giedroyc. The topical show aired for an hour across nearly five weeks, but was not re-commissioned. Recently, he has returned to radio with various one-off shows for stations such as BBC2.

Personally, Hammond's most riveting TV ventures have been two enthralling specials recorded with Evel Knievel and Stirling Moss. The former was a lengthy interview pieced together from numerous meetings with the all-time most famous daredevil stunt rider. Knievel was a childhood hero of mine and, being the same age as Hammond, it was as if he was asking all the questions that I would have wanted to put forward, had I been lucky enough to meet him. At the time of these meetings, Knievel had already been diagnosed with the diabetes and idiopathic pulmonary fibrosis that eventually killed him. Hammond was respectful and yet confident enough to ask difficult questions of a man not renowned for suffering fools gladly.

Initially he was visibly nervous on meeting his childhood hero and the entire programme was fascinating to watch. It later transpired this was Knievel's last interview before his death in November 2007. When Hammond interviewed racing legend Moss, recovering from a horrific fall at home that broke both his ankles, some bones in his feet and several vertebrae, his respectful reverence was also apparent.

Having started his career in regional radio (and with an academic background behind that), speaking as a fan this is an area that I personally would love to see Hammond investigate further. His *Top Gear* caricature is highly entertaining, but is there a limit to the amiable cheeky chappie persona? Although his own topical magazine show didn't get renewed, Hammond is at his best when serious, investigative and passionate about his subject. If you asked his co-stars what The Hamster's best non-*Top Gear* TV work has been to date, no doubt they'd say his adverts for fresh fish at Morrisons! Interestingly, he himself admits that he is not always so amiable, telling *www.timesonline.co.uk* that, 'There is a bit of Italian in my family and I do have a short fuse. I tend to explode and have a huge temper tantrum, but then it is all gone and I'm happy and smiling two minutes later.'

One fact about Richard Hammond that his co-presenters make no secret of finding absurd is that gradually he has become more of a sex symbol, perhaps not something the shy primary school Hamster might have expected. After he grew his hair much longer, his slightly expensively dishevelled appearance seemed to be a hit with female viewers (when May was named 'Worst Celebrity Haircut' in a 2007 Brylcreem poll, Hammond's longer locks triumphed in the 'Best' category). As far back as 2005, he topped *Heat* magazine's list of 'Weird Celebrity Crushes'. Having said that, his main 'rivals' in that unlikely chart included Bob Geldof, Derren Brown and believe it or not, Boris Johnson. In his acceptance speech, with tongue planted firmly in cheek, Richard said: 'So, I'm the best of a really bad bunch – hoorah! I'm still a little sceptical about all this. After all, I'm the short bloke who was always ignored at school discos. I used to pitch up in a badly matching flowery shirt and tie, stand on the side of the dancefloor and wait for a girl to come and talk to me – and they never did. Now I'm top of a Z-list nookie league.'

Perhaps more graciously, he went on to say that he thought if women fancied Clarkson, it must be a perversion. In fact, his lanky *Top Gear* colleague has enjoyed some of the apparent reflected *Top Gear* attractiveness: a 2008 poll of 'Men I Secretly Adore' placed Jezza third, behind only Jonathan Ross and Philip Schofield! On hearing the news, he complained about not coming first.

A diminutive 5'7", Hammond has the unfortunate job of working alongside a towering Clarkson, which undoubtedly makes him look far shorter than he actually is. However, he genuinely doesn't seem to mind: 'As a pecking order it works quite well,' he told *Times Online*. 'If I wasn't shorter than him, it would just look like two blokes having an argument.' Of course, Clarkson relentlessly mocks his fellow presenter's height, most famously by putting pictures on the 'Cool Wall' out of Hammond's reach when they disagree. With stunning *Top Gear* directness, Richard likes to point out that he's still taller than George Clooney, Tom Cruise and Hitler: 'In my mind, I look like Clint Eastwood – tall, scary, strong and silent – but women just think I'm fluffy and inoffensive. I'm not cute: I'm miserable, I have a mean, dark heart and I'm sinister!' He went on to suggest his wife would not call him a romantic, although he once bought her a Harley-Davidson for her birthday. 'I fancy girls on motorcycles' was his selfless reasoning for the two-wheel purchase!

Hammond admits that since he's appeared on television, he is frequently approached by 'a certain type of girl', something he finds hilarious and obviously unappealing: 'I'm very lucky [my wife] trusts me. But if I wasn't happily married I'd be on a non-stop rampage, exploiting my victory ruthlessly. I'd be on one long, shallow, celebrity-driven shagfest.'

One can only imagine how May and Clarkson would have laughed on hearing the news of the 'Weird Celebrity Crush' survey. Others were less surprised. Writing in the *Mirror*, women's editor Caroline Jones said, 'With his cheeky grin, his reassuring voice, but most of all that naughty twinkle in his eye, the appeal is obvious. What's not to love? You don't have to be interested in motoring to recognise a racy little model when you see one. And he's certainly got our engines revving.' Indeed, the fact that Hammond was happily married with two kids and doted on his family made him all the more adorable in many women's eyes.

Of course there's a wider issue here: Hammond in particular has made *Top Gear* a programme that women watch. With the greatest respect to Clarkson and May, they are far more improbable sex symbols, something they themselves might readily admit. Suffice to say, *Top Gear* was for many years the motoring equivalent of 'the football': 'It used to be the programme your fella watched while you had a bath,' wrote Jones, 'all boring men in cardies banging on about Beetles and BMWs. Now it's funny and sexy. Richard's enthusiasm makes you want to understand the difference between oversteer and understeer – even though you don't care.'

CHAPTER 15

James May, Part II

For much of the 2000s, James May lived in Hampton, a very genteel town on the outskirts of London, where house prices are exorbitant and there's a tangible whiff of sedate Englishness in the air: so, perfect for him then. He has been with his partner – the dance critic Sarah Frater, who writes revered pieces for such publications as the *Evening Standard* – since 2000. Speaking to the *Mirror*, May described her thus: 'I like a bit of rusticity in my women. Sarah's an eccentric. She won't mind [that description].'

May appears to represent the quintessential English bachelor, albeit one with a long-term partner: 'Some people just don't get married and I am a late developer. Sarah and I have never really talked about living together, we just never have. And it's practical. My house isn't terribly big ... [in fact] my house is f***ing horrible. Sarah likes to go back to her Notting Hill flat – she's happy how it is. As for children, I don't yearn for them, but I don't rule it out,' he continued.

Speaking to the *Independent*, he admitted to being hopeless about keeping a nice house: 'I can't make a house homely – my house just looks like a garage or a shed. I'm not untidy, but it just looks so uninviting.' He has since moved to Hammersmith in west London, where his house boasts a garage (unusual for that busy area of the capital). It's not clear where he keeps his fleet of cars, motorbikes and aeroplanes, however.

However, he's not averse to romantic gestures. 'When we went to Istanbul recently,' he told *The Times*, 'we were walking near the Blue Mosque one night when a figure in traditional clothes sidled up and whispered, "Make her happy. Buy her carpet." And then disappeared. He wasn't trying to sell me one, just offering advice. So I asked the owner of the B&B and he suggested a place that had antique rugs at decent prices. I bought a runner with a threadbare patch for twenty quid, and yes, it did make her happy. So thanks, mate.'

The couple share a dog, a rather wild-sounding creature called Fusker, named after a form of internet theft. May describes the mutt as 'stand-offish and grumpy, just like me.' Fusker was a gift from Hammond's wife Mindy (and Sarah has told him, 'You get the pet you deserve!'). Like Clarkson, May is not unknown to make fashion faux pas, having been filmed in a selection of numerous questionable sweaters and lurid shirts. He states simply: 'normal bloke is my style.' This is slightly misleading because he has been known to spend quite a lot of money on clothes, but proudly hails his ability to 'make them all look rubbish' – this from a man who likes velour and bemoans the extinction of the 1970s' beaded door curtains in cars.

When he's not filming, he loves to relax with Sarah at home, sometimes venturing into the kitchen to cook nice meals, or if he's feeling sociable he prefers to go for a few quiet pints with his mates and play darts down the pub. He is a devoted bitter drinker and enjoys sampling real ales. If it's raining, he might sit in and watch an old movie, preferring classics such as *The Battle of Britain* or *Where Eagles Dare*,

May's personal garage is maybe not so understated as you might expect. Admittedly, over the years his fleet has perhaps predictably included a Bentley T2, Triumph 2000, Rover P6, Alfa Romeo 164, 1971 Rolls-Royce Corniche, Jaguar XJS, Range Rover, Fiat Panda, Datsun 120Y, Vauxhall Cavalier, a Mini Cooper, Citroen Ami, Mazda MX-5 and numerous classic motorbikes. But don't be fooled by the Captain Slow tag: he has also owned his fair share of supercars such as a Ferrari F430, an Aston Martin V8 Vantage and even the monstrous Lamborghini Gallardo LP560-4. Coincidentally, like Hammond, he often uses a Brompton folding bicycle for city commuting.

James freely admits to being what some would call a 'tinker', a person who loves to mess about with engines and machines: he says he can't walk past a hardware store because it's full of nuts and bolts, tools, penknives and other cool stuff. He once revealed that one night he was happily messing with a piece of an old Honda engine for hours when Sarah popped her head around the garage door to ask: 'Is there any chance you can come inside and behave like a normal person for a while?'

'Normal people' also go on holidays, something May has said he's not very good at. However, his globe-trotting escapades with *Top Gear* have clearly made him travel-hardened: 'I'm not very good at planning them,' he told *The Times*. 'For years, I used a bucket shop in Kilburn. Whenever I had a week free, I'd go in and say, "What have you got for a hundred quid?" And he'd say, "Cairo, tomorrow", so I'd say, "Fine". That's the way I like to travel. You soon learn that unless you're heading for the Arctic or the Amazon, when you arrive there will be toothpaste, toothbrushes and hotel rooms. And if there aren't, well, you can always sleep on the central reservation. I've done that enough times to know it isn't the end of the world.'

As mentioned earlier, May is also a qualified pilot: 'Aeroplanes were something I was interested in as a small boy,' he told the *Independent*. 'I get bad vertigo and I never thought I would be able to afford to do it. I was a bit lucky. I only went down to the airport for a trial – I just kept going and ended up with a pilot's licence.' So he admits that he spends nearly all of his cash on cars, classic motorbikes, planes and fuel. Sounds like the perfect life!

Like his two co-presenters, *Top Gear* has long since stopped being May's only television role. However, his shows are invariably more cerebral than the rather more explosive programmes often made by his counterparts. So, we have him presenting shows such as Lifestyle's *Road Rage School*, co-hosting coverage of the 2006 London Boat Show and bizarrely beating Gordon Ramsay at eating animal penises on an edition of the verbally caustic Scottish chef's *The F Word*! Unsurprisingly perhaps, both men ended up being sick. It began as a bit of fun, with Ramsay daring May to eat one and he was so confident that the mild-mannered *Top Gear* presenter wouldn't be able to eat any of these 'delicacies' that he then offered to match every one himself. Having already stirred up controversy by serving horsemeat on his show, Ramsay didn't shy away from the inevitable headlines.

Although the unlikely duo had great fun together, Ramsay was rather less forthcoming about May's actual cooking skills: 'The worst [celebrity chef] ever would have to be James May, with his fish pie. Even though he won, which was extraordinary. He was drinking a bottle of red wine throughout the challenge, so I thought it was in the bag. And Geri Halliwell as well – disaster zone! You won't be seeing either of them opening a restaurant.'

However, May's best TV show other than *Top Gear* is easily the intriguing *James May's Toy Stories* for the BBC, which features classic toys from yesteryear, including some of his personal favourites. But he didn't just look at the toys from his childhood, he super-sized them: he reconstructed the banked track at Brooklands raceway using Scalextric, tried to build a life-size Airfix model of a Spitfire and even submitted a garden to the RHS Chelsea Flower Show made entirely from plasticine. (Note: controversy is never far away from the *Top Gear* presenters: a group gathered outside the BBC to protest at the cost – allegedly £500,000 – of letting a well-paid presenter live out his childhood Spitfire fantasy).

Most notably, May built an entire full-size house from Lego in August 2009 (he was a self-confessed 'Lego fiend' as a child). The location was Denbies Wine Estate in Surrey and it was estimated that he used 3.2 million bricks to complete the building. Such was his popularity by this point that nearly 3,000 people turned up to see him start the build. Sadly, although Lego themselves hoped to move the house, brick by plastic brick, to their flagship theme park near Windsor, the cost of dismantling and rebuilding was simply uneconomic at £50,000 – even with 1,000 volunteers. James and the *Top Gear* website tried to find a buyer for the house, alas to no avail. A month later, the Lego building was demolished after the wine estate reluctantly had to reacquire the land for its next harvest. It later transpired that a Lego cat, built by a fan and called Fusker in honour of May's own pet, had been stolen from the house by persons unknown.

Sadly, James's attempt to break the longest model railway record failed amid claims that vandals and thieves had tampered with the 10-mile track. It was to stretch from Barnstaple to Bideford in Devon but was broken up in places by thieves and coins dropped on the line destroyed the special battery, which was later stolen.

May explained to the *Daily Mail* that from the age of five he had wanted to fly a Spitfire and eventually he did just that for the episode where he built the life-size Airfix replica. Surprisingly, he found the experience of flying the actual World War II legend unrewarding: the cockpit smelt of oil and dust and he was freezing. Although he said that he much preferred the staggering technology of the Eurofighter, this is a man who admits to a blind spot for electronic technology: he once took his annoying mobile phone into a field and shot it with a Beretta shotgun: 'If technology annoys you, I highly recommend shooting it to death. It's very cleansing. I've been tempted to shoot the dashboards of many cars.'

Elsewhere, James has travelled alongside wine connoisseur Oz Clarke for *Oz and James's Big Wine Adventure*: as a confirmed bitter drinker the experience seismically changed his habits and he admits to often phoning Clarke for advice when he's standing in the supermarket wine aisle. It was during one such wine outing with Clarke that May's concert-standard musicianship was briefly exhibited, albeit on the lowly recorder with a troupe of Morris dancers!

Weirdly, James has written one jingle for a major car manufacturer (he is contracted not to say which one), which he composed on a Casio keyboard, waltz-style. On *Top Gear*, his musical tastes are often ridiculed and he certainly hasn't helped himself: after spending several days recording the engine notes of various cars, he played back his awful, atonal version of the show's theme tune on a small ghetto-blaster in the studio to guffaws from both colleagues and audience alike.

He has also presented programmes about the moon landings, sharks, great inventions and science fiction being implemented in real life. Like Hammond and Clarkson, James has also written several very popular books although unlike his co-stars, he has yet to enjoy a No. 1 bestseller.

He says that although he occasionally watches his own performances he prefers not to do too much of this as 'it's painful' and he is eager not to be over-exposed on TV, telling the *Independent*: 'I do try to resist the urge to become a tart. I've never wanted to be on television for the sake of it, I suppose because I'm not one of life's natural presenters – I'm not an actor. If my frock isn't blown up by a particular idea, I do turn it down.' The very same journalist reported that May's persona in the flesh was so laid-back, 'he appears forever on the brink of yawning.' Of course, this is a caricature just as Clarkson's motor-mouth persona is not how he lives 24/7, but that's the nature of blipvert modern TV: it's all about soundbites, snapshots, quick fixes.

James May is lower down the 'Weird Crushes' rankings than Richard Hammond, but still receives more than his fair share of love letters, despite the loud shirts with pictures of jet fighters on them. Some fans have routed him out at his local pub, leaving gifts, albeit not panties or bras but fruitcakes, a smoked haddock, sweets and spam. His Lord Byron-esque shaggy locks and ramshackle look are a teenage dream he can now indulge. Oddly, when he first joined *Top Gear*, May was asked if he'd mind trimming his shaggy barnet but the haircut is now so synonymous with his TV image that the good folk at the BBC ask him not to cut it off.

In fact, James May is perhaps something of a dark horse in the *Top Gear* stable. Although his fellow presenters may have a more obvious profile, May's quiet, laconic style and passionate interest in his subject matter has made him what the *Independent* calls, 'the most in-demand presenter on British television.'

CHAPTER 16

Jeremy Clarkson, Part III

Like his two colleagues on *Top Gear*, Jeremy Clarkson's profile has seen him work on a proliferation of other TV shows, as well as numerous articles, several hugely popular DVDs and a dazzling array of best-selling books. He has published many bestsellers, with sales of several of them running into the hundreds of thousands. In fact, his success in the book world has even led some literary observers to credit Jezza with increasing literacy among the young male population, so popular are his titles with the younger reader's market.

Clarkson's non-*Top Gear* TV work is similarly prolific and equally successful. His aforementioned chat show ran across 27 half-hour episodes between November 1998 and December 2000 and saw him interview a variety of famous faces from the music, showbiz and political worlds. However, perhaps not surprisingly, the series is best remembered for controversy, most obviously when he offended pretty much every Welsh person on the planet (and a few Scots for good measure). During one show, he put a plastic map of Wales in a microwave and then proceeded to incinerate the entire country, only pausing to add that he hadn't put Scotland in there, 'because it wouldn't fit.'

Another early diversion from *Top Gear* came as the presenter of the UK version of BBC's *Robot Wars* and we have already talked about *Jeremy Clarkson's Motorworld* and *Jeremy Clarkson Meets The Neighbours*. Other shows have included *Jeremy Clarkson's Car Years* for BBC2, but he also frequently digresses into another passion in his life – engineering. Having been awarded that meringue-tainted honorary degree by Oxford Brookes University for his long-standing support of engineering, Clarkson has also showcased the same on such programmes as BBC2's *Inventions That Changed The World*, featuring fascinating studies of the gun, computer, telephone and television, among others.

Like his fellow presenters, Clarkson is a poplar chat show-guest and he's even taken effortlessly to the *Have I Got News For You* hot seat during the period of rotating hosts, the programme having dismissed regular host Angus Deayton in October 2002. And most appropriately of all, Jezza has made many hilarious contributions to the *Grumpy Old Men* BBC2 TV series. Perhaps reflecting his political interests which we noted earlier, he's even been a consummate and cerebral guest on BBC1's *Question Time*. By 2007, despite his many detractors and the countless headaches he causes the BBC, Clarkson's long-standing, varied and prolific career was recognised at the prestigious National Television Awards with a 'Special Recognition Award'.

Of course, such a lengthy TV career and sustained high profile means that Jeremy Clarkson – whether he likes to think so or not – makes an impression on the nation's TV-watching population. So we have what is termed 'The Clarkson Effect'. This was first witnessed with something as superficial as his choice of trousers.

His penchant for wearing blue Levis was attributed by some to a fall in sales of that particular item, the theory being that no one with any fashion sense would want to be seen wearing the same clothes as the presenter. Lorna Martin, features editor at the fashion trade magazine *Draper's Record* has said: 'Denim was in a big slump. Jeremy Clarkson personified the problem and became legendary.' Why spend millions of dollars on male models to make grainy black-and-white adverts as art statements when a ten-minute clip of Clarkson leaning against a Vauxhall, tutting, can undo all the hard work? Although this is harsh, it's not particularly something which Jeremy himself loses any sleep over.

Indeed, he makes no claim to be a fashion guru. His dress sense is, at best, questionable. People have tried to improve Clarkson's style, such as the ever-tactile Trinny and Susannah, who attempted to give him a makeover on a celebrity version of *What Not To Wear*. Previously they had derided his fashion sense as that of 'a market trader' and invited him onto their show as a potential candidate for the 'Worst Dressed' award. Perhaps not entirely surprisingly, their valiant efforts to re-style Clarkson failed miserably and he went so far as to state he'd rather eat his own hair than go back on the programme.

When the fashionista presenters appeared on *Top Gear* as the 'Stars in a Reasonably Priced Car' two years later, Clarkson said it was payback time! He pointed out that he had previously been voted the sixth worst dressed celebrity but after appearing on their show he'd been 'promoted' to second worst dressed famous face, only behind Graham Norton. Trinny and Susannah retaliated and pointed out that girls' attitudes to clothes were like men's to cars – it was all about impressing people so they laughed at Jeremy's Ford GT40, dismissing it as the equivalent of a floral dress midlife crisis. At times there seemed to be a genuine frisson of tension in the studio.

But getting back to The Clarkson Effect in regard to fashion, it is unlikely that the demise of Levis sales was his fault alone but you can see where the theory comes from. When he tested the brutal Koenigsegg CCX, given the beauty of the car he was trying out at the time, Jeremy's choice of clothes for this piece truly proves that he appears to have pretty much no interest in fashion. He stood next to one of the most desirable cars ever made in a particularly horrid combination of the infamous light blue jeans and a very worn-out Che Guevara T-shirt.

Some see The Clarkson Effect in more serious tones. As we have seen, almost universally the environmentalists and climate campaigners, Transport 2000, the motor industry workers and safety campaigners abhor some of Clarkson's comments and attitudes because in their opinion his massive public profile and popularity make him by default a role model. Like footballers, sportsmen and rock stars, many will argue that whether Clarkson likes it or not, his actions and opinions have a deep impact on large chunks of the population. Campaigner Emily Armistead of Greenpeace does not accept that his remarks have no consequence: 'Clarkson is a problem because he has represented some climate-sceptic views and for someone to be on national television saying [such things] is quite alarming.'

It's a charge Clarkson vehemently denies; he refutes that he is a role model and plays down the impact of his rants. He believes people have minds of their own and are not so easily led. Perhaps conflictingly, following the aftermath of the banana-meringue-in-the-face incident, Clarkson also said this: 'I want to be the champion of ordinary people – who seem to be lectured to all the time. Look, there are two sides to the argument. I do listen, constantly, to their side of the argument. And every time they're presented with my side, they shove pies in my face.' He went on to say, with a cheeky grin, no doubt:

'They get together to discuss things, these people, eating their nuclear-free peace nibbles, and they're just never exposed to the other side of the argument ...'

Even his employer, the BBC, has gone on record to state that he is 'not a man to give a considered opinion.' Clarkson himself has been quoted saying, 'I don't have any influence over what people do ... *Top Gear* is just fluff. It's just entertainment – people don't listen to me.' Indeed, it's a position he takes up with some regularity: 'Even if I thought for a moment that anyone paid any attention to anything I say – and I have figures to prove that they don't' – I'm sorry, I'm not employed to think one thing and say something else.' The figures he refers to are car sales volumes, as former producer Jon Bentley explains: 'Jeremy has always said we did a wonderful review of the Renault GTA and they sold about three (well, actually more, but not many more). Then we did a terrible review of the Toyota Corolla, likening it to a washing machine, and that went on to sell millions.' (And this despite the manufacturer's refusal to send any more cars to *Top Gear* for some time). Similarly, the Ford Orion was one of that company's best-selling models ever, even though Clarkson repeatedly berated it. There may be some truth in this but there is, as ever, another viewpoint in relation to the power of *Top Gear* (rather than Clarkson personally): 'I'm sure we did often have an influence,' ponders Bentley. 'Particularly with some of Quentin's best used car pieces that talked positively about a used car bargain. There was the phrase that went round the trade: "*Top Gear*, Thursday, Top Price Saturday."' Fast-forward several years and Clarkson now frequently makes the Top 100 lists of Britain's most influential and powerful media figures.

On an episode of *Top Gear* in 2002, Clarkson made some comments about testing cars around Wales, saying the country was largely empty because no one wants to live there (he's made similar remarks about driving through 'boring' Lincolnshire). Predictably the BBC were bombarded with complaints that he was encouraging speeding, including one letter from the Clwyd West AM Alun Pugh written to BBC Director-General Greg Dyke; Clarkson flatly denied his remarks had encouraged fast driving and a BBC spokesman insisted such suggestions were 'nonsense'. The following week, a man in Flintshire was caught speeding at 137mph and JC's words were picked up on by the media covering the police action. However, North Wales Police denied there had been a clampdown on motorists since Clarkson's comments on the programme.

There are other, even more simplistic examples of his influence. For instance, he pretty much put the phrase 'flappy-paddle gearbox' into the lexicon. Ask yourself this: what is that type of gear-changing system *actually* called? *Exactly*, it's a flappy paddle ...

But let's not forget, his influence is not necessarily always a bad thing. When Clarkson became a patron of Help For Heroes, the charity later received a cheque from an anonymous donor for £50 with the message, 'Clarkson made us do it'. The campaign organiser was delighted: 'When he put his weight behind us, it became acceptable to support the soldiers without implying that you were necessarily supporting the war.' Over the years, Jeremy has helped the charity prodigiously.

Unfortunately, whatever he says to try and diffuse his words and avoid controversy, there will always be people who detest The Clarkson Effect. Due to his proliferation of negative comments about Norfolk, some residents of that county have started a 'We Hate Jeremy Clarkson' club.

Despite his extremely high profile, away from our screens Jeremy Clarkson is a relatively private family man. Save for what scant biographical information we have about Clarkson and his own newspaper columns too, there is a relatively modest amount of material on him in the public domain. If you strip away all the quotes, the controversies, the programmes and so on, he is essentially a private person. He usually refuses interviews, even when his co-presenters Richard Hammond and James May have already agreed to them.

He met his wife, Frances Cain, when she was working as a recruitment consultant (she is now his long-standing manager, highly respected within the industry). 'We had mutual friends and ended up in the same restaurant one night,' Frances told *www.timesonline.co.uk*. 'We had an argument about whether it was better to be a man than a woman.' The chemistry was ignited and they've been together since, marrying in May 1993.

Frances is the daughter of the Victoria Cross hero Robert Henry Cain. A VC is the highest medal for gallantry awarded to British and Commonwealth forces and was given to Cain in commemoration of his valour in the Battle of Arnhem. Although Frances' father died of cancer in 1974, long before Clarkson married his daughter, both are extremely proud of Cain's bravery and in 2003, Jeremy presented a BBC documentary on his father-in-law and fellow VC-winners. In October 2005, he visited the British troops stationed in Iraq; he has also written and then presented a documentary about World War II's Operation Chariot, *Greatest Raid of All-Time*.

The family home is a beautiful manor house near the idyllic Cotswolds market town of Chipping Norton and Clarkson is currently the town's most famous resident. In 1987, comedy genius Ronnie Barker retired from TV to Chipping Norton and ran an antiques shop called The Emporium. Previously, The Who's Keith Moon owned the Crown & Cushion Hotel in the High Street. Clarkson once told the tale of an elderly Rover driver who had been stationary for 15 years, confused by the complicated double roundabout in the town centre.

In Series 6, the *Top Gear* team actually filmed in Chipping Norton for a spoof feature about Jeremy helping the local community. It was reported his presence had been requested by the Mayor to open a refurbished open-air swimming pool. Clarkson said he was delighted to help as his own children had learnt to swim in that very pool (he also takes a dig at Hammond, saying he'll open anything, even a crime scene). Jeremy duly glided up in a Mark 1 Rolls-Royce Silver Shadow from 1976, chosen in honour of the various rock stars frequenting the sedate town during that decade of excess. However, the car had seen better days – like many of the worn-out old rockers of yesteryear – and Clarkson carried out some ad-hoc repairs, including repainting the wheel arch with a silver paint that bore no apparent resemblance to the original colour. For some bizarre reason, he also ended up eating some ultra-expensive American car wax he'd been given.

The climax came when Jeremy arrived at the 'ceremony' to open the pool, drove straight through a fence and plunged the Roller straight into the swimming pool, à la Keith Moon. It was a great example of a really silly *Top Gear* moment – there was no real point, no real car review, no big message or technological insight, just a bit of fun in Clarkson's home town.

Speaking to *The Times*, his wife revealed a few insights behind the gregarious front that JC presents on TV: 'Yes, he's opinionated and, yes, he does have habits which annoy me, like leaving soggy cigarette ends by the sink, abandoning his socks under the sofa and not replacing the loo roll. But he is a total pussycat underneath – very sensitive and caring.' It's common knowledge that Clarkson is also a devoted family man and proud father to his three children – Emily, Finlo and Katya – who are separated by only four years. Given his predilection for fast cars, he even aims to teach them to drive in the grounds of his house in their early teens so that when they finally hit the road, they will be more than capable and therefore safer.

Also, don't be fooled by the slapdash comedy that the presenter promotes when reviewing cars or leading features: his preparation is second to none. When Clarkson reviewed the Veyron racing from Italy to London, he explained on-screen that before attempting the top speed of 253mph, you had to stop the car, release a button in the door frame and run a series of precise checks – he then proceeded to give the rear tyre a Laurel and Hardy-style kick before shrugging his shoulders as if to say, 'That'll do'. Yet it's a known fact that behind the scenes, Clarkson knew *everything* about the Veyron before he even got into it. It's not unknown for him to return home at midnight after a long day's filming only to re-write pieces that he and Andy Wilman have been talking about ready for reconsideration in a production meeting at 9am the next day. According to Wilman, Clarkson is the 'engine room' of *Top Gear*: 'It's Jeremy's show. No question, because it can't be a democracy – it's Jeremy's vision. We've all got drive but his drive is noticeably amazing.'

But in the cold light of day, away from the studio lights and the headlines, is Clarkson really the Beelzebub of ecology, is he as bad as some people like to make out? His close friend AA Gill revealed in the *Mirror* that this might not necessarily be the case, saying that at home Jeremy carefully separates his rubbish ready for correct recycling. JC has actually gone on record to say that hydrogen cars may be the way forward; further, as an avid fan and supporter of British engineering, he has nonetheless criticised the efforts of twentieth-century engineers, saying they are merely refining the gargantuan genius of nineteenth-century minds. By way of example, he says the fact that we still drive cars by means of 'small explosions' is proof of this and he has belittled the car industry's inability (or perhaps reluctance?) to invent an alternative method of fuelling vehicles.

When it was revealed that Jeremy recycles, some critics – not wishing to let him off the hook so easily – denounced him as a hypocrite but he retorted that the problem was exacerbated by the inevitable polarisation that occurs when green campaigners denounce people as either 'completely green or not green at all'. The lack of a middle ground frustrates him and he blamed this on, 'lunatics who want everyone to live in crofts and Facebook trees.' Clarkson uses a much-maligned patio heater but reserves the right to complain about wastefully individually wrapped lumps of sugar in expensive restaurants and howl at supermarkets for using too much packaging. He highlights US packaging mountains in landfill as an example, saying that he's not convinced that man's 3 per cent contribution to the carbon dioxide bank affects climate and also states that he's not entirely convinced that a rise in global temperatures is necessarily a bad thing although he did back this up by saying a parrot would make a more interesting Cotswolds garden species than a sparrow. So, the problem with Clarkson is sometimes you never know if he's being serious or not, and he knows this and loves it.

Later he also admitted that he grows his own vegetables, eggs and barley, although he qualified this statement by saying 'a man' actually grows them for him on part of his land. So, he's not exactly Felicity Kendal in the seventies BBC sitcom *The Good Life*, but perhaps a start has been made. What's more, he reveals that he composts with old issues of his long-standing enemy, the *Guardian*. Yet this is also the man who refuses to buy Fairtrade crisps. He's a total conundrum.

His argument is that he hates the methodology of the environmental movement, but 'loves the destination'. The end result is something he completely sees the validity of, but the approach and means of getting there drive him wild.

Worse still, in a survey conducted by car rental firm City Car Club of the 'Top Ten Most Polluting Celebrities' not only did Clarkson not come first, he didn't even beat The Hamster, who came in two positions above him at eighth (James May did not make the list). Jenson Button, whose own personal cars had an average carbon emission of 383.1g/km, nearly three times the average output of a typical family car, was the worst offender. Also in the list were Simon Cowell and Gordon Ramsay, with JC scraping in at No. 10.

Speaking of personal cars, The City Car Club quoted Jezza's private collection as containing: a Lamborghini Gallardo, a Volvo XC90, a Ford Focus, a BMW M5, an Aston Martin V8 Vantage, a Mercedes-Benz SL55 AMG, a Mercedes-Benz CLK AMG, a Range Rover TDV8 Vogue SE, two VW Sciroccos, a BMW Z4, a Toyota Land Cruiser Amazon and a Mitsubishi Lancer Evolution X. Clarkson has several favourites and contends that you're not a true petrol-head until you've owned an Alfa Romeo. He long admired the Ford GT, a road version of the legendary racing car and bought one only to find it was so unreliable that he returned it for a full refund just a month on. Later he changed his mind and bought the car back, despite telling fans that he had never been able to complete a single journey in the vehicle. Back in the old *Top Gear* years, Clarkson had been unable to road test the Ford GT40 because he was too tall to fit in the driver's seat of that particular (smaller) version. The considerably shorter Noel Edmonds took his place and went on to buy one for his own personal collection – a very rare car at the time.

In Series 1, broadcast in 2002, Clarkson tested his very own Mercedes SL55 AMG round the track ... at about 5mph. Although this was the fastest automatic car in the world at the time, he wasn't about to ruin it by treating the vehicle with the same brutal testing antics as other people's cars! As an aside, during this piece he can be heard talking about difficult days at work before saying, '*Not* that I've ever had a hard day at work!'

Clarkson's new Ford GT was eventually sold off to make room for a Lamborghini Gallardo Spyder – the car that he reviewed and then bought for himself in Series 8. So, what is his favourite of all? Well, he obviously has several dream supercars that he has enjoyed but the vehicle that he repeatedly flags up as impressive is, oddly enough, the Volvo XC90.

Over the years, Jeremy has been blatantly 'anti-Porsche'. When reviewing a Ferrari, there is always an element of personal bias – he just loves that Italian marque. However, with Porsche he finds them all a little clinical, too precise. He is repeatedly critical of the iconic 911's rear-engined set-up although he does on occasion complement Porsche's technical prowess, but his reviews are usually muted at best. There have been rare exceptions to this: he almost bought a 2003 911 GT3 and later reviewed the German manufacturer's fastest-ever model, the hypercar Carrera GT, in glowing terms.

This lengthy list is just some of the vehicles that he *has* owned at some point, rather than all at once; nonetheless it's a beautiful selection of cars. At the same time, by virtue of owning them he has consigned a number of classic vehicles to the 'Uncool' side of the Cool Wall, that prerequisite of any machine owned by any of the *Top Gear* presenters. And finally with regard to machinery, he once put an EEL F1A jet fighter in his garden but this was subsequently removed after a request from the council, who didn't believe his claim that it was a 'leaf blower'.

Jeremy Clarkson's self-deprecation is often missed and it would be foolish to think he is as exaggerated in real life as he appears on the screen. Back home, among his family and his idyllic country life, the former local reporter is a man who has become one of the world's most successful television faces in recent times. From being a humble Paddington Bear salesman, it's no mean feat.

CHAPTER 17

The Crash

'I'm so alive, I'm so alive!'

Richard Hammond, speaking from the cockpit of the jet car after the first test run

I'd been away for a few days abroad and as I walked through the airport departures lounge, I caught sight of a one-day-old copy of the *Sun* with the headline: 'TOP GEAR STAR IN 315MPH CRASH'. I must admit, my blood ran cold. Having been overseas, I'd heard nothing about the accident, so to suddenly see Richard Hammond's face next to such a frightening headline was chilling. Suddenly, all the *Top Gear* fun, the high-jinx, the knockabout humour, all seemed instantly out of place: we all knew they did these crazy stunts and tricks, but they'd never really get hurt, would they? *Would* they?

It was not unheard of for celebrities to have accidents while filming TV shows. In 2006, pop star Ms Dynamite crashed at more than 100mph while filming *The Race* on Sky but was okay after precautionary hospital checks. On the same show, Ingrid Tarrant flipped a truck earlier in the week but was also unhurt, albeit understandably a little shaken. Over on *Fifth Gear*, touring car champion and presenter Jason Plato was badly burnt when the Caparo T1 he was testing caught fire on the track. In the USA, on WLS-TV, a car actually crashed into the TV studio while the news was live on air! Richard Hammond himself had previously only suffered minor injuries throughout his *Top Gear* career, with a broken thumb and a cracked sternum being his most serious afflictions to date but there had never been anything so traumatic and frightening as what happened to him in 2006.

The day was 20 September 2006. *Top Gear* was at Elvington Airfield, just a few miles southeast of York, filming for an episode in Series 9 that was due to be screened in early 2007. The plan was to have Hammond drive a jet car with the aim of exceeding 300mph. Remember the 'Ideas Board' in the *Top Gear* office? Well, around 2004, Richard had posted a note on it saying that he wanted to 'go really, really fast, faster than supercar fast'. Over the years, he has made no secret of his attraction: 'I love speed,' he once told the *Guardian*, 'I don't know why. I think the desire to move fast comes from man running after an antelope with a spear, it comes from the need to catch stuff.' He was about to get his chance. Internally the project was to be called, 'Vampire – The Need for Speed'.

Now you might think that if Captain Slow can take a Veyron – with nice leather seats and electric windows – to 253mph, then it's not a big deal to go that little bit extra. However, Bugatti spent millions developing the Super Sport, which increased the maximum speed of the 'standard' car by only five miles an hour so to surpass 300mph takes you into the realm of cars that are effectively four wheels with a rocket strapped to the seat. Dangerous stuff.

The *Top Gear* production team are used to organising complex and dangerous challenges and this was no exception. Initially a company who specialised in jet powered cars (and was indeed owned and run by two of the world's finest jet-car racers) contacted the programme to suggest it might be a fun feature to film their attempt on the land speed record, set for July 2006. *Top Gear* was not in the habit of covering such events in this way but the show's production team did like the idea of putting a presenter in a ludicrously fast jet car. It was perfect *Top Gear* territory – so, who was going to drive this beast?

Why, Captain Slow – James May, of course. The production team were aware that Hammond already had a lot of excellent features for the forthcoming series and felt it appropriate for May to be the man behind the wheel of the car, particularly given his nickname. Then quite late in the day, it proved impossible to organise James's hectic diary around the schedule and so Hammond got his chance to drive 'really, really fast' after all.

The car to be used was called the Vampire, a jet-powered modified racer and holder of the British land speed record at 300.3mph, set in 2000 at Elvington itself. This type of car accelerates with such ferocity that forces of 6G are commonly recorded, akin to that in a state-of-the-art jet fighter. The car was owned by Northants-based Primetime Landspeed Engineering (PTLE), revered experts in the field who would also provide the training for Hammond (it was normally driven by Colin Fallows, holder of the speed record).

PTLE was a collaboration between its principals, Colin Fallows and Mark Newby, and they were very much leading experts in this area. They had been working together since 1994 and had a stable of three such jet cars; interestingly, one of these – named 'e=motion' – is powered by electric batteries. Fallows himself was a renowned racer and also worked as an engineer at Santa

Pod raceway; he had been in teams who built drag cars, which often used former Red Arrows' Rolls-Royce Orpheus jet engines.

Hellbender and Vampire were both well-known cars on the British drag/jet car circuit until Hellbender was involved in a fatal accident at Santa Pod in 1986, when it suffered a suspension failure in a side-by-side drag race. Colin Fallows subsequently bought Vampire and various advanced upgrades and state-of-the-art modifications were made. The company stated that Vampire had made in the region of 3,000 runs without incident, a truly remarkable record: this was a team and a car at the very top of their sport.

The track at Elvington Airfield was a site that PTLE were very familiar with, having previously made several land-speed record attempts there. It's a well-known airfield, principally famed for the huge air show it hosts every summer; another advantage is that it's not an operational airfield. The track itself is 3km long and as such, is perfect for air shows and aircraft exhibitions. It has also been used for testing Formula 1 cars, land yachting and even police driver training.

The *Top Gear* team's preparations were exhaustive and meticulous. On the day itself, there would be onsite medical teams who were fully conversant with motor-sport incidents, the training from PTLE would be thorough, a specialist company (Racelogic) was brought in to host the telemetry, no film crews were sited along the runway and a *Top Gear* race consultant was sent in advance to meet the team at PTLE and prepare a briefing for the programme's team and Hammond himself. Indeed, the consultant visited PTLE's Northampton premises on 18 June and was happy with what he saw. In his subsequent briefing to Richard, he explained the controls and gave other detailed advice about driving a car at such speeds. A full and detailed Programme Risk Assessment (PRA) was completed, then referred to the ORM department (Operational Risk Management) for extra certainty. This procedure was not always used for filming such events, which reflects the extent of the *Top Gear* team's planning – notes later showed that great emphasis was placed on Hammond receiving sufficient time for training and that he was not to be rushed under any circumstances. The event was months and months in the planning. An internal Programme Risk Assessment stressed in very clear terms that they had to be certain that in the event of an accident, Hammond could be rushed to the appropriate medical facilities as fast as possible.

On the actual day of filming, the same meticulous measures were taken. The track was painstakingly walked to check for any debris and other fine detail precautions were taken. A course was marked out ending in two large green cones, which represented the braking point for Hammond to shut down the engine and engage the primary parachute. The length of the course was intended to allow him to get near to a speed of 300mph.

Measured runs were scheduled to be completed in one direction only along a pre-set course and the speed would be measured by advanced GPS satellite telemetry. The intention was to record a maximum rather than an average speed over two runs across a measured course (the latter being how they would have qualified for a land-speed record attempt). But a speed record was not what *Top Gear* was after: they wanted Hammond to go exceptionally fast and then describe the experience. Andy Wilman was later revealed to have vetoed an official land-speed record attempt because he felt it was too complex and risky. Yet more caution.

Clearly, although Richard Hammond is a very accomplished driver, this was a whole new world. That is why it was organised for PTLE's two principals, Mark Newby and Colin Fallows, to train him on the morning of filming. Specialist as this type of racing is,

Hammond was not the first non-professional to take the wheel of the Vampire: in fact, members of the owners' families and one journalist had previously been trained to drive it. When Colin Goodwin drove the car for *Autocar* magazine in 2001, he said that he'd found PTLE to be exemplary trainers and that a seasoned driving journalist could train to a safe standard in one day.

Richard was in excited spirits and learned fast, showing a natural aptitude for the training he was being given; he also admitted that he felt very confident in the preparations and the team around him, so he was not fearful at all: 'You become in a suspended state of concentration, thinking about what you're going to do, but there's no fear.' In breaks between training, he was relaxed and made the on-site team giggle with his spoof stunt-driver impressions of the 'Silver Flash', resplendent in a Formula 1-style flameproof suit. Joking aside, his helmet, gloves and race suit were of the highest standard and as worn by Formula 1 drivers. Although he did not wear the HANS head restraint as sported by F1 drivers, he had a very strong foam neck collar to assist with any potential whiplash.

Training was complete just after lunchtime, as was some filming of the car and other general footage. This was not a normal vehicle, so Fallows's lengthy expertise was crucial: there is no clutch, no accelerator, you set the engine and then to move forward, you took your foot off the brake. In addition, Colin Fallows first did a so-called 'shake down' run in the jet car with the afterburner ignited to check everything was working on the vehicle and with the film and data capture crew ('on the jet car's side is a sticker saying 'Real Race Cars Have Afterburners'). For each run, Hammond would have to sit in the tiny cockpit, strapped in with ultra-strong belts to the point of being barely able to breath; it was in fact a racing specification five-point Simpson safety harness. If the arms are not kept tight in a cockpit, in the event of an accident it has been known that the driver's limbs are sliced off. To get the right amount of tension for safety, an instructor would actually force his knee into Hammond's chest to make certain he was completely secured. It was an uncomfortable and claustrophobic environment.

Richard began his first actual speed run at 12.54pm, but not before an extensive list of checks had to be made, all of which were recorded. Once the star began his test runs, events proceeded to plan. Initially his speed was relatively modest, although that's all relative as the first run went to 206.1mph. After each run, he was filmed to capture his reaction.

As he became more comfortable with the controls, the speeds accelerated and it was clear from fairly quickly on that he was capable of going very fast indeed. They broke for lunch after the third run, which had reached 220.4mph. It was now decided that Hammond was doing sufficiently well to be able to engage the afterburner. In total, he would complete six runs, with the afterburner only being used on runs four, five and six – although on run four it did not ignite properly after he had not pressed the igniter switch for long enough and so the run was aborted after less than a kilometre. It was after using the afterburner successfully for the first time that he said those prophetic words: 'I'm so alive! I'm so alive!'

The penultimate run of the day, his sixth, was a complete run with the afterburner on full-length. With the afterburner on, the car was generating 10,000-brake horsepower – that's the equivalent of *10* Bugatti Veyrons, or *18* Ferrari 458s, or *100* Ford Fiestas. The Red Arrows could generate up to 3500lb of thrust when using Rolls-Royce engines fitted to the car; however, with the afterburner lit, this was increased to a mind-boggling 5000lb of thrust.

The sixth run registered 314mph, although Hammond was not

told of this speed in order to be able to capture his elation on-camera later on hearing the news; a member of PTLE was overheard saying, 'That was highly impressive!' It would have been a British record. As mentioned, however, the correct stringent monitoring procedures were not in place (this was not an official attempt, as the *Top Gear* team had repeatedly pointed out) and so the achievement did not qualify.

The run was originally scheduled to be the final attempt as the shoot was provisionally planned to end at 5pm, partly to keep noise levels limited, but it was decided to gain an extension to the booking to allow one final run to capture footage of the Vampire's afterburner being lit. Part of the reason seems to be that the team were worried about wet weather the next day and no one was prepared to send Hammond out in the Vampire in such treacherous conditions. With the prospect of the second day's filming being rained off, they decided to take one more run: this final extended run, the seventh of the day at 5.25pm, was the one which nearly cost Richard Hammond his life.

He later said: 'I suppose it's like when you were playing outside as a kid and then your mum called you in for dinner. You'd always stay out for a bit longer,' to which Clarkson responded, 'And that's when you'd always fall out the tree!'

Exactly 14.25 seconds into the seventh run, after a distance of 1,120 metres had been covered and with the Vampire travelling at 288mph, the front right tyre blew out. The car veered off sharply to the right, and dug into the grassy outfield, before turning over and rolling several times. Finally, it flipped over end-to-end, then travelled forwards (while upside down at 230mph) and came to rest inverted, perpendicular to the line of the track and over 60 metres from the runway.

In seconds, the medical teams were on the car. Former fire

fighter Dave Ogden, owner of Event Fire Services, was one of the first at the scene – footage later showed the medics arrived within 10 seconds. He told the BBC news team. '[The car] went onto the grass and spun over and over before coming to a rest about 100 yards from us.' Indeed, it was upside-down and 'dug in' to the grass. Ogden immediately felt for a pulse and could hear Hammond breathing, although at this point he was unconscious.

Eventually, once it was clear that Richard was safe to move, the emergency crews righted the car and began the delicate process of cutting him out with hydraulic shears. As they did so, he began to regain consciousness although Ogden also said he 'drifted in and out a little bit'. The air ambulance reached the site in an astonishing 15 minutes and once he was safely in the helicopter, it was reported that he became a little agitated as he wanted to do 'a piece to camera' about the crash.

Hammond was airlifted to Leeds General Infirmary's neurological unit, where he was listed as critically ill. It was reported that he had suffered superficial facial injuries due to the dirt which had dislodged the visor and been forced inside his helmet; there was a minor eye injury (some dirt was also forced up his nose) but most worry of all, he had suffered bruising and swelling to the brain due to 'head acceleration effects', also known as 'shock loading'.

The hospital spokesman would only reveal: 'He has seen some improvement overnight but remains in a serious, but stable condition.' He went on to say that Hammond's wife was at his bedside and at the request of the family no more information would be released.

When the news of the horrific crash broke, the BBC was inundated with thousands of well-wishers sending Richard their thoughts. The website alone received over 10,000 messages from worried fans wishing him a speedy recovery. Donations of £50,000+ were sent in to the Yorkshire Air Ambulance, who had got the presenter to the neurological unit in just 12 minutes. All the newspapers ran front-page coverage and television news crews had regular updates; some of the pieces focussed on the fact that he'd wanted to do a piece to camera even as he lay on a stretcher. It seems bizarre now and makes me think of the stuntman in *The Simpsons*, who attempts all sorts of insane daredevil escapades which see him get mangled and battered to within an inch of his life only to somehow always lift a thumb up afterwards to alert the crowd that he is alive … just. But this wasn't a cartoon, it had actually happened and it was anything but funny.

However, *The Simpsons*' character is not some comical creation based on mere fiction; research suggests serious head-injury victims often have distinct moments of clarity in the instant aftermath of an incident before the physiological reality hits home. In this instance, Hammond's professionalism came to the fore: he instinctively believed that if they missed the chance to get a piece to camera with his genuine reaction, the feature would be not as good.

Initially the watching world was told that Richard's recovery would take fifteen months in hospital; incredibly he went home after only five weeks and the doctors treating him advised that he was on course for a 100 per cent recovery. Speaking at the time, James May seemed optimistic about his colleague's chances for a full recovery: 'He's fit and he's a very simple mechanism,' he told the *Daily Mail*, 'It would be like trying to break a tin-opener – you can't really break a tin-opener. I suspect Hammond was a handy scrapper at school.'

Of course this was an endearing brave face: behind the scenes, the *Top Gear* team were all shocked and deeply shaken by the trauma. Clarkson also visited his friend frequently and the story goes that at one of his first visits, less than 48 hours after the accident, Hammond sat up in bed and asked why he was there. Clarkson told him that he'd been in an accident, to which Hammond is reported to have replied, 'Was I driving like a twat?' May visited frequently too and even took the recuperating star a Lego tractor and plough. There was a hidden poignancy to this gift – Richard had once revealed that as a kid he used to watch old *Top Gear* and afterwards, make Lego models of the cars he'd just seen on the show.

Hammond suffered from post-traumatic amnesia, a common result of brain injury. One story he later recounted was asking the nurse for a cottage pie and then when the food arrived, he said, 'That's great! It's my favourite, how did you know?' Immediately after being moved from the critical ward to recuperation at Bristol's BUPA hospital, Hammond was chatting to his wife Mindy and suddenly said, 'You're lovely, but I've got to stop talking to you because I've got to go back to my wife – she's French.' Yet at all times he could remember the number plate of his first-ever car, that Shelby-liveried Toyota Corolla. Even more bizarrely perhaps, his childhood Birmingham accent returned for a few days. Later he described his head as being like 'a bag of snakes' from the trauma and Mindy has confirmed that she would often find him crouching on the hospital bed, clutching his head in agony.

'If I look at my best friend,' says neuroscientist Dr Kerry Spackman, 'there's part of my brain that tells me they're a man, another part tells me that they're a good mate, another part tells me what they do for a living, another part tells me their name and who they are and how I know them; all these connections are stored in different parts of the brain, not just in one place – there's not a "best friend" place. So this is where you can get some very bizarre things [happening after brain injury] because you can know somebody but not know your relationship to them, or perhaps you can know the relationship, but not know their name.

'The original circuits that were connected to all the parts of who his wife was – in fact, the whole *personality* of some of those circuits – might have been damaged permanently and what's happened is he's grown new circuits around them to make up for that. So, basically he's had to relearn some of those tasks and that's why he'll feel he's not quite the same: he'll still be Richard Hammond but there'll always be some parts of him that will be ever so slightly different.'

Nonetheless, he continued to make great progress and was indeed discharged from hospital after five weeks. His first post-crash interview was with the *Daily Mirror*, for whom he also writes a column, and he revealed the extent of his immediate danger when paramedics rushed to him while he was still trapped in the wreckage. Speaking from 'a secret hideaway' where he was recovering with his wife and daughters, Richard said: 'Doctors use a point system: fifteen is normal, three is a flat-line; I was a three – I was that close to being dead. I was in a bad way when they came to get me. The air ambulance guys were amazed I was still breathing.' (Trivia fans note: the surname Hammond has its roots in Norse history and the William the Conqueror era, but is generally understood to mean 'protected'.)

Hammond seemed remarkably philosophical about his near-death experience. His most high-profile TV interview shortly after the crash was actually on *Friday Night With Jonathan Ross*. 'There was a sense of "Oh, bugger,"' he told Ross, in typically light-hearted fashion. He also said he could not recall asking to do the piece to camera in the helicopter, or for that matter 'the first few weeks.' What's more, it soon transpired that he had very little recollection of the crash itself – again, not uncommon –

instead saying that he recalls getting into the jet car and then his next memory was waking up in hospital. Speaking to Sir Stirling Moss on their one off interview show, Hammond revealed that as his car went out of control, he felt no fear, instead having some strange feeling that there was a 'To Do' list he'd ticked off that day and dying in a crash was next on the schedule.

David Coulthard – who nearly lost his life in a fatal plane crash in 2000 – confirmed to this author that in any such high-speed accident, people's experiences can be very subjective and each incident is different: 'Sometimes you hit a wall before you know it, your mind is on the next corner and it goes but other times you feel it going, you try to recover, you do all the instinctive things that you would do and you never give up until the accident comes to a halt. But it depends on the incident, of course and also on the individual: for example, other people tell me that when they've had crashes the noise is terrible but in all the many racing incidents I've had over the years, I don't hear anything. In my experiences of car and plane crashes, I believe that my hearing shuts down so that my brain can focus on the senses that are needed to recover the accident or come out of the situation safely. Other senses take priority.'

Two separate investigations were launched into the exact circumstances of the crash – normal procedure for such a devastating accident, particularly one being filmed. They were by the Health and Safety Executive and the BBC (who also fully co-operated with the H&SE). All the *Top Gear* presenters and production staff were confident of their preparations and maintained all safety procedures had been followed diligently.

Former *Top Gear* producer Jon Bentley was involved in the programme years previous to the new safety legislation being introduced: 'I do remember Health and Safety coming in – I wrote most of the generic risk assessment myself. I managed to argue against some notion that film crews would all have to wear high-visibility jackets while shooting at all times: we all thought, "Aaargh!" I managed to think up a reply to the Health and Safety people along the lines that the prospect of three or four people standing by the side of the road dressed in high-visibility jackets and pointing a camera would cause huge alarm to the average motorist and would be more likely to cause accidents than prevent them.

'I was directing the first shoot after the legislation came in. As it happened, we were doing a potentially quite dangerous stunt, attempting to break a world record for the "flaming dominoes". We had twelve cars standing vertically on end, we then set fire to them and a veteran stunt driver in a Jaguar was going to drive through them all and knock them down. We managed to break the record and nobody was hurt. I don't think Health and Safety stopped us doing anything.'

The Health & Safety Executive has become something of a pariah in modern British culture, berated as a killjoy organisation that ruins the fun things in life such as driving fast cars or playing conkers (with, or without caravans). Indeed, *Top Gear* has had a fairly terse relationship with the H&SE, with regular on-screen jibes about their demands. Timothy Walker, director-general of the Health and Safety Executive, has been quoted in the media as saying: 'I am sorry Jeremy Clarkson believed that health and safety was the "cancer of a civilised society". I do not think the families of over 200 people killed at work each year would share his view.'

Regardless of individuals' opinions of the H&SE's validity – or lack of – there's no denying that the report compiled after the crash investigation was so phenomenally extensive and detailed as to highlight the exact purpose of such an organisation so it is perhaps ironic that *Top Gear* has helped to show the H&SE has a very important role to play in society in general.

The investigation was led by principal inspector Keith King, who appears to have been exhaustive in his attention to detail: he interviewed every principal participant, from the *Top Gear* staff, the PTLE owners, people on site on the day to technical experts and even Richard Hammond himself, who met with him to discuss the crash in mid-December.

King's report focussed on a number of areas, but three in particular: the planning and preparation undertaken by the BBC and other parties involved, the training given to Richard Hammond and a technical examination of the vehicle and its tyres. Having read all the staggering minutiae and technical detail of the full Health and Safety Executive Report into the incident, I came away with the feeling that this was, above all, an *accident*.

No stone was left unturned by the H&SE. For the examination of the car, specialist evidence was obtained within the organisation on ergonomic issues, complemented by expert advice from the Transport Research Laboratory about the tyres, as well as information from the North Yorkshire Police regarding the vehicle itself and the crash scene. The BBC also appointed their own consultant to examine the tyres.

The detailed examination of the car by the H&SE showed that many of the safety features were in excellent working order: the roll bar had worked, the harness performed perfectly, the chassis was relatively undamaged and the fuel system had no leaks. The left side front wheel and brake assembly had sheared off as they were designed to do and were found some 80 metres away from the car; the crash helmet was highlighted by the report as suffering no 'significant structural damage ... There were two impact damage marks to the right and to the rear of the crown of the helmet', which the report suggested was the result of being 'struck against a bar-like object'. PTLE later said they had seen crashes at higher speeds that received less helmet damage and suggested this may have been caused by the camera clamp being used to film cockpit footage (a fact acknowledged by the H&SE as a possible 'exacerbating factor').

The wording of the report's summary was very precise and included this note about the BBC's preparations: 'The investigation also identified failings in the BBC's safety management systems relating to risk assessment and the procurement of services from others, and by PTLE in their risk assessment for the services they provided to the BBC at Elvington. These failings and other recommendations are being pursued with the two parties involved. However, when viewed against H&SE's enforcement criteria, none of these failings merit prosecution.' The report also stated that Colin Fallows was 'a consummate jet propulsion engineer' and that his knowledge was 'encyclopaedic'. Further, that PTLE 'operated at the extreme end of the automotive spectrum', which necessarily carries a higher risk. Ultimately, the investigation stated that it had identified, 'omissions by two of the parties involved, but finds no grounds for prosecution.'

Although the report highlighted a minor number of areas of concern, it went on to say that several factors were vital in probably saving Hammond's life: these included the Vampire's roll bar and immense structural strength (the cockpit area was left completely intact), the driver's restraints that Hammond found so suffocating to have put on him, the crash helmet and the rapid response of the entire team present when the crash occurred.

The BBC's own cockpit footage clearly shows a tyre blow-out on the front offside wheel. Telemetry later revealed that Hammond was not braking at the moment of explosion – in other words, he was unaware of a problem in advance. The H&SE report confirmed 'catastrophic failure' was the 'immediate cause' and the speed when the incident occurred was confirmed at precisely 288mph. Close forensic examination of the tyre revealed it had been damaged as a result of an object (or objects) entering the sidewall immediately adjacent to the edge of the tread during the previous run. Although a blister was visible in the tyre's outer side, this appeared to have subsided and was not visible to the naked eye as they prepared for the final run. It was therefore a ticking and hidden time bomb.

In the H&SE report it was also stated that Hammond's reaction to the blow-out was, 'that of a competent high performance car driver, namely to brake the car and to try to steer into the skid. Immediately afterwards he also seems to have followed his training and to have pulled back on the main parachute release lever, thus shutting down the jet engine and also closing the jet and afterburner fuel levers. The main parachute did not have time to deploy before the car ran off the runway.'

This confirms the parachute was deployed by Hammond, a fact that he revealed was highly reassuring as he'd previously felt enormous guilt (both as a married man and father) that somehow he might have 'cocked up'. Not so. The report went on to say that he, 'displayed considerable presence of mind, and to have managed to deploy the parachute following the blow-out ...' Analysis of the telemetry showed that even if Hammond had reacted with the fastest reflex humanly possible, the accident might still not have been avoidable, even by an experienced jet driver.

In interviews after the crash, Hammond made light of his driving ability, playing down the complexity of the car, and it was also noted he'd driven a Renault F1 car, which appeared to be a far more complex task than the jet car: '[Vampire] has got less knobs and buttons than a Nissan Micra – it's great. All you do is get in and press a button, literally ... you take your foot off the brake and just set off down the track with unbelievable acceleration.'

However, he is being overly modest: in effect, what the report was saying was that Hammond's driving ability was so acutely developed that outside of the realms of a racing professional or indeed a jet-car professional, his reaction times could not have been better. Even then, his reaction and decision-making was so adept and swift that the difference between his reactions and those of a jet-car racer's was small. In other words, there appears to be a clear implication that but for this innate ability, he may not have survived the crash.

Speaking in 2010, the original Stig Perry McCarthy said that although all three presenters were very capable drivers, Hammond probably just edged the other two in terms of talent and skill. The Formula 1 legend David Coulthard, who has appeared on *Top Gear* a number of times and is a fan of the show, concurs all three presenters are extremely competent behind the wheel, as he told the author for this book: 'I would imagine that with that huge amount of industry knowledge and experience, you can't help but be good drivers. Being a good road driver and being a good circuit driver are two different things altogether. I'm a good circuit driver, but I'm not a particularly good road driver – those three are clearly able to do elements of both.'

The renowned neuroscientist Dr Kerry Spackman has worked in motorsport, including for Formula 1 teams such as McLaren and Jaguar, for years now. He said that it appears Hammond's driving ability was indeed exceptional: 'When it's under pressure, the brain will do whatever is automatic, consciousness is too slow. Consciousness takes you time, it's a big overhead. That's the difference between a good tennis player and a bad tennis player: for example, I have to think about all my shots and what I'm doing, whereas for a professional tennis player, it's all automatic: you don't have to think about how to walk, you just get up and your legs do what they do. But a baby has to think about that process, which is why it stutters and stumbles, and its legs are all out of control. So that's the first point: consciousness is very, very slow.

'So, when you're under extreme pressure – for example, in an accident when the world's not working and you're about to die, the brain just relies on automatic reflexes. [Hammond's reaction] is a remarkable achievement and whether [it's because] he had mentally rehearsed the things or was really well briefed … but it's extraordinary and the average person would have got it wrong.'

Speaking on BBC Radio 5 Live, the world land speed record holder, RAF fighter pilot Andy Green, said this: 'It's a very brave thing of Richard to do to step into a very skilled, very specialist sport, pretty much from cold. He would obviously have had some practice but he hasn't lived with this, he hasn't developed the car, he hasn't been part of it for a long time.'

At such a high velocity, the complex engineering is mind-boggling: drag increases exponentially with speed, so at 300mph even the dirt on a car can cause drag. At that moment your world is travelling at nearly 450 feet per second: that Hammond was able to react in any way that might have contributed to lessening the crash's impact is remarkable.

As we have seen, *Top Gear* has always attracted a wealth of criticism from various quarters and Richard's accident was a golden ticket for some of the show's more critical observers. Long before any investigation had been completed, fairly predictable calls of recklessness were hurled the BBC's way, even though preparations had clearly been meticulous.

When Richard was critically ill, Andy Wilman said there would be no more *Top Gear* without the three presenters' full line-up; he also quashed rumours that the accident might mean that they would have to tone down the show's more outrageous features (it's the *Two Fat Ladies* mentality again). No doubt, the inevitable calls for the show to be dropped didn't help Hammond's recovery. When talk inevitably turned to the actual footage and his job as a *Top Gear* presenter, many media observers felt it would be ghoulish and inappropriate to show footage of the crash. But *Top Gear* disagreed and on 28 January 2007, for the first episode of Series 9 they broadcast both the crash and a full interview with Hammond, explaining what happened and what it had felt like. For his part, although the presenter admitted to being apprehensive, he insisted that he felt it would be 'irresponsible' if they didn't broadcast the film and address the aftermath. Inevitably, the critics' barbed pens were sharpened ready for action when he returned to the programme in what seemed a remarkably quick time.

Rather than shy away from the accident, though, *Top Gear* confronted it full-on. Alongside features on the new Jaguar XKR, the Aston Martin Vantage and roadworks, the team interviewed Hammond on the crash. They started by mentioning that even with their 'limited knowledge of television, they knew not to show the crash footage until the end of the show, otherwise everyone would just switch over and watch the finale of *Big Brother*.' Clarkson then made a gag about Hammond becoming Princess Diana – it was good to see nothing had changed.

They then said that Richard had insisted they didn't make a fuss and with a deep note of sincerity behind Jeremy's introduction of, 'I didn't think I'd ever be saying this at one point,' Hammond was given a champion boxer's entrance, complete with dancing girls, a grand staircase and fireworks. To a rapturous welcome he came into the studio and said his introduction was the most embarrassing thing that had ever happened to him.

He appeared to be normal, so Clarkson then asked what he contends is the big question: 'Are you now a mental?' Following this, May offered him a tissue in case he started to dribble. Perhaps not entirely surprisingly, afterwards there were some complaints. A spokesperson for Headway, the brain injury association, said: 'There are survivors with brain injuries who dribble following their accident and this is not something to joke about. It really was offensive and insulting to all those people living with brain injuries and their carers.'

Meanwhile, Hammond made light of his injuries, saying, 'The only difference between me now and before the crash is that I like celery now and I didn't before.' Clarkson then selflessly offered to do all the supercar challenges in future! After a moving thank you from Hammond to the nurses, hospital, well-wishers and *Top Gear* fans, the show simply moved on to resume 'normal service' and in this case, a side-splittingly funny feature about roadworks.

It is not until the end of the show that the trio sit down on their old leather car seats to talk about 'the little fella's car crash'. Hammond joked that the fuel pump was from a concrete mixer and the gear box came out of a Reliant Robin. It's then that the most prophetic TV presenter intro ever was broadcast: Hammond was shown sitting in the cockpit, talking about the 10,000bhp that will be behind him if he presses the afterburner switch which might lead, he adds unwittingly, to 'the biggest accident you've ever seen in your life.' Then again, Colin Fallows is seen strapping Hammond in, 'in case he goes upside down.'

When he first fired up the jet engine, Hammond said it was terrifying. He somehow managed to commentate on his first run almost all the way down the runway, despite doing 220mph. For the first afterburner run, he was noticeably quieter, his eyes a deep-set focus of concentration (he nearly cried). Not surprisingly, as this was actually 314mph. They then showed the crash, which was met by stunned silence in the studio. Even so, much merriment follows – Clarkson says he could have held it – before Jezza makes an endearing and genuine toast to The Hamster, welcoming him back.

In fact, Hammond's doctor had been somewhat apprehensive about his patient seeing the video footage, but Hammond's own view was that it hadn't killed him, so why should it be a problem now? He has also pointed out that many of the challenges on the show contain an element of risk and that all three presenters are accustomed to this: 'We spend our lives minimising risk, so that's what I couldn't believe – that it had actually gone wrong.' Naturally, they were bound to have some fun on the first show back, but at the same time the show was eager to make it clear there was nothing funny behind all the japery: 'Just because we make light of it on the show,' said Hammond later, 'don't think for a second I make light of it myself because I don't – it was bloody horrible.'

Both he and the team rightly point out that although there had been criticism of the *Top Gear* challenges, in fact although the tyre blow-out led to the hideous crash, preparations went to plan: the car's safety equipment worked brilliantly, the medical team were on the scene in seconds, they had the correct equipment to deal with the incident, the helicopter was able to take him to a hospital within minutes, the crash helmet did its job, and so on. 'I'm living proof that safety works,' he insisted.

Although Hammond and his team promised on that particular show that the crash would never be mentioned again, of course this has not been the case. In fact, it cropped up in 2009, when they were discussing Felipe Massa's near-fatal F1 crash that year, it was mentioned after a review of a Bentley and most comically of all, it was referenced hilariously when the trio were buying cars suitable for teenage boys and spent an afternoon in the *Top Gear* office phoning around insurance companies while pretending to be seventeen. At one point, Hammond is asked by the call centre if he's had any accidents in the past five years ... cue a cheeky raise of the eyebrows and a pause before he said, 'Er, no.'

The surprise at his remarkable recovery was widespread; however, eighteen months after the crash, Richard revealed that in fact the longer-term effects were much more invasive than he'd at first realised. Speaking to the *Daily Mail*, he admitted that he still suffered emotional problems and memory loss issues – for example, one day he forgot all the PIN numbers to his cards. He said that he struggled 'mortally with depression' and still spoke regularly to a psychiatrist; he then went so far as to say that his brain needed to re-wire itself to fully recover. The physical swelling and immediate physical damage had gone but internally, there was still much to recover. He'd damaged the part of the brain that controls spatial awareness and revealed that he now finds it difficult to park his car.

Neuroscientist Dr Kerry Spackman is not surprised: 'I'm not sure of the severity [of his head injury] but it appears to be a mild traumatic head injury. This is not actually 'mild', it's severe but this term just means his skull didn't crack open and his brains didn't come out. In this instance, where [the person has] effectively banged their brain around, it is a common and well-known occurrence that depression happens. It's not that a person is down, it's actually that they've given the brain such a rattle that part of that whole protective mechanism [kicks in]. It's nothing to do with the person's mood or anything like that, it's just what happens. So, a lot of people with bad head injuries will have some kind depression, couple that with the fact he's had a very severe head injury ... it really depends, it's the luck of the draw.'

Dr Spackman also points out that when the head is decelerated at such a velocity, it's really a highly precarious and dangerous time: 'If, for example, I run straight into a brick wall face first and my head jerks forward, sometimes the damage is at the other side of the brain, at the back of your head because all the fluid runs forward and that squashes forward and pushes the head backwards, so you get a bang at the back of the head, even though you've run into something at the front. When the brain gets banged around, it's a horrible business and it's not obvious where the damage is going to be. Particularly if [as with Hammond] a car has rolled and bounced.'

Richard also admitted that on reflection going back to the show only four months after the crash was 'much too early'. Speaking in the *Daily Mail*, he said: 'I thought I was better when I went back to work, but now I don't remember going back. I was really having a bloody hard time, I had to evolve new strategies for coping.' He went on to say: 'I damaged all the complicated bits of the brain to do with processing and emotional control. I was prey to every single emotion that swept over me and I couldn't deal with it, I had to relearn things from scratch.' This necessity to re-learn how to cope with life means that the majority of victims of injury to the brain find the simplest things very testing indeed.

The impact of the crash on Hammond's life has been deep and lasting. Poignantly, he is now vice-president of UK children's brain injury charity, The Children's Trust. In July 2009, he met with children and staff at the opening of the charity's state-of-the-art £7 million project in Tadworth, Surrey. The *Top Gear* presenter was escorted by thirteen-year-old Chas, who had been severely injured in a skiing accident in 2008, and told reporters present: 'I know only too well the challenges people face following a severe brain injury but for a child, there are extra dimensions because their brains are still developing.'

Talking about his own accident is always a mixture of seriousness and levity; it's a tricky balance for Hammond to get right. At times, The Hamster cannot avoid making light of the situation and once joked in the *Mirror* that he was disappointed not to have any long-lasting or more dramatic scars: 'Do you realise how annoyed I am that I've got no marks on me? Absolutely nothing at all, nothing for the pub! There are people who fall off their trikes at the age of four who've got better injuries than me. I've been through hell and I've got nothing to show for it except a chipped tooth! I'm gutted.'

And did he have any mementos from the crash? Well, not the helmet – the manufacturer asked if he'd kindly return it to them as, 'they told me that it's the fastest test [they've] ever put it through.' He's requested that they return it one day so that he can put it on a plinth on his office wall.

Ultimately, it was for Richard to decide when he was ready to return to *Top Gear*. Reflecting on the incident that nearly killed him and his lengthy recovery since, he is still convinced that the programme had attempted to do all the right things. His stance is that if one boy racer thinks twice about how badly cars can go wrong – even in the ultra-safe world of television – then that same speeding teenager might pull back on the pedal a little ... and how could that be a bad thing?

CHAPTER 18

Supercars and Top Gear

One criticism often levelled at the new version of *Top Gear* is that they tend to focus on cars that 99 per cent of the population could never afford. Initially, the old generation of the programme was very much a 'normal' motoring show and as such, they regularly featured 'cars of the people' such as Escorts, Mondeos, Metros, and so on. However, if you scan through the new *Top Gear* archives, there is a clear predominance of supercars and high performance machines being filmed and reviewed.

The obvious way that the show features these stunning machines is on the 'Power Lap' board. Regardless of the way a car is tested, whether it's driving across Europe, ploughing down a snowy mountain, thundering around the Highlands or careering up a circular multi-storey, at the end of each piece the cars are usually brought back to the trusty *Top Gear* test track and handed over to the tame racing driver. Once The Stig has thrashed a vehicle around the track, the show returns to the studio where the presenters and audience await the time with baited breath.

There are regulations for Power Lap Times on the track: the car has to be road-worthy, commercially available and able to negotiate standard speed bumps. For this reason, the laps completed by the Aston Martin BBR9 (a Le Mans car), the Ferrari FXX (slick tyres) and the Renault F1 car (it's a Renault F1 car!) and the Caparo T1 (too low-slung) did not qualify, nor did those by the Radical SR3 and the Sea Harrier. Conversely, manufacturers (and The Stig) are allowed to alter suspensions and gear shifting to their most aggressive set-up and traction controls can be switched off. As we have seen, at the time of writing it's perhaps not surprising that the Veyron Super Sport has the fastest lap time of 1.16.8.

In a direct response to the on-going criticism of supercar bias, Clarkson announced in Series 6 that they would therefore review the 'cheapest' Ferrari available, the stunning 430. As a fan of the marque, this was a shoe-in for a good review but in fact Clarkson could barely contain his joy, thrashing it around the circuit with lashings of superlatives, comparing the engine note to a symphony orchestra. A startling statistic with this car is that Ferrari claim any driver can take the new 430 around their test track only one second slower than their own test driver, such is the technological brilliance of the machine. Clarkson agreed and declared it a masterpiece, although he added that you could always sell your left leg for £3,000 if you wanted to buy the flappy paddle gear shift as you wouldn't need a clutch foot.

My own favourite part of this exuberant review is when Clarkson points to the 'snow and ice' button on the steering wheel – bringing to mind the months and months of high-tech wizardry and boffin-like development injected into that safety setting and the world-leading technology it possessed – only for him to dismiss it by saying, 'That's irrelevant!' (Note: James May enjoyed the 430 so much that he went out and bought his own.)

Going back to the review of Pink Floyd drummer Nick Mason's F60, the Enzo, after all the shenanigans and fooling around with the musician's new book, Clarkson's review of this landmark Ferrari was superb. His hyperbole was without limit as he said he'd never known such 'savagery' and at one point clearly cannot think of anything clever to add, instead just relying on his emotional instinct and saying, 'I wish you were here.' And that's another part of *Top Gear* that we love – we all wish we were there too. Often the presenters say exactly what you might be thinking while watching them at home. This happened again at the end of the piece, when Nick Mason left the Enzo behind and flew home in his helicopter and, as Clarkson himself asks, 'Why would you do that?'

Jeremy's Ferrari love affair was first seen way back in 1995 when he appeared on *Jeremy Clarkson's Motorworld* and called the red supercars 'sex on wheels'. But he wasn't a brand snob. In Series 5, it was hard to ignore the pure exhilaration he obviously felt when testing the madcap Ariel Atom. This ingenious piece of British engineering from a company with only seven employees unleashed a brain-distorting burst of acceleration, largely thanks to having its chassis on the outside of the car, a mechanical exo-skeleton which made the end car almost literally as light as a feather. In fact, such was its lightweight purity that it actually boasted more bhp per ton than even the Enzo. This left the car with a 0–60 time of just 2.9 seconds.

When Clarkson reviewed it, he began by saying, how many middle-aged men died on motorbikes purchased as some kind of mid-life crisis impulse buy? Instead, why not buy the Atom, a genuine four-wheel alternative to a superbike (likewise, with no roof and no windscreen)?

Notably, the Ariel Atom is one of the most popular *Top Gear* trading cards because on it is a brilliant picture of Clarkson's face almost literally 'melting' as the brutal acceleration pulls his cheeks back to behind his ears. It makes for hilarious viewing as Jeremy shouts that he looks like an alien or The Elephant Man. Aside from the gags, he *loves* the car; it even qualifies for a Power Lap time because it's commercially available and can negotiate all standard speed bumps. The Stig's lap time – *sans* any music as there is no stereo – was a blistering 1.19.5, second only at that point to the Enzo and even somewhat quicker than Porsche's flagship hypercar, the Carrera GT. Clarkson eventually declares that he has never known acceleration like the Atom and that it's the most exciting car he's *ever* driven. For all his controversy, it's hard to see how a compliment like that can't be anything other than a huge boost to the tiny car manufacturer. (Note: *Top Gear* later released a radio-controlled toy version of this mad vehicle.)

Another classic high-speed lap for Clarkson came in the aforementioned Caparo T1, a road-legal racing car designed by the same people who developed the legendary McLaren F1. The car had a registration plate and lights, as well as indicators and, in theory, space for a passenger so the *Top Gear* team felt it was worth a power lap to see if the T1 could beat the then-Power Lap leader, the bonkers Koenigsegg (1.17.6). Like the Atom, there was no stereo for the tame racing driver's tunes but unlike the Ariel, this particular beast cost a massive £2,235,000.

However, the Caparo T1 was not a car with a simple history: its mechanical development was plagued with problems because the team behind it were trying to achieve an engineering feat that had rarely been rivalled: to put Formula 1 speed and power on the British roads. As mentioned, when the car was tested by rival show *Fifth Gear*'s Jason Plato (a touring car champion), the engine had set on fire and Plato suffered burns to his face and arms. Clarkson made light of this chequered history by saying the *Top Gear* emergency team usually consists of 'a van with sticking plasters and aspirin in it' only for the camera to pan across to a fleet of ambulances, paramedic motorbikes and even an air ambulance helicopter! He wore an F1 safety suit and helmet and was clearly a little apprehensive.

And he had good reason to be cautious – the car had 575bhp (more than most Ferraris) but weighed 'less than a patio heater' according to Clarkson. This meant that its ratio of bhp per ton was *double* the Bugatti Veyron and the 0–60mph time was equal to that superlative VW engineering masterpiece. Sure enough, Clarkson was blown away by the speed, saying he had never felt acceleration like it. The speed was akin to the Atom, but he criticised the T1's handling as carrying way too much understeer and even went so far as to say that on the roads this issue, mixed with the seismic power, could prove highly dangerous. After several repairs and numerous lightning quick laps, Clarkson was energised but with reservations; they then unleashed the Stig in the T1.

Back in the studio, Jeremy reveals the mind-boggling lap time of 1.10.6, a full seven seconds faster than the mad Koenigsegg ... only to immediately take the car back down as it was incapable of going over a speed bump. Clarkson said the nose was so low, it couldn't even run over Gandhi.

In Series 2, the *Top Gear* team had already lapped without incident in the 'modest' standard Koenigsegg but since then, matters moved up a notch. This unique supercar manufacturer is the brainchild of its namesake founder, a Swedish multi-millionaire who made his first million importing frozen chickens into Estonia and was inspired to create the car when, as a five-year-old, he watched a movie about a local bicycle repairman who made his own racing car. Koenigsegg was very serious about speed: when his standard Koenigsegg achieved a top speed of 242 mph, it beat the world's previous fastest production car (a record that had stood for years) – the McLaren F1's 240mph; then the Bugatti came along and smashed the Koenigsegg's fastest, so the competition was on for yet more speed.

When Koenigsegg delivered the souped-up version known as the CCX to *Top Gear* in Series 8, the lack of a rear wing meant the car did not have sufficient downforce to lap the track at high speed without spinning off – as The Stig found out when he bowled into a tyre wall. This incident attracted criticism for the show's treatment of the cars themselves. The tabloid headline, 'TOP GEAR YOBS WRECK £1 MILLION CAR', fuelled a series of articles saying the team were essentially 'road thugs' for having mashed up the brutally fast Koenigsegg CC8. Behind the scenes, the Swedish manufacturer shipped the car back home and fitted it with a small rear spoiler, then dutifully flew it back to the UK. Rumour has it that The Stig suggested this modification and he was proved correct. And the result was a brand new lap record of 1.17.6. (Note: Koenigsegg say the faster time was a result of more than just this one alteration.)

The fastest-ever lap around the track, however, was in a Renault Formula 1 car: the French F1 team had been watching the *Top Gear* Power board time grow faster and faster, usually hovering around the 1.20 minute area for most supercars and so they contacted the programme to say they could get their 2005 F1 car – as used by Fernando Alonso to win the Driver's and Constructor's Championship – around in *under a minute*. Who better to drive at the helm than The Stig? The feature was a fascinating and clever foil to allow *Top Gear* to describe the technology and engineering brilliance behind a F1 car: we were told that they needed 16 engineers on site just to start the car up and given a long and breath-taking list of performance stats.

With more than half the lap at full throttle, The Stig took the car round and pipped 183mph on the straight. In as much as The Stig is a mysterious character, this piece also reminded viewers that he is a phenomenal race driver too. Even though the track was greasy, the car went round in a ridiculous 59 seconds dead. Back in the studio, Clarkson asked Hammond to take the Renault's leader board-topping time down because it was ineligible, but The Hamster was unable to reach it.

On the subject of Renault Formula 1, Hammond himself has driven one of their cars around a track. Although he was seen spinning and initially struggled to even pull away from the pits, don't be misled into thinking he wasn't doing exceptionally well. Dr Kerry Spackman has worked in Formula 1 for years, including at McLaren and Jaguar, and he explains why such a car is deceptively difficult to drive: 'For a while Richard couldn't even drive it fast enough to get to the point where it was working properly: he couldn't get the tyres up to temperature, it wasn't driving fast enough for the wings to work and he was crashing the car and sliding off the track, it just wasn't in the operating zone. In an F1 car everything is just so much faster, it's like facing my tennis serve as against facing Andy Roddick's tennis serve. In an F1 car, you are walking on a tight rope.' This is an opinion backed up by many former racers, such as Sir Stirling Moss who told Hammond in their one-off interview show that, 'there's a very big gap between the best amateur and the poorest professional.'

While driving the F1 car, Hammond could also be seen and heard shaking and sounding as if he was being 'roughed up'. This is no surprise to Dr Spackman: 'It's hard to appreciate the sheer violence you experience in a Formula 1 car, it's unbelievable. If, for example, you are going down a normal road and you jam on your brakes as hard as you possibly can so that everything in the backseat flies forward and your tyres are screaming, that's probably 0.8 of a G, if you're lucky. Formula 1 racing cars routinely pull 5 to 6G under braking, so the driver's body weight goes to half a ton. At that point, their head is the equivalent weight of someone sitting on it, but at a right angle, and that weight is bouncing on you. It's banging you from side to side while you're trying to do the most delicate actions and yet drive at the highest speed; it's like being shaken around and beaten up while trying to do brain surgery. They didn't have time to explain all that in the episode when Hammond drove the F1 car, it's just a whole different thing.'

Unlike the old *Top Gear*, the new generation rarely ventures into the world of competitive motorsport. Where its predecessor enjoyed a close relationship with rallying, for example, and regularly reported on F1, the new *Top Gear* typically only dabbles in this area when famous racing drivers come on the show or world champion drivers help them with their stunts (for example, Mika Häkkinen teaching Captain Slow to rally).

Perhaps one of the oddest but most entertaining motorsport features was when Richard visited a man who'd built a monstrous drag racer from scratch in his kitchen, but he couldn't actually get out. Along came *Top Gear* to help him axle-grind the wall off his kitchen and extract the car with a mini-digger and some precarious-looking ramps.

It was all good fun but on a more serious note, the most direct involvement of the new *Top Gear* in actual racing came when the team took part in the Silverstone Britcar 24-hr Race in Series 10, Episode 9. Previously, they had made some bio-fuel by planting rapeseed, but James allegedly bought the wrong type of seed and so they produced a vast quantity – 500 gallons – far more than they needed. Rather than risk the wrath of eco-campaigners by throwing this fuel away, they chose instead to enter the race at Silverstone to use it all up.

The trio had thought the race was an amateur's paradise, a good old bit of British stiff-upper-lip racing, a spot of lunch maybe and jolly good fun to be had by all. However, when they arrived at the circuit Clarkson was horrified to find a mélange of supercars, Le Mans-style hypercars and motorhomes that would put the Formula 1 paddock to shame. Immediately, they knew that they'd massively underestimated the challenge. Officially, they were the only 'Novice' racers on the track and as such had to have a sticker on their rear bumper to declare this, presumably to alert the multitude of overtaking cars. As he pushed his helmet on ready for qualifying, Jeremy said it was unquestionably the scariest thing he'd ever done.

Initially, all went well and Clarkson and Hammond completed some strong flying laps; then James May went out and forgot to do a third lap, therefore failing to time. In desperation they sent out their secret weapon – The Stig – who ensured they were not in last place, much to the delight of the team.

Further setbacks hindered them, with their car being rebuilt so late in the day that they had to start from the pit lane, but eventually they made it to the start ... just! In the first hour, The Stig made up twenty places and then it was over to Clarkson who, for once, did not clown around at all, not even for a second. This was serious stuff and his usual jovial remarks were missing. Later he explained that there was so much to think about, to concentrate on, that he couldn't make any remarks or even contemplate being a TV presenter, it was so demanding. After a sterling effort by James, Captain Slow pulled into the pit as he was getting dangerously tired; he handed over to Hammond, who only a year or so after his near-death experience in the jet car was initially brilliant, but then crashed again – fortunately this time with no injuries or dramas other than a massive three-hour rebuild of the car. When he limped into the pit, the engine refused to restart and there was a long list of damaged parts. By the time the fixed BMW rejoined the race, they were in last place.

So they sent The Stig out again and he made great progress, before Clarkson brought the BMW home in a highly emotional state, tears trickling from his eyes as he crossed the finishing line. It was all compulsive *Top Gear* stuff and made the viewers at home think that perhaps they should do more of those serious pieces.

Notably, this particular race was an example that Richard later gave of how he was still recovering from his horror smash in the jet car. Previously, he'd joked that his exemplary driving skills were insufficient for him to cherish designs on being a racing driver himself: 'I'm too polite. I say, "After you" – I'm a bit rubbish! Most racing drivers are nuts.' But the reality of this particular *Top Gear* challenge was more striking for him, personally. He said that at the Britcar Race, he felt that he'd reacted more unpredictably than he might have prior to the jet-car crash. To be fair, given that he'd almost lost his life one year previously, hurtling around a track at high speed and in the dark would test the most resilient of nerves. But Hammond believed there was more to it than that: 'I was scared and nervous. It was making me argumentative, angry, thinking I wasn't good enough for the job; feeling awful.'

Perhaps of all the many *Top Gear* supercar and sportscar features, one stands out above all else. In Series 1, the team set themselves a challenge to find out which nation builds the fastest supercar. Why, Britain of course! And the car in question was a rusty old Jaguar XJS. To be fair, they actually fitted the old banger with nitrous oxide canisters (known as 'noz'), which added a colossal 500bhp extra! Still, the ensuing drag race saw the Jag leave a Porsche 911 Turbo, a 360 Ferrari and a Corvette in its wake. So, who says Britain doesn't make great cars?

CHAPTER 19

The Polar Trek

Without doubt one of *Top Gear*'s most ambitious, entertaining and as it turned out, controversial shows was 'The Polar Special', broadcast in July 2007. By their own definition the show had come up with a true 'epic' this time.

Their aim was simple, if a little lunatic: Jeremy Clarkson and James May would race Richard Hammond in 24-hour sunlight to the Magnetic North Pole. The original intention was to coincide with the annual Polar race but eventually it was just filmed independently. This time the duo's weapon of choice was a heavily modified Toyota pick-up truck (*that* car again!), with Richard racing against his fellow presenters using only a sled pulled by a team of 10 Canadian Inuit dogs. The car-bound pair also genuinely planned to (and indeed, *did*) use the car's SatNav System, even though the Magnetic North Pole is not a fixed point and had in fact moved 100 miles since 1996 (the True North Pole is some 800 miles further north). Essential modifications were made to the truck, such as raised wheel-arches, adding 38-inch ice tyres, an auxiliary fuel tank and some tinkering with the gear ratios. In all, 240 man-hours were spent making the cars fit for the incredible trek ahead.

The logistics of this particular show were way beyond the usual demands placed on the production team. There was a very real possibility of death in temperatures that regularly sink below -65°C. No one underestimated the challenge ahead and the team spent months preparing the show, which according to their own production notes was, 'our most technically challenging and scariest film ever.' It was also the first episode of *Top Gear* to be shown in high-definition.

By their own admission, the trio were not exactly polar-hardened explorers. Clarkson said he'd been on bi-annual ski-ing trips a few times and Hammond had done nothing that might prepare him for the trek, although May took reassurance from the fact that he'd once built a really big snowman on his own. Weeks before the trek itself, the three presenters had to be specially prepared for the arduous journey ahead, flying out to Austria to undergo a harsh-weather training boot camp. There, a crack squad of polar explorers and survival experts taught them how to survive in temperatures that can kill an ill-prepared person in minutes. One piece of advice was to take a shovel and a gun, if they needed the toilet. As well as the film crew, they were accompanied by a doctor, a mechanic and also a member of the Special Forces. Guns were taken as the Arctic is home to over 60 per cent of the global polar bear population.

Hammond had to fly out a week earlier to take a crash course in dog sledding and he would also need to ski for long sections of the trek. He paired up with American Matty McNair, an experienced Polar explorer, and both were equipped with mini snowmobiles, known as 'skidoos'. The entire production crew was initially based at a town called Resolute in Nunavut, said by many to be the coldest inhabited place on earth. From this starting point, they were set to race across approximately 400 miles of icy tundra, frozen oceans and mountains of giant ice boulders.

The first three days went well but as the teams encroached further north, conditions became shockingly bad. Along their way, Clarkson and May came across a crashed C-47 aircraft, which was riddled with bullet holes: the accident had taken place in 1949 and the crew suffered only minor injuries. The story goes that subsequent bullet holes were made by decades of passing explorers, although internet conspiracy theorists had other ideas ...

The trek also revealed that the famous on-screen bickering between the three presenters is only partially for the camera. Admitting the on-screen characters are slightly exaggerated from their real-life ones, May revealed that on the polar trip he came close to hitting Clarkson, who he finds 'brash' (Jeremy thinks James is pedantic). One particular topic of argument was Clarkson's iPod choices: King Crimson, Genesis, Guns N' Roses, all served with a garnish of Jeremy talking over the top: 'We drove each other insane. I wanted to bash his head in with a shovel. But you know, we are blokes so we didn't dwell on it and ultimately no harm was done. Fundamentally, we are good mates. Mostly.'

So, what stopped the bickering? A terrifying moment when the thin crust of ice their Toyota was balanced precariously on seemed about to break and plunge them into a fatal -50°C ocean. 'That was the most scared we've ever been,' James has admitted. 'Every muscle in my body was primed for death. There was a hammer in the car for breaking the window in the event of going under, and I'd loosened it so that I could free it with one finger. I was rehearsing it in my mind ...'

The race was harder for Richard, although at one point his sled overtook them while they were crossing the first of two fields of ice boulders. Neuroscientist Dr Kerry Spackman gave some insight into the very real dangers the trio faced on their trek to the Pole: 'If you're sitting at rest, one third of your total energy is used by the brain, so even though you have your liver, your kidney, your muscles, your heart, your digestive system and so on, your brain takes one third of the energy. The brain has a very narrow operating window of how much oxygen it needs, what temperature it needs and it is really very delicate. That's why a lot of your body's function is to keep the brain at exactly the right temperature and with the right amount of oxygen. If you take twenty quick breaths, you feel dizzy because you've just changed your oxygen and CO_2 levels in your blood, you haven't really done a lot yet – you feel terrible!'

So, when the trio travelled to the Pole and the temperatures were so extreme, for all their joking about, this was dangerous territory. Spackman continues: 'Changing the temperature [so dramatically] just completely upsets the whole biochemistry, it's a really delicate thing. All sorts of things happen: the brain basically goes into preservation mode when it's under stress with low oxygen or low temperature. The brain is selfish: it says, "Look after me first, give me everything I need to keep functioning!" When you are operating in severe cold, the brain basically starts shutting down many of its functions and what that means is the body's reactions get slower and slower, attention levels go, the ability to focus disappears, the ability to think about things, concentrate, prioritise, all those things just go out the door. You can stop blood going to your arm for a short while but it will come back okay; stop blood going to your brain for a few seconds and those neurons will just die. People can die.'

It was the furthest north that any humans had ever driven a car but sadly this was perhaps not what the fabulous episode will be best remembered for. It was just after safely negotiating that about-to-crack ice sheet that May and Clarkson did something that was to backfire massively when they returned to the UK: they poured themselves a celebratory gin and tonic. The ride was understandably bumpy, so at one point James asked Jeremy if he could, 'slow down while I cut the lemon.' Given they were on top of a frozen ocean, Clarkson even said to camera. 'Don't write in to complain about us drinking and driving, because we're sailing!' In fact, given there are no roads in that part of the Arctic, they were not actually breaking any laws. Also, the gin drinking was part of a running gag where May and Clarkson laugh about how much easier their challenge had been than Hammond's (who was far more exposed to the elements).

With Clarkson and May at the finish line and tele-communications between the two teams erratic at best due to the inclement conditions, the production team decided it was unfair to insist Hammond also finished, not least because he was so far behind. Emil Grimmson is chairman of Arctic Trucks in Greenland, the company who modified the trucks for the programme, and he was impressed, saying Clarkson and May, 'did quite well for novices.'

The three presenters were then taken to ice runways and sent home on specially adapted snow planes. Life was not so comfortable for the rest of the crew and support team, however, who had to do an about turn and trek back through 400 miles of ice and snow!

A nice flourish to this brilliant piece of television came at the end, with a ritual the team often employ for specials: they changed the end credits. In this case, their first names were replaced with 'Sir Ranulph'. It was a fun gimmick that the show had employed before: for the Winter Olympics special, everybody was called either Björn, Benny, Agnetha or Anni-Frid in honour of ABBA; for the American road trip, they took suitably redneck names such as Cletus Clarkson, Earl Hammond Jr., Ellie May May, and Rosco P. Stig (all the crew were renamed Billy-Bob); the African special, they replaced their first names with Archbishop Desmond, Vietnam saw them rechristened Francis Ford (as in Coppola), and for the Sport Relief special, 'Top Gear Ground Force', they were renamed Alan Clarkson, Charlie May and Handy Hammond. According to some sources, the only time this gimmick has featured in a regular episode is in the final show of Series 8, when they were roadies for The Who and ran the 'Transit van Challenge' and so took the names Lee, Wayne and Terry in honour of van drivers the world over.

On their safe return home from the icy world of the Pole, however, trouble was afoot. As May and Clarkson sipped gin and tonic thousands of miles from home, they couldn't have known that their actions, when broadcast, would cause a flurry of complaints. One viewer was so incensed about the 'blatant use of alcohol while driving' that he took the matter to the BBC complaints division.

The scene which showed them drinking was done as a comic device only, with no intent to stir up trouble, unlike some of the show's more obviously confrontational moments. However, although 4.5 million viewers watched the programme – a great ratings success – and only a handful complained, the BBC Trust's editorial complaints division was duty-bound to investigate. Bizarrely, some viewers also complained about cut-away shots of the race being 'staged' and misleading, complaints that were subsequently dismissed. There was also a complaint (also dismissed) about the shot of a frost-bitten penis.

Unlike with Clarkson's Nazi salute/Polish SatNav gag, in regards to the drink-driving accusation, the Trust did uphold the complaint, saying, 'the scene of drinking whilst driving was not editorially justified in the context of a family show pre-watershed.' This broke guidelines and was thus criticised as it could be seen to glamorise the misuse of alcohol.

The normally mellow James May was clearly angered by the Trust's decision. Speaking to newspapers from his London home, he insisted that they had deserved the drink: 'It's bloody hard work driving to the Pole and having a nice gin and tonic was something we totally deserved,' he told the *Daily Mail*. 'We were in the middle of nowhere – literally in the middle of the sea, and we were neither in any danger, nor posed any danger to anyone or anything for hundreds of miles.' He also pointed out that they were far from drunk, but merely enjoying a drink.

Andy Wilman and his team have always been resolute defenders of the programme if they feel any controversial footage or comments are justified and in response to the BBC's criticism, the production team's statement said: 'The item was filmed in an uninhabitable area of the North Pole, in international waters and they weren't shown to be drunk or not in control of the car.'

But the furore wasn't over there: Greenpeace plunged into the fray. As we have seen, the show and environmental campaigners have previously locked horns over various features on the programme. This time, Greenpeace were appalled, describing the Polar race as 'beggaring belief' and said it was 'highly irresponsible'; they also criticised the BBC as a public service broadcasting channel for screening the footage. Emily Armistead of Greenpeace was quoted as saying: 'The Arctic is one of the areas most endangered by climate change. Perhaps Clarkson and his cronies felt that climate change wasn't destroying the Arctic quick enough, so they decided to do this. It's quite astounding, really. They are taking some of the most polluting vehicles on the road to spew out far more CO_2 than is necessary in an area that is suffering the worst damage from climate change. It does matter that *Top Gear* keeps on doing things like this.'

Back in Chipping Norton, seven climate protestors proceeded to dump horse manure on Clarkson's lawn, with a banner saying, 'This is what you're landing us in.'

Other times, however, *Top Gear* has confronted the

environmentalist campaigners head-on with its features. Typically, these are riddled with sarcasm and irony, though: for example, we have James May in Series 10, Episode 3, saying the world is becoming more and more crowded and there is increasing pressure from environmentalists to have a small car. Cue one of *Top Gear*'s funniest-ever features. This personal favourite is the episode which sees Jeremy Clarkson drives the world's smallest car to work ... literally *into* work, taking the Peel P50 into the *Top Gear* offices themselves. The 1963 car was built on the Isle of Man and cost only £918; it boasted a 49cc moped engine capable of 100 miles to the gallon. Measuring only 54 by 41 inches, it was recognised by the *Guinness Book of World Records* as the smallest production car ever made, which meant that for the 6' 5" Clarkson, just getting inside presented a challenge in itself.

Eventually he crammed himself in and set off for the BBC's west London offices in the little beauty. An interesting aside was that as he was driving along in the minute car, he pointed out the *Top Gear* camera crew's car was Congestion Charge-free as it was a Lexus hybrid. Arriving at White City, Clarkson pulled the car into reception before driving into a lift. Newsreader Fiona Bruce also got into the lift and then helped him out (the P50 doesn't have a reverse gear). As she walked off, Jeremy made another one of his 'accidental' quips when he said she had a nice bottom and then added, 'I said that out loud, didn't I?' It's a gag we know well by now, but it's still very funny.

While various *Top Gear* staff looked at the car and the news presenter, and revered journalist John Humphries even drove the P50 around the corridors, Clarkson was seen 'phoning' Hammond and apparently asked him why he doesn't clean his teeth more often – he was astounded that it might cost £4,000 to have them whitened. It was another of the running gags that makes *Top Gear* at times more akin to a sitcom than a factual car programme.

Then Jeremy headed off in the vehicle to an important BBC meeting, sitting in the car at a table ready for a meeting tabled as 'How to Reduce the Carbon Footprint of Our Ethnically Diverse Disability Access Policy for Single-Parent Mothers'. The camera panned across the table of attendees, showing all sorts of ethnic minorities: so we had a hippy, a white man, a black man, a dwarf, a Sikh, a Japanese woman and then JC in his tiny car. It's brazen, it's blatant ... the team know it will offend certain viewers but they don't really care, it's all done for humour. After driving past the background of the newsroom and announcing the P50 is the future of city driving, Clarkson was then left stranded by newsreader Dermot Murnaghan, who turned him the wrong way round on the main road outside the BBC. Classic *Top Gear*!

And there have been other features which *Top Gear* could claim to promote environmental issues. In Series 12, Episode 7, James May fronted a piece about the new Honda FCX, a vehicle that he described as, 'the most important car in 100 years.' The Los Angeles' test highlighted the stunning potential for Honda's new hydrogen car, whose only emission was water. It's an electric car but one with no batteries, instead it uses a hydrogen fuel cell. James started to explain the technology behind the miracle car and even suggested viewers could switch channels while he did the boring science bit. Indeed, as he droned on, even the cameraman scanned across a beach where they were filming to focus on a bunch of busty, bikini-clad girls playing volleyball. But the piece was not just a jest: May harshly derided previous electric cars as 'appalling little plastic snot boxes' but passionately championed the hydrogen Honda. The feature closed with James looking down on LA, while lamenting the forthcoming energy crisis: 'This,' he said, was 'the car of the future'.

In Series 10, *Top Gear* ran a piece that proved you don't need a car at all in a modern city. It wasn't perhaps their intention, but that's ultimately what they did prove. They staged one of their most preposterous races in Episode 5: James May was ostensibly showcasing the brand new Mercedes 'Chelsea Tractor' 4x4, Richard Hammond was to cycle across town on a state-of-the-art carbon fibre racing bike, while Jeremy Clarkson was to take a powerboat up the River Thames and The Stig would use only public transport.

They were to start in west London and the finishing line was City Airport, right across the capital in the East. The Stig got himself an Oyster Card so that he could hop on and off buses and tubes without needing to mess about with change, although we were told the card is, 'useful if you have no understanding of money.' Surprisingly, the normally laid-back James May soon becomes irate in the ludicrous London congestion and even called one particularly aggressive driver a 'bullying bus-driving Nazi', words perhaps more likely to come from Clarkson's mouth.

At first, Hammond was flying along and appeared to be an easy winner, but The Stig and Clarkson began to catch him. For good measure, they threw in a red herring about The Stig's identity: when he sat on the Tube, he picked up a discarded newspaper but when he saw the sports-page headline, 'LEWIS ROARS TO F1 GREATNESS', he threw it down in disgust, which suggests that maybe he could be a rival F1 driver after all or even Lewis himself double-bluffing.

Eventually, Hammond and his bike was declared victor, but Clarkson was gutted – not just for losing the race but also because of what the result said about the petrol engine. He chastised Richard, saying, 'You've ruined *Top Gear*!' and suggested this would now have to be the last-ever show. The Stig arrived next, beating James May's car by 15 minutes. Single-handedly, the team had proved that for city living, you don't need a car – a final insult to the combustion engine.

CHAPTER 20

The Stig Versus Top Gear

*I*n retrospect, all the speculation about the true identity of The Stig seems odd ... because in Series 4, the real Stig actually appeared in the studio, without his helmet on, in full view of the public. So, who was he?

The BBC never wanted us to know. It was rumoured that initially only three people (Andy Wilman and two other producers) knew the true identity of the second Stig; apparently the presenters were also kept in the dark at first. However, in 2010 the man behind the white mask decided to publish his memoir with HarperCollins, which led to a bitter and high profile wrangle in court. The BBC and the *Top Gear* production team reacted angrily to news of the impending publication and announced an immediate attempt to gain an injunction to prevent its release. Perhaps the most anger came from an always-vocal Andy Wilman, whose blog told it as he saw it, saying the BBC had a right to protect the character's anonymity 'from a bunch of chancers' who were 'hoping to cash in on it'. He also described The Stig's identity mystery as 'one of the best and most harmless TV secrets', a passionate summary that was hard to argue against.

The legal discussion was rightly held in private – as the court stated, to make it a public hearing would completely defeat the object of the anonymity issue – and the process took over a day and a half. Eventually it was announced that the judge had rejected the BBC's call for an injunction and The Stig was free to publish his work. Indeed, this had always been HarperCollins' argument: that he had a 'perfectly legitimate right' to release his book. However, the BBC stated that the driver in question had signed a confidentiality agreement and to reveal his identity would ruin the enjoyment of millions of *Top Gear* fans.

And so The Stig was revealed as Ben Collins, aged thirty-three from Bristol, a former Formula 3 driver and stuntman. The secret was out.

Several weeks later, on 5 October 2010, the judge explained his decision to allow HarperCollins to publish The Stig's memoir, saying his identity was in the public domain. In a public ruling, Mr Justice Morgan said: 'In the present case, the identity of Mr Collins as The Stig is in the public domain. If that has caused and/or will cause harm to the BBC, I do not see how any further harm will be caused to the BBC if Mr Collins is not allowed to publish his autobiography [*The Man In The White Suit*] in time for the 2010 Christmas market.'

Ben Collins actually attended court for some of the proceedings but was not seen in the public areas – again, with some speculation suggesting he was The Stig, a sighting would have defeated the object of the court case. In numerous TV interviews, he himself later pointed out that his name had first been mentioned as a possible Stig two years previously in the *Radio Times*. In the H&SE report into Hammond's crash, Ben

Collins was referred to as someone who, 'worked closely with *Top Gear* as a high performance driver and consultant', which perhaps didn't leave much to the imagination.

In January 2009 some newspapers had legitimately obtained company documents from Ben Collins' business files at Companies House, which showed he had provided 'driving services' to the BBC and some cited this as evidence of his Stig-iness. The timing of this original invoicing documentation – just a month after the first sighting of the white Stig on the show – was further evidence, it was claimed. The *Telegraph* claimed he was said to earn between £5,000 and £10,000 per show. However, the BBC freely admitted that Ben Collins often supplied himself as well as other drivers for both the programme and *Top Gear* Live shows. The *Daily Mail* later mentioned him in an interview with James May in the summer of 2009, but he laughed it off, saying it was in fact himself.

When news of the failed injunction bid broke, the BBC issued the following press statement: 'The *Top Gear* audience has always made it clear that they enjoy the mystery surrounding the identity of The Stig and the BBC felt it important to do all it could to protect that anonymity. The BBC brought this action as we believe it is vital to protect the character of The Stig which ultimately belongs to the licence fee payer.' It was in direct contrast to HarperCollins, who also highlighted the same funding issue by saying it was 'disappointed that the BBC has chosen to spend licence fee payers' money to suppress this book.'

While I respect HarperCollins' decision to publish his memoir as a choice he has made, as a fan of *Top Gear*, I have to admit to being slightly saddened that I now know the identity of The Stig. I'd heard so much about him over the many series that I actually started to believe that he was indeed made of metal, his heart ticked like a clock, that he was terrified of ducks and Lorraine

Kelly has a restraining order out against him. Standing back from the furore for a moment, it's a striking indication of the success of *Top Gear* and The Stig's character that a side-part in a BBC2 show about cars could become headline news in every household across Britain.

For their part, in the aftermath of losing the application for a court injunction, the *Top Gear* presenters reacted with a mix of dismissive comedy and outright anger. Shortly after the news broke, James May appeared on Richard Bacon's *Radio 5 Live* show and was inevitably asked about the court case. He appeared to stumble and stutter before he finally revealed that he had in fact been The Stig from 2005 to only four weeks ago, before lambasting HarperCollins' book as therefore containing about four weeks of material alone: 'Obviously I'm now going to have to take some legal action of my own because I have been The Stig for the past seven years and I don't know who this bloke is, who's mincing around in the High Court, pretending it's him.'

The publishers' victory was not met with any humour by Jeremy Clarkson, however: quoting his words in a later *Sun* newspaper column, he said public school had taught him that, 'you never rat' – an attitude to life that his close friends say makes him an immensely loyal friend.

A reflection of the sheer size of The Stig scandal can be ascertained by the way in which Jeremy reacted and the subsequent series of events thereafter. As a famous local resident, he was attending a charity auction in Chipping Norton lido shortly after the court case, where he gave an interview to the west Oxfordshire local community station, Witney TV. A regular viewer, Clarkson was happy to talk to them about the recent legal wrangle. In the resulting video, he lambasts Ben Collins for being greedy, saying, 'You may remember a film called *Wall Street*, in which Gordon Gekko said greed was good and greed works. It doesn't: if you're watching this children, greed is bad, he's just decided he'd rather be ... put it this way, he's history as far as we're concerned!' He went on to say that the programme has 'thousands of people queuing up to be whatever it is we create. I've spent the last three weeks doing nothing but trying to work out what to do instead.' He went on to insist: 'We'll get somebody, don't you worry! *Top Gear* is damaged, but not out.'

The direct interview was quickly picked up by a media anxious to get the scoop on Clarkson's views on The Stig case and via the internet and word-of-mouth on fan sites, the piece went global in a matter of hours. Within a day, news sites as far afield as Australia were reporting on Witney TV's scoop. According to one source, Witney TV is, 'pulled together on Apple Macs, without a wealthy backer'; their news is released via a website, on YouTube, as downloads, and is also available on iPhones.

The original impetus for the station was that in their opinion the mainstream multi-billion pound news corporations do not offer local coverage of any quality (and frequently not at all, as in the case for the Abingdon area where Witney operates) and so the grass-roots model was designed to meet niche demand. Their usual stories are upbeat, with a strategic decision made to cover only 'positive' news, so horrific disasters are never featured. The formula proved highly attractive and with over 100,000 hits, the station was now paving the way for alternative news, not least with the global Stig scoop, the biggest entertainment story of the week.

Ben Collins' book reveals many fascinating insights into his life as The Stig. He never parked in the same place twice, he didn't talk about his role to anyone other than the small inner circle who already knew his identity, he always left any identifying documents, phones or credit cars, etc. locked in his car in case someone invaded his dressing room, he wore a balaclava on his face when driving home from the *Top Gear* test track (often as far away as eight miles, in case prying paparazzi lenses were following him) and he would never, ever appear in his white suit without the helmet on.

However, the subterfuge became increasingly difficult to keep up and Collins later revealed that he would often chat to people he'd met when dressed as The Stig but forget that he was not supposed to have met them before. He revealed that Mark Webber knew he was The Stig because of the way he stands, having raced against him many times in Formula 3. Also, *Dragons' Den* entrepreneur Theo Paphitis walked past him in his civvies and said, 'Hello, Stig', something that still baffles him. How did *he* know?

Jeremy Clarkson placed an 'advertisement' for a new Stig via an article in the *Sun*, which included such requirements for the successful candidate as 'hating Boy Scouts, being able to punch a horse to the ground and having eyes that blink sideways.'

So, how exactly had The Stig been unmasked as early as Series 4 then? For years, there had been rumours about his true identity but a long time before he was finally revealed, Ben Collins actually made an appearance, both in a challenge and subsequently in the *Top Gear* studio without any helmet or form of disguise. This came in Series 4, when the team wanted to attempt a tricky and dangerous stunt: getting a parachutist to land from a plane and into the back of a convertible, speeding at 50mph.

The feature is set at the *Top Gear* track and we are first introduced to Tim, a parachutist expert. Then the camera pans to his side and we are told this is Ben, 'his racing driver mate'. It was in fact The Stig, unbeknown to everyone watching at the time.

Once the stunt began, it became obvious why Ben needed to wear no helmet. Time after time, the parachutist descended from the skies and attempted to land in the back of the Mercedes soft-top. Meanwhile, Ben was driving along at 50mph, with a microphone and headpiece so that he could be in constant contact with the parachutist. Furthermore, he was always looking up to the skies to see exactly where the human bird was. Of course, neither task could have been achieved wearing a full-face helmet.

The stunt proved to be extremely difficult and it was only after many attempts and with the light fading and the wind picking up that they finally managed to land in the passenger seat. Cue James May skipping across the runway and Ben Collins – aka The Stig – doing doughnuts on the track. We even hear The Stig/Ben talk, as he said 'Good effort, my son, well done!' to his parachutist 'friend'. The feature then flicks to the studio, where both Tim and Ben (again, with no helmet on) are introduced to an admiring crowd. The Stig was among them and they didn't even know it. Collins was also visible in Series 10, driving a Honda Civic Type R against Clarkson, and raced alongside various British Touring Car drivers in a five-a-side car/football sequence.

Perhaps not entirely surprisingly, Ben Collins no longer works for *Top Gear* and has instead signed up for the rival show, *Fifth Gear*. On his first episode of that show, Vicki Butler-Henderson introduced him as, 'A world famous driver who's recently found himself out of a job and his name rhymes with The Twig.' Ben was then seen on camera, unmasked and says, 'Yes, I can speak and it's a massive pleasure to do so. I've spent too long trapped inside a stormtrooper's outfit for my liking.'

Whatever the aftermath of the court case (still pending at the time of this book's publication), the fact remains that everyone now knows the identity of The Stig. Indeed, it's a shame because it wasn't just the BBC who enjoyed all the pretence: the media and the viewers did so, too.

With the extensive powers of modern-day investigative

journalism, which exposes corrupt politicians and drug-runners every week, it's highly likely that Fleet Street might have discovered the true identity of The Stig, had they wanted to. In fact, it has been suggested that many journalists already knew him, but chose to keep quiet. Like a TV motoring show version of Santa Claus, the real fun was to be had joining in the ruse.

CHAPTER 21

Nothing Changes, Nothing Stays the Same

As the first edition of this book was going to press, the court case between Ben Collins and *Top Gear* was quite literally still being decided and daily TV headlines and newspaper front pages chronicled the story being played out. Since that time, however, the high profile of the whole controversy feels rather odd. After the headlines subsided, Collins moved on to work for *Fifth Gear* on a single series and later, among other things, as a stunt driver for the new James Bond film *Skyfall* (2012). His former colleagues at *Top Gear* had long since moved on, too. In fact, the manner in which the *Top Gear* team dealt with the whole Stig/book controversy enabled them to effectively nullify any negative impact Collins' unmasking might otherwise have had.

At first, some media spectators questioned how *Top Gear* would cope – if at all – without the *bête noir* of The Stig, who as we have seen had become such an integral part of the show's massive global appeal. Initially, James May did his best to continue his ruse of claiming to be The Stig and regularly repeated this deliberate misinformation in his column for the *Daily Telegraph*. He also 'revealed' that when he finally decided to stand down from the role, his replacement would be none other than another Mr Collins, albeit the Apollo 11 astronaut, Michael Collins.

There were dozens of different internet rumours about The Stig being written out of the show altogether but the BBC steadfastly maintained that no decision had been made as to The Stig's survival. One fact was clear: the public's thirst for the character remained strong. Back in 2008, one online poll claimed the search entry 'Who is The Stig?' was the most frequently asked question on the entire web. In the immediate aftermath of the Collins' court case, there seemed to be no real dilution of this interest; although that incarnation of The Stig had been exposed, the character still seemed to hold an affectionate place in the nation's hearts. Another online poll by the *Guardian* found that 64 per cent of respondents to the question 'Do we need a Stig?' replied in the affirmative. More practical speculation began to wonder who would play the new Stig if his character was continued, with highly qualified names such as F1 drivers Heikki Kovalainen and Anthony Davidson being early favourites. Meanwhile, the BBC entered the fray in refusing to rule out a female replacement.

Then ahead of the forthcoming *Top Gear Live* tour and with a canny sense of fun, clips were posted on the show's official website showing footage of a 'Stig farm' somewhere in the remote English countryside, including several multi-coloured Stigs. The Stig farm was apparently free range and GM-free and located in a secret (what else?) rural part of Britain near the B4073 (for the record, that runs through Painswick, near Gloucester). The suggestion was that *Top Gear* was simply going to grow a new Stig.

Previously, Clarkson had been particularly scathing of Collins and when he opened one of the *Top Gear Live* shows that autumn, he wasn't about to let go. Pointing out that some observers saw 'Stig-gate' as the end of *Top Gear*, he insisted, 'Not so, barely a blip', before showing a longer video of the Stig farm. Set to funky music, a rainbow of Stigs was seen wandering aimlessly about a mucky farm, at one point herded by a farmer in wellies. The comic video was all good fun but in fact cleverly diluted the impact of the loss of 'white' Stig by showing so many new multi-coloured Stigs, which also served to remind the viewers that this mysterious racing driver was in reality a fictitious character. There was one more dig, too when Clarkson said, 'Some Stigs decide to write books, but that's never a good idea.' After the video of the Stig farm had ended, Clarkson introduced the 'new Stig' to a rapturous crowd as a Ferrari 430 Spider skidded into the arena, driven by a conventional white Stig, identical to the one portrayed by Collins.

Top Gear never shied away from mentioning the controversy on the show itself either. In the 'US Road Trip' Special, December 2010, the trio branded The Stig a 'Judas Iscariot' and then proceeded to test out firearms against a dummy of the white-suited 'traitor' driver. Notably, in that episode, film director Danny Boyle became the only person *not* to be trained by The Stig for his lap, instead being coached by 'Emergency Stig', namely former racing driver Tiff Needell. The show must go on ...

While the world was clearly enjoying the rumours of the 'new' Stig (and seemingly still unperturbed that his successor's identity had been revealed), the very first Stig also revealed a surprising side. In a 2011 interview that was widely quoted by dozens of fascinated national publications and regional magazines, the original 'black' Stig, Perry McCarthy, stated what anyone inside of motor-racing knows is true: that despite the best efforts of *Top Gear* to vilify the humble caravan, those ridiculed vehicles are in fact an essential tool for many an aspiring race driver. 'Caravanning played an important part when I was racing,' he was quoted as saying in the *Shropshire Star*. 'Actually I used motorhomes ... the advantages of being on-site, at the edge of the race track are immeasurable.' He also pointed out that all the top drivers use motorhomes. It's a bit of a jump from the million pound motorhomes populating the F1 paddock to a lowly caravan, but McCarthy went further and revealed that in fact he was actually a card-carrying member of The Caravan Club – 'Answer this truthfully, can you really get excited about a holiday which starts at either Gatwick or Luton Airport? There's also a kind of pioneering spirit to it, too, and I like that.' He went on to champion the 'luxuries' offered by modern caravans as against the anodyne anonymity of a hotel chain. McCarthy also told reporters that he could now look back and be proud of his time on the show: 'I was part of the biggest motoring show on the planet and it was great fun to do.' Clearly very happy with his role, he also quipped, 'As Sinatra sang, "Regrets, I have too few to mention," and none of them are becoming a racing driver or being The Stig.'

* * *

Fairly quickly after the court case, it became apparent that *Top Gear* was going to emerge from the Stig controversy with barely a scratch. Another clever piece of the Stig 'revival' came in the hilarious Christmas Special, which saw the trio replicating the journey of the Three Wise Men by driving from northern Iraq to Bethlehem – hardly the safest route to select. They made their trip even more dangerous by buying cheap, old convertibles for the journey, including a Mazda MX-5. In fact, the actual route taken by the Three Kings was simply too dangerous in the modern day, and so the intrepid trio had to opt for a more long-winded path but nonetheless one that was still filled with genuine danger. While they disguised one car as a Bedouin tent, tested out how to bullet-proof car doors and fitted Hammond's Mazda with a stereo that constantly played Genesis and couldn't be switched off, James May was in for a rougher ride when he fell backwards onto a rock and knocked himself unconscious, suffering a rather nasty and bloody gash to his head. When the 'Three Wise Men' finally arrived at the 'Nativity' scene in Bethlehem, they clustered round the newborn son of the Lord only to find out that he was in fact a suited, helmet-wearing Stig baby. 'I wasn't expecting that,' said James May somewhat obviously (at least they had some decent gifts: a fake gold medallion, a bottle of hotel shampoo called Frankincense and a Nintendo DSi).

The first episode of Series 16 continued to confront the Stig issue head-on when James explained that Stigs grow very quickly, revealing the baby Jesus Stig was now fully formed and ready to drive any car they sat him in. So, within three months of the Stig controversy supposedly threatening to make *Top Gear* implode, the show was up and running as usual and all the fuss seemed a relic from the distant past. This was helped by the fact that out on the *Top Gear* track, the new Stig seemed to set very similar times to what the presenters took to calling 'sacked Stig'.

And in keeping with the mythology surrounding the former Stig, the urban myths and cultural misinformation about the character continued. He was always introduced using exactly the same wording as their 'tame racing driver' with surreal facts about his personality or life; he appeared in the background of computer driving games; his helmet and overalls could be bought as add-ons for Gran Turismo 5 and Forza Motorsport 4 console games and Google Street View images picked him up at various locations in the background, such as the A82 by Loch Ness (for added mystery) and even three times inside Legoland in Berkshire. In Series 18, the deification of the character continued unabated, with The Stig being referred to as the show's 'Senior Cornering Solutions Consultant'.

By the summer of 2011, some water seemed to have flowed under the bridge when Richard Hammond and Ben Collins both attended a fundraiser for a military amputee charity. When he came to introduce his former colleague, Hammond told the crowd to welcome 'ex-Stig Ben Collins'.

Aside from resurgence of The Stig, elsewhere for *Top Gear* the controversy never seems to subside. In late 2010, the media regulator Ofcom had censured Jeremy Clarkson over what was deemed 'discriminatory' language, which had the potential to be highly offensive to some viewers. This was following a review of the Ferrari F430 Speciale in which Jezza stated that it was 'a bit wrong – that smiling front end – it looked like a simpleton – [it] should have been called the 430 Speciale Needs.' Ofcom received two complaints and in announcing its decision offered that it had taken into account *Top Gear*'s 'irreverent style and sometimes outspoken humour and studio banter' but ultimately found against the show – 'In Ofcom's opinion, while obviously intended as a joke and not aimed directly at an individual with learning difficulties, the comment could easily be understood as ridiculing people in society with a particular physical disability or learning difficulty.' The BBC responded to the censure by removing the reference from all future repeats, as well as the BBC iPlayer online service.

CHAPTER 22

Headlines and Heat

If 2010 had been the year when Stig was unmasked, then 2011 was in some ways an even more difficult one for *Top Gear*. Although they had cleverly and almost seamlessly negotiated the Stig controversy and forged a future with the same white-suited driver playing an identical role, both on screen and away from the cameras, this was not a great year for some of the team.

Jeremy in particular continued to attract headlines. The New Year had started very well – in late January 2011, the programme scooped the 'Best Factual' gong at the National Television Awards but the crew were not able to celebrate for long. Just seven days later, the fairly average opening episodes of Series 16 were overshadowed by yet another 'foreign friends' controversy, following comments on the show about Mexicans, which solicited an official complaint from that country's ambassador to London. The on-screen conversation between May, Hammond and Jezza expounded the theory that national characteristics and generalised personality traits were reflected in cars from specific countries. Among the choice cuts of this particular exchange was the following foray into international diplomacy from Hammond: 'Mexican cars are just going to be lazy, feckless, flatulent, overweight, leaning against a fence asleep, looking at a cactus with a blanket with a hole in the middle on as a coat.' Mexican food was referred to as 'refried sick' and the trio even tipped a wink at any possible forthcoming complaints, with Clarkson saying it was highly unlikely as the Mexican Ambassador would be asleep.

Well, the Ambassador wasn't asleep and he was none too happy either. The most senior Mexican official in Britain fired off an official complaint to the BBC objecting to the 'offensive, xenophobic and humiliating' comments. 'The presenters of the programme resorted to outrageous, vulgar and inexcusable insults to stir bigoted feelings against the Mexican people, their culture, as well as their official representative in the United Kingdom ... [which] only serve to reinforce negative stereotypes and perpetuate prejudice against Mexico and its people.' The BBC apologised and Jeremy offered a serious discussion in his *Sun* column suggesting if all humour is stripped of any material that may offend someone, somewhere, then there is no humour left at all. As if to underline the point, he rounded off with another gag about Mexicans. Once more, *Top Gear* ended up in political hot water when a cross-party group of six MPs said: 'This level of ignorance is far below anything expected from anyone in the public eye and illustrates a serious lack of judgment by the programme-makers.'

By now, *Top Gear* had become an example held up by its many critics for all that was politically incorrect and offensive about certain types of British television. By way of defence, Clarkson suggested it wasn't his show that was of concern, but the creeping and insidious atmosphere of humourless PC campaigners aiming to make all TV inoffensive. Speaking at those National Television Awards a few days earlier (which was set against a backdrop of *Sky Sports* presenters Andy Gray and Richard Keys being sacked for alleged 'sexist' comments), Clarkson made a reference to the famous Monty Python 'Spanish Inquisition' sketch, saying, 'We've arrived at a stage where you actually can be busted for heresy by thought, which is a terrifying place to live.' James May took a slightly more light-hearted approach on that awards night, collecting the trophy and saying he'd like to thank 'the girl who tucked our microphone cables down our trousers' – a reference to a comment made by Andy Gray that had contributed to his dismissal by Sky. Clarkson opined that if the same rules that had applied to Keys and Gray were set out for *Top Gear*, then he and his brace of presenter pals would have been sacked 100 times! (Notably, half of the *Top Gear* production crew is female.)

If it wasn't comments on the show or in interviews that caused problems for the *Top Gear* trio, then later in 2011, it was elements of Jeremy Clarkson's private life that caused the spotlight to once again fall on him. Clarkson was the subject of countless newspaper headlines after a super-injunction which he had issued was lifted and numerous publications subsequently chose to run articles about his private life. This latest legal development was set against a context of the now infamous Ryan Giggs 'super-injunction' story, where it eventually transpired that the married footballer had been having an affair and had used the expensive super-injunction procedure to keep this fact a secret. A phone-hacking scandal was also erupting around the *News of the World* that would eventually lead to the Leveson Inquiry and so celebrities' private lives and the role of the media was very much a hot topic. While the far-wider argument continues to rage about the privacy of famous faces as against what the media – rightly or wrongly – considers to be a justification of public interest, once more the heat on Jeremy seemed to dissipate quite quickly and he was able to get back to the business of filming for *Top Gear*, whose ratings it should be noted seemed totally unaffected.

However, a much greater fury was soon heading Clarkson's way. In December 2011, while public sector workers were striking en masse on the streets of Britain in protest at proposed changes to their pensions (with an estimated two million people out on strike), Jeremy went on the early-evening magazine programme *The One Show* for an unrelated interview. When the chat moved on to the inevitable topic of the strike, he made a joke that would soon see him on the front page of most tabloids and become, yet again, a media target. Initially pointing out the lack of public services had made the streets quiet and easy to commute through, Jeremy warmed up and delivered this joke: 'We have to balance this, though, because this is the BBC. Frankly, I'd have them [the strikers] all shot. I would take them outside and execute them in front of their families. I mean, how dare they go on strike when they have these gilt-edged pensions that are going to be guaranteed while the rest of us have to work for a living.' In fact, many people took greater offence towards the end of the interview when Clarkson questioned why trains have to stop when someone jumps in front of them, with his point being – again seemingly in jest when you see the clip – that delaying the train is not going to help that person.

Nonetheless it was joking that he would execute the strikers in front of their families that seemed to cause most offence. Cue outrage from the unions amid calls for Clarkson's immediate sacking over what were described as 'appalling' comments; according to some unverified sources within a few days there were over 30,000 complaints made to the BBC. One union spokeswoman said: 'The excuse that this has been said in humour is completely and utterly unacceptable.' Dave Prentis, UNISON's general secretary, was quoted in the *Mail* as saying, 'While he is driving round in fast cars for a living, public sector workers are busy holding our society together: they save others' lives on a daily basis, they care for the sick, the vulnerable, the elderly.'

The BBC itself was moved to publish the transcript of the interview but their action did little to dampen the growing and vociferous criticism. Clarkson issued an apology, in which he said, 'I didn't for a moment intend these remarks to be taken seriously – as I believe is clear if they're seen in context. If the BBC and I have caused any offence, I'm quite happy to apologise for it alongside them.' The BBC was also moved to try and temper the outrage by saying, '*The One Show* is a live topical programme which often reflects the day's talking points. Usually we get it right, but on this occasion we feel the item wasn't perfectly judged. The BBC and Jeremy would like to apologise for any offence caused.'

Some political commentators pointed out that Clarkson is a personal friend of Prime Minister David Cameron and that these 'light-hearted' remarks were perhaps more damaging than just a joke. When confronted with his pal's comments on ITV's *This Morning*, the Prime Minister firmly brushed the issue aside, saying it had been 'a silly thing to say ... I'm sure he didn't mean it'; Labour leader Ed Miliband was less conciliatory and said the comments were 'disgusting'. UNISON even went so far as to invite Jeremy onto a hospital ward to join a healthcare assistant for a day at work. Previously they had said they were seeking legal advice about whether his remarks could be referred to the police, although they later welcomed the apology.

The BBC, it seemed, was clear in its position. Director-General

Mark Thompson said: 'I don't intend to sack him. I believe it is absolutely clear to anyone who watches the clips, perhaps not who reads a section of the transcript, these remarks are said entirely in jest and not to be taken seriously. In my view Jeremy Clarkson's remarks were absolutely and clearly intended as a joke.' He went on to say, 'There are many millions of people who very strongly support and enjoy Jeremy Clarkson,' and also that the complaints have 'to be balanced against a couple of flippant remarks in one programme. Well over 20 million people watch *Top Gear* in a given season. It gets a very high rating from the public for quality. People watch that programme expecting often outspoken humour from Clarkson.' BBC Trust chairman Lord Patten went even further in his defence, saying of *Top Gear* that, '[It is] probably one of the leading "cultural" exports of this country. A lot of people would be disappointed [if he was sacked].' Clarkson later flew out of the country, while it emerged that the BBC had also received 341 messages of support for him. Others pointed out that the number of complaints received was less than 2 per cent of the people claimed to be on strike.

* * *

Clarkson wasn't sacked and the show continued. He still had a Christmas surprise for his critics, though, when a New Year Indian Special featured a number of comments about the country's culture that were likely to raise eyebrows. These included jokes about food, trains and a Jaguar car fitted with a toilet seat on the boot. This time the number of complaints was tiny compared to *The One Show*, numbering less than 200, but a diplomatic spat was potentially around the corner when the Indian High Commission complained formally to the BBC for what it considered 'offensive' remarks and 'toilet humour'.

This controversy came at the end of a quite ordinary year of *Top Gear* shows. Series 16 and 17 had run throughout 2011 and had perhaps been some of the weaker episodes in the show's otherwise strong canon. To some media observers and members of the public alike, many of the challenges seemed a little repetitive or tired and there were relatively few spectacular highlights. Aside from making their own snow plough out of a combine harvester and the first return to the 'Cool Wall' for two years, a fascinating verbal tussle with former deputy Labour leader John Prescott and Jezza was the best moment of Series 16. Perhaps most obviously the classic fourth episode featured the finest sequence in Series 17 when the trio set out to prove train travel can be made cheaper and more accessible.

Clarkson pulled a carriage with a 1980s Jaguar XJ-S convertible converted to run on train wheels, while Hammond and May used an Audi S8 to pull several caravans (predictably perhaps, they eventually caught fire). Another highlight was the eminently affable double Formula 1 World Champion Sebastian Vettel at the top of the F1 drivers' leaderboard, with a Suzuki Liana time of 1.44.0m. But otherwise it was only a modestly entertaining pair of series, with several lulls when the comedy and larking about just swamped any serious car talk at all. All this was largely overshadowed by the on-going controversies swirling around the show and its presenters. And this is a crucial fact – among all the media and personal controversy, it is sometimes hard to forget there is a TV show about cars at the centre of the story. Fortunately, with the spectacular 18th series of *Top Gear*, the team delivered the perfect reminder of exactly why they were the most popular automotive show on earth.

CHAPTER 23

Back in the Game

With all the press furore surrounding Clarkson's comments about strikers still fresh in the memory, the opening episode of *Top Gear* Series 18 was guaranteed to be watched even more closely than usual. Cynics suggested this was exactly what Clarkson was doing when he made such comments, that these 'controversies' often seemed to arise when he was promoting a DVD or a new series. However, he makes comments that some people find offensive at other times, too and it just so happens that when he is promoting a new series or project he has to appear on radio and TV and other interviews, which means he has to chat, which means he tends to speak, which in turn means he sometimes offends people. For him, it's a Catch-22. And it's not as if Jeremy Clarkson is a new talent to our screens who will catch you off-guard by making risqué jokes – if you find his opinions offensive, there's always the remote control.

With the poor Series 17 long forgotten, even by ardent fans of the show, the opening episode of Series 18 was aired on Sunday,

29 January 2012. If this new episode offered any hint that the trio were past their prime, that the format was looking a bit tired as some critics suggested or that the viewer was getting bored, then this would surely be the nail in *Top Gear*'s coffin. This was, after all, the sixth most complained about programme on all TV channels in 2011!

There was an added frisson of interest because this was the 'tenth' anniversary of the modern format of *Top Gear*. The speech marks reflect the uncertainty of that actual celebration, a fact pointed out by none other than producer Andy Wilman, who revealed in *The Sunday Times* that 'one thing that *Top Gear* maths isn't, is accurate.' He explained that ordinarily this means a car with, say, 480bhp actually ends up having '500bhp' on screen and any top speed in the upper reaches of 180–190mph is often given out as 'nearly 200mph'. So, by his own admission the tenth anniversary was a date which he said 'I can't be sure' of. The logic went that the first show of the new format aired in 2002, but if each year was counted up then that made 11! It was not the first time this had happened – it wasn't until the team were working on the 105th episode that someone in the *Top Gear* office pointed out they'd already missed the 100th episode milestone. Whoops!

However, to what must have been hugely annoying to the show's many snipers, that first episode of Series 18 was an absolute classic! Unashamedly focussing on cars that only a tiny percentage of the population can afford, the trio took the entirely hypothetical premise of which supercar would you choose if you *didn't* want to buy the scintillatingly beautiful new Ferrari 458. Having previously reviewed this car and its main competitors, you could almost see them sitting in the *Top Gear* trailer trying to think of a clever way to get another run out in these beautiful machines.

It was a fascinating premise as the 458 was launched in 2009 to such acclaim that many motoring journalists felt it comprehensively nullified its competitors. Always keen to explore an opportunity to drive around Europe in supercars, the trio obviously felt it was their public duty to find out if this was true. Arriving in Italy with a Noble M600, a McLaren MP4-12C and a beautiful brand new Lamborghini Aventador LP 700-4 this was always going to be a high-octane opening show.

In many ways, the programme was a microcosm of why *Top Gear* has proved so popular, but perhaps more to the point why it can *remain* popular in the future. It was almost like a check sheet of all the best points of the show – without ever feeling like the production team and presenters had been quite so prescriptive and deliberate. There was the presenter's boyish joy at seeing and driving supercars; the jokes at each other's expense, that school-yard gang spoken about earlier in this book; the risqué jokes about foreigners, such as the hilarious sight of Hammond trying to get so much as a 'Hello' out of an overweight Italian vehicle recovery man, who talked on his phone for an age before driving off without helping; more gags about the ludicrous chaos of Rome's city driving; great challenges as they thundered their machines first around a bumpy race track at 200mph; expert driving and incisive car reviews; and genuine tension as they took to the infamously lethal Imola racing circuit to push their cars to the limit.

This was genuine danger too, not just an on-screen dramatised version. When they took the cars to the Nardo Ring circuit to test the top speeds, there was no tomfoolery, no over-acting, just sheer steering wheel-clutching adrenalin as the trio attempted to outpace each other on a race surface that was sorely lacking. Apart from one aside about Hammond not having a particularly good outcome the last time he tried to drive so fast (see Chapter 17), this was clearly very serious stuff. And let's be honest, regardless of crash helmets and cameras, if you lose control of a road car at 200mph or more, there's a very good chance that you will be going home in a box. There are some realities of high speed racing that even prime time TV cannot sterilise. It was all entertaining stuff. Wilman was clearly proud of that opening episode, calling it 'proper telly', and he'd be right. He said it was 'special' and it was.

The next instalment of the new series followed up on the early promise, too. It was almost as if the *Top Gear* team wanted to give us an opener of pure petrol-head heaven, without all the controversy and quips, but somehow couldn't resist being a little bit naughty. This time it was two of the world's economic powerhouses in the firing line: America and China.

Richard Hammond is a huge fan of NASCAR and so the boys sent him off to America to film a feature on the hugely popular motorsport, which despite being ostensibly a batch of cars going round in circles for hundreds of laps, still manages to attract upward of 250,000 people to each race. Is it better than F1? Well, that was what Hammond was sent out to prove. (Previously in the 2010 Christmas Special, the trio had 'invented' Old Testament NASCAR after romping around a sandy circuit inside a 2,000-year-old chariot stadium.)

NASCARs are 900bhp of brutally raw power, with no electrical aids, not even a fuel gauge, so in essence they are the polar opposite of the space-age technology found in F1 vehicles. Hammond revels in this purity and at the event he was chosen to drive the parade car for the running start to the race; later, he even drove a few laps at full pelt himself, albeit with only one other car alongside him.

The real fun in this second episode of the 18th series came with the sense that James May and Jeremy Clarkson were increasingly unable to keep their famously risqué humour at bay.

Cue several jokes at the expense of the USA, including references to fat people, pronouncing 'aluminium' wrong and World Wars. They are, according to Jeremy, a nation that is apparently 'easily amused' and capable of turning dreary sports into spectator festivals. With no small dash of irony, that week's Star in a Reasonably Priced Car was American actor Matt LeBlanc from *Friends*, who proceeded to post the fastest lap ever at 1.42.1, a tenth of a second faster than the previous record holder, Series 17's Rowan Atkinson.

After a brief flurry of politically incorrect news – including Clarkson making a gag about the Elephant Man complete with his version of John Merrick's heavily impeded speech – the show moved swiftly to the Far East. While Hammond had been mixing with rednecks and 'putting cheese on everything', May and Clarkson travelled to China to discover if that country actually made good modern cars. Seemingly not, according to the duo.

The opening salvo was a gag about Chairman Mao and a buffalo. However, after this cheeky start and as suggested by Andy Wilman in *The Sunday Times*, there was a very noticeable delivery of cold, hard facts in this feature – cut-away shots of the two presenters rattling off stats, such as China selling 38,000 new cars a day, etc. But yet again the real fun was when the comedy kicked in. At the race track, The Stig's Chinese cousin smashed through a door and proceeded to attack both presenters and crew with a flurry of martial arts moves (The Stig's Italian cousin had made an appearance at Imola the week before). 'Attack Stig', as he was christened, could only just be penned into the car and even stopped halfway around one lap to kung-fu kick a steward (at the end of the piece, Attack Stig lunged at May and kicked him in the testicles). May and Clarkson weren't done with their opinions either, implying Chinese crash tests were ludicrously lax and making the point that counterfeiting was rife in the country, including in the car industry, where 'lookalike' models of Western vehicles were commonplace. And according to Clarkson, most Chinese cars only have to have enough headroom for someone who is 5'3". The show closed with three Chinese *Top Gear* imposters back in the studio saying they were coming to take over the West's car industry. So, America and China lambasted in the same 60-minute slot. *Top Gear* was back on form! I myself knew the show was back to its best because the morning after the second episode, I checked the news channels to see who had complained about what.

In fact, quite the opposite happened late in February 2012, when the TV watchdog Ofcom cleared Jeremy Clarkson of breaking broadcasting rules over his infamous 'strikers' comments before Christmas. They said the remarks, while 'potentially offensive' were justified by the context but were unlikely to encourage viewers 'to act on them in any way'. They added that viewers would expect Clarkson to be controversial due to his 'well-established public persona' and that 'his comments were not an expression of seriously held beliefs,' going on to point out that *The One Show* had ended that particular programme with an apology. By Series 18, the trio were even relaxed enough to make light-hearted references to the controversy during one particular show's 'News' piece about people who make fraudulent insurance claims for whiplash.

The forthcoming series shows no signs of losing the momentum that the scintillating opening episodes injected back into *Top Gear*. Ludicrous but unmissable highlights include an attempt to film a car chase for the re-make of *The Sweeney* and trips to the frozen landscape of Sweden to test drive a – what else? – Ferrari FF and a new Bentley, of course! And Richard fires up a rally car in a race to the finish with a man in a flying suit.

It was important to note the deliberate tactic that producer Wilman had highlighted: the new series was far more factually informative than the show had been of late, essentially in recognition that petrol-heads may enjoy the thrills and spills of a madcap test drive or 'special' show, but at the root of their penchant for tuning in is a fascination with cars (as I have mentioned so frequently in this book). Otherwise the programme is just a series of comic sketches. Thankfully, *Top Gear* haven't overdone this more practical approach in Series 18 and turned the programme into some kind of *University Challenge* for car freaks; despite the more serious approach to some factual parts of the show, they still revel in ensuring that every episode has, as Wilman puts it, 'a drizzle of nonsense'.

CHAPTER 24

The Best Job In The World!

As we have seen, between 2009 and 2011, there was a fair barrage of criticism aimed at *Top Gear*, with several media critics suggesting the long-serving motoring show was perhaps finally running out of steam. There were suggestions that the famous banter between the presenters had grown too forced and scripted – something they vehemently denied – and that the features were becoming either ludicrous or predictable. Fortunately, the brilliant Series 18 defied all the naysayers but nonetheless some of the core challenges for Clarkson and his colleagues remain.

It seems that the producers and presenters of the new *Top Gear* are sometimes damned if they do and damned if they don't. After originally eschewing the old format of fairly serious reviews and magazine pieces, the latest version of *Top Gear* took on board ever more madcap stunts and odd challenges with gusto, but as the years have passed this approach has increasingly attracted more and more criticism, with detractors accusing them of veering away from being a car programme and simply evolving into a straight entertainment show. But this is not necessarily a bad thing, surely?

Top Gear is nothing if not self-aware. For example, in one show during Series 6, the trio apologised for the previous week's 'boring' reviews of Cabriolets and Chevrolets in Iceland and said they'd decided to go back there and film something far more exciting. What could be less dull than Hammond taking a seat in a bonkers 1,000bhp Icelandic off-road jeep? This insane vehicle was normally used for driving (literally) up cliff faces, but here, it was turned to driving across a lake instead, hoping to rely on its huge tyre grips to provide buoyancy. The task needed a constant nitrous oxide injection, which was successfully achieved – no mean feat of engineering that. Richard then went in with a champion jeep driver who, incredibly, succeeded in racing the vehicle across the surface of the lake without it sinking. The point of mentioning this small clip is that it's a classic example of *Top Gear* being aware of its own pitfalls and reacting quickly to remedy any valid criticism.

When they do find themselves with no choice but to review a 'boring' car, however, they will inevitably spice up the test with all sorts of insane challenges. As inferred earlier in this book and picking up on a point Andy Wilman himself has made, the art of car design is so honed in the 21st century that a majority of commonplace cars are very solidly built, well designed, cleverly thought out, and to be frank, unlikely to attract a terrible review.

A great example of a 'non-review' of a car was in Series 11, when they tested the Daihatsu Terios. This was a compact 4x4 that had won various awards, including '4x4 of the Year' by *4x4 Magazine*. It had decent performance for its 1.5 litre engine, superb economy and cost only £75 a year to tax, due to its low emissions. Though it boasted a spacious interior, it was shorter than a VW Golf, with lots of extras as standard, even offering reverse parking sensors on all models, and yours for about £14,000.

There's not much you can say about a car that ticks so many boxes in certain areas. So, *Top Gear*'s approach was simple: don't say anything. Clarkson instead had the livery painted in faux fox fur and took the little 4x4 out into the country for a spot of hunting. Or rather, being hunted. With a small rag soaked in fox urine attached to a rope on the bumper, the Terios was then chased by a pack of salivating foxhounds around the English countryside, followed closely by the huntsmen and, some way back, Richard Hammond, teetering about on a horse and trying his best not to fall off.

In the whole test, Clarkson barely mentioned the actual car or its performance. The most obvious statistic was the 0–60 time he offered but otherwise the piece was all about not being caught by the hungry hounds or moaning ramblers. 'If anybody does have an objection to what we are doing here,' said Clarkson, as he ploughed through a hedge and pleasantly wooded glade, 'do please feel free to keep that objection to yourself!' In his defence, he did get out of the car to shut a gate after himself at one point. Oh, and he also said the car was lighter than a buttercup and that the ride was bumpy, but to be fair, this was said as he was hurtling across a ploughed field. The strange – and clever – part of the test is that the viewer comes away thinking the Terios is actually a cracking little car.

There is another theory expounded by critics about the show's shelf-life. The trio of presenters' 'every man' personas mean you really relate to their view on a car. When Clarkson gets out of a Lotus Elise and points out his belly is a bit heavy to get out with any style, you feel for him and understand the point he is making. And when Hammond drives a Porsche with child-like enthusiasm around the power track, even though most viewers could get nowhere near his lap time, somehow you know that's how *you* would feel driving it. It's like your mates down the pub trying out all these fast cars and filming it – and that's a big reason why *Top Gear* works.

Critics say therein lies a possible time-bomb for the successful formula: the three presenters have (rightly) become very well-known and extremely well paid, so apart from their interest in cars, they really don't bear much resemblance to 'the man on the street' anymore. Therefore, like legions of rock stars before them, will they start to 'lose touch' with their core audience? I don't believe they will, but to be objective you have to accept it's a possibility. It's an analogy that has been thrown at *Top Gear* more than once – that of a visceral, exciting grass-roots phenomenon that becomes massive over the years but in so doing loses contact with the reasons why it became popular in the first place. And it's the same for the millionaire rock star whose first album was bedsit poetry but finds it hard to write the same quality of material sitting in his multi-million pound crib. Each presenter now has a beautiful home, boy toys galore, solo projects such as books and TV shows, fame, money and all the trimmings.

Reassuringly, when viewers' comments citing several of these criticisms were aired on the *Points of View* programme, the Controller of BBC2, Janice Hadlow, rejected them and backed the show fully. Wilman and Clarkson, ever the realists but also perennially confident of their show's uniqueness, have not over-reacted to the recent criticism. Writing on his fascinating blog, Andy Wilman has suggested this incarnation of *Top Gear* is 'nearer the end than the beginning.' He explained that although they felt they had recently produced some good features, they also felt rushed and had been exhausted for long periods of time during some of the latter shows. Notably, the ratings for the 2009 series were down, too – although at five million, they were still superb for BBC2. This may simply have been due to the time slot moving later to 9pm to avoid clashing with ITV's *X Factor*.

Wilman also revealed that when they had filmed a feature on Lancias, they had all experienced what he phrased as a 'wake-up call' in that they felt they were getting back some of the original spirit of the show before its exponential success. Wilman's blog closed by saying that if there was to be an inevitable end, 'our job is to land this plane with its dignity still intact.' 'It will end,' Wilman told the *Guardian*, 'because we are a one-trick pony, as all good shows are, and at some point we will run out of ideas or the public will go, "We've got the point now."'

Controversy and *Top Gear* go hand in hand, that much is clear. If there comes a time when stunts, fast cars, provocative comments and high-speed jinx become old-fashioned and fall out of vogue, then the programme is done for. Should it change and dilute these staple ingredients to curry favour, however, it would no longer be *Top Gear*.

But if the current *Top Gear* line-up might be heading towards its Indian summer before retiring off into the pit lane of TV motor shows, what's next around the corner? James May already has plans: 'The discussion I have with Jeremy is that one day we'll have a pub,' he told the *Daily Mail*. 'I'm quite interested in beer, Jeremy likes wine, we both like eating, so when we stop doing the show we're going to have a *Top Gear* pub. Not as a branding exercise where you turn up occasionally like Gordon Ramsay – this would actually be us serving you, all the time: beer, wine, pies, fish-finger sandwiches. We'd live upstairs.'

However, any whispers that *Top Gear* is past its prime are ill-founded. At the time of writing, the series remains one of the world's most-watched television programmes. *Baywatch*-esque, it has expanded across the globe and conservative estimates now confirm that a staggering 350 million do indeed watch each episode. It is rumoured to be the most-pirated TV show on earth. YouTube clips regularly attract millions of viewers, there are multiple translated versions and it is broadcast in territories as far-flung as Australia and Latin America. To date, however, there are just three 'international' versions, namely shows completely re-made for an overseas market: Russia, Australia and America. The Australian version was run by Channel Nine, who won the rights after a competitive bidding process that reflected the popularity of the show Down Under (the channel's parent company was publisher of *Top Gear* magazine in that territory, too). Indeed, in 2008, a joint venture between Jeremy Clarkson, Andy Wilman and the BBC was structured, which meant both presenter and producer were now more formally part of the vast empire.

In the UK too, there have been permutations of the *Top Gear* formula, albeit for charity. *Top Gear* has helped Comic and Sport Relief on three occasions to date: *Stars in Fast Cars* in 2005 came first, then *Top Gear of the Pops* (2007), with appearances by Lethal Bizzle, Travis, Supergrass and McFly, who were asked to write a song including the words 'sofa', 'administration' and 'Hyundai'. Richard Hammond played his trusty bass and performed alongside Justin Hawkins of The Darkness fame, singing a passable version of Billy Ocean's 'Red Light Spells Danger'. Finally, they filmed the 2008 special, *Top Ground Gear Force* for Sport Relief, with 'new' gardening presenters 'Alan Clarkmarsh', 'Handy Hammond' and 'Jamesy Dimmock May' all teaming up to butcher Olympian Steve Redgrave's garden.

So, it's an international show that has created a global media empire. Viewers have witnessed some of the most challenging, hilarious, dangerous, unique and mind-boggling stunts, races, tests and treks that modern TV has ever seen. Is this what makes

Top Gear such a success? Of course, there have been a number of competitive motoring shows on TV: notably Channel 4's *Driven*, ITV's *Pulling Power*, Granada's *Vroom Vroom* and BBC World's *India's Wheels*. And then there's the motorsport reality show, *Roary The Racing Car*. But it's *Top Gear* that easily rules the roost and why is that?

At the start of this book, I suggest that the allure of the motorcar is a major factor in the show's appeal. And so it is. Also, the team attempt stunts and feats that no right-minded person would ever try and this mixes in a little Vaudeville suspense with the factual analysis. But having reviewed the brilliant TV that the *Top Gear* team have been making for all these years, there's one over-riding and potently important factor: the chemistry of the three presenters is arguably the magic ingredient. Other motoring shows perform stunts, too, and also have similar challenges, journeys, and so on but no one else has Jezza, Captain Slow and The Hamster himself. As Simon Cowell might say, that's the X factor. F1 legend David Coulthard agrees: 'They are incredible TV personalities, who have mastered the art of comic timing. Even when the dialogue is quite clearly scripted, they perfect the timing; add to that the fact that they are clearly very knowledgeable presenters, then it all makes for a brilliant show. I actually can't watch most shows on repeat, but I'll happily sit there and watch *Top Gear* on [satellite channel] Dave. I think the viewer can identify with them because although at times they are acting, they are only really acting *themselves* and they are doing that in a very journalistic way that's very interesting to watch. I think what they do takes a great deal of skill: to be able to handle a TV presentation like that, to be so knowledgeable in your chosen field and master the comedy, too.'

Part of the appeal of the trio's chemistry is that it strips back their, no-doubt, more complex off-screen characteristics into cartoonish caricatures. Perhaps that's why the show has increasingly attracted both old and young to its ratings. Certainly, my eldest loves to deride Captain Slow for driving old posh cars at a snail's pace while also saying The Hamster will dare to try anything once – all in the same eight-year-old breath as laughing at Spongebob and trying out exercises by Sporticus. To him, they are effectively from the same cartoonist's brush. Wilman himself has joked that *TG*'s viewers are either school boys or prisoners!

Watching the series in sequence now, you notice the team's growing confidence and the presenters' characters blossom, even when exaggerated. Their schoolboy attitude permeates everything that *Top Gear* sets out to do (the production office describe this approach as 'ambitious, but crap' ideas). Time after time, it's impossible not to snigger with them and you can almost see a nine-year-old Clarkson in short trousers sitting at the back of a class at Repton arguing with Wilman as to whether a certain hair-brained challenge can be done. Hammond, chuckling to himself, once said: 'I love setting off with deliberately childish and innocent and wide-eyed hopefulness and I think people enjoy that.'

A *Top Gear* editor went further when he was quoted in the *Guardian* as follows: 'Thick people doing thick things is not funny. Clever people doing clever things is not funny. But clever people doing thick things really is funny.' Meanwhile, James May is not so sure: 'A lot of people put the success down to the chemistry between the three of us but I think that's being rather generous. Basically, I see it as a sort of cross between *That's Life* and *Last of the Summer Wine*. We actually address some pretty big issues on our programme – sociology and so on – but through the medium of cars.'

Ever the technician, James has simplified the formula even further: '*Top Gear*: three blokes pushing the boundaries of automotive acceptability.' BBC Worldwide's director of content and production Wayne Garvey has observed: 'What's interesting about *Top Gear* is that everyone thinks it's about cars. It isn't. It's about men and their relationships, and that's a universal theme.'

And yes, it's all about being part of the gang. One of the finest examples of the team's state of suspended school years came during a throwback to Hammond's radio days in Series 8, when the trio are put in charge of BBC Three Counties Radio drivetime show. Everyone involved was fearful of Jeremy Clarkson's famously outspoken views being allowed free reign live on air, and so it proved to be. While Richard Hammond tried valiantly to organise the show (albeit after a stuttering start), Jezza was left in charge of the travel news, during the rush hour no less. As the nervous faces of radio staff turned to horror, he proceeded to expose bad driving and even give out types and colour of cars causing jams. This included one suggestion to actually shoot the driver! He was also heard to use the words 'ginger' and 'Welsh' in a less than positive light and there was a tense moment when they clearly upset the station's sports reporter, who was livid about their lack of knowledge about cricket rules.

Eventually, while roads around the Three Counties region ground to a halt, angry listeners phoned in after their disastrous drive home, many of them disgusted by the content. Realising they had perhaps overstepped the mark, the team put on a nine-minute song and ran off. As they fly down the stairs and out of the station, you can't help but see them as naughty schoolboys scurrying away after they've flicked chewing gum at a teacher. Watching this hasty retreat and the cringe-worthy incident with the sports reporter, it's hard not to feel as if you too are at the back of the class, sniggering along with them.

And it's not just petrol-heads who find it funny. To achieve the colossal success that *Top Gear* has, the net needs to catch a wider demograph. On holiday, my wife (not averse to *Top Gear* per se, but like many females not about to watch it on purpose) was relaxing with a gin alongside us three boys. Clarkson was in a car (I don't recall which one), berating the designers for some schoolboy error about headroom while fiddling with the controls in a primary pupil attempt to snap them off when, horror of horrors, my wife laughed! Out loud. Then she thrust her hand in front of her mouth and said, 'Oh my God, I just laughed at *Top Gear*!' This is a woman who drives so slowly she can do 70,000 miles on one set of brake pads and is the only person in the Western world who goes 150 miles without needing to use the brake pedal. And she laughed. But that's part of the huge appeal of the show: it's not just for petrol-heads.

There's no doubt that a major part of the appeal is the vicarious nature of what you are watching. On countless occasions, I have said to myself, 'They must have the best job in the world!' To be fair, they have said so themselves on screen. Don't be fooled, though: at times, the schedules can be exhausting and of course if you race your fellow presenters across Europe, you are away from home for long periods and it can be hard to be away from loved ones, especially if you have a young family. Also, shooting can sometimes be time-sensitive or highly compressed: on one occasion, the *Top Gear* presenters worked 76 days in a row without a break. Nonetheless, it's *still* the best job in the world.

And maybe, just maybe, it's the best TV show in the world, too ...

Appendices

Appendix I: 'Old Top Gear' Presenters

Angela Rippon (1977–79)

Noel Edmonds (1979–80)

William Woollard (1981–91)

Chris Goffey (1981–97)

Tony Mason (1987–98)

Tiff Needell (1987–2001)

Jeremy Clarkson (1988–2000)

Quentin Willson (1991–2000)

Michele Newman (1992–98)

Steve Berry (1993–99)

Andy Wilman (1994–99)

Vicki Butler-Henderson (1997–2001)

Julia Bradbury (1998–99)

Brendan Coogan (1999)

James May (1999)

Kate Humble (1999–2000)

Jason Barlow (2000–01)

Adrian Simpson (2000–01)

Appendix II: 'New Top Gear' Presenters

Jeremy Clarkson (2002–present)

Richard Hammond (2002–present)

James May (2003–present)

Jason Dawe (2002)

Appendix III: Guests on New Top Gear

SERIES 1

Harry Enfield

Jay Kay

Ross Kemp

Steve Coogan/Richard Burns

Jonathan Ross

Tara Palmer-Tomkinson

Rick Parfitt

Sir Michael Gambon

Gordon Ramsay

SERIES 2

Vinnie Jones

Jamie Oliver

David Soul

Boris Johnson

Anne Robinson

Richard Whiteley

Neil Morrissey

Jodie Kidd

Patrick Stewart
Alan Davies

SERIES 3
Martin Kemp
Stephen Fry
Rob Brydon
Rich Hall
Simon Cowell
Sanjeev Bhaskar
Rory Bremner
Johnny Vegas
Carol Vorderman

SERIES 4
Fay Ripley
Paul McKenna
Jordan
Ronnie O'Sullivan
Johnny Vegas/Denise Van Outen
Terry Wogan
Lionel Richie
Martin Clunes
Ranulph Fiennes
Patrick Kielty

SERIES 5
Bill Bailey
Geri Halliwell
Joanna Lumley
Jimmy Carr/Steve Coogan
Christian Slater/Tim Harvey/Matt Neal/Anthony Reid/Rob

Huff/Tom Chilton
Cliff Richard/Billy Baxter
Roger Daltrey
Eddie Izzard
Trinny Woodall/Susannah Constantine

SERIES 6
James Nesbitt
Jack Dee
Christopher Eccleston
Omid Djalili
Damon Hill
David Dimbleby
Justin Hawkins
Tim Rice
Chris Evans
Davina McCall/Mark Webber
Timothy Spall

SERIES 7
Trevor Eve
Ian Wright
Stephen Ladyman
Ellen MacArthur
Nigel Mansell
David Walliams/Jimmy Carr

SERIES 8
James Hewitt/Alan Davies/Trevor Eve/Jimmy Carr/Justin
Hawkins/Rick Wakeman/Les Ferdinand
Gordon Ramsay
Philip Glenister

Ewan McGregor
Michael Gambon
Brian Cox
Steve Coogan
Jenson Button/Ray Winstone

SERIES 9
Jamie Oliver
Hugh Grant
The Stig's African Cousin
Simon Pegg
Kristin Scott Thomas
Billie Piper

SERIES 10
Helen Mirren
Jools Holland
Ronnie Wood
The Stig's African Cousin
Simon Cowell
Lawrence Dallaglio
Matt Neal
Anthony Reid
Tom Chilton
Mat Jackson
Jennifer Saunders
James Blunt/Lewis Hamilton
Keith Allen
David Tennant

SERIES 11
Alan Carr/Justin Lee Collins
Rupert Penry-Jones/Peter Firth
James Corden/Rob Brydon
Fiona Bruce/Kate Silverton
Peter Jones/Theo Paphitis
Jay Kay

SERIES 12
Michael Parkinson/ The Stig's Lorry Driving Cousin
Will Young
Mark Wahlberg
Harry Enfield
Kevin McCloud
Anthony Reid
Matt Neal
Gordon Shedden
Tom Chilton
Boris Johnson
Sir Tom Jones
The Stig's Communist Cousin

SERIES 13
Michael Schumacher
Stephen Fry
Michael McIntyre
Usain Bolt
Sienna Miller
Brian Johnson
Jay Leno

SERIES 14
Eric Bana
Michael Sheen
The Stig's Vegetarian Cousin
Chris Evans
Guy Ritchie/Ross Kemp/Tom Chilton/Matt Neal/Mat
Jackson/Gordon Shedden/Anthony Reid/Stuart Olive
Jenson Button
Seasick Steve
Margaret Calvert

SERIES 15
Nick Robinson
Al Murray
Peter Jones
Peta
Johnny Vaughan
Angelina Jolie
Louie Spence
Amy Williams
Alastair Campbell
The Stig's German Cousin
Rupert Grint
Rubens Barrichello
Andy Garcia
Tom Cruise
Cameron Diaz
Jeff Goldblum

Appendix IV: Top Gear Trading Cards

As a father of two petrol-heads under the age of eight, I am very familiar with the *Top Gear* trading cards collection. I love them! And I admit to spending far too much money on them, but how else am I going to get the prized Stig Sub-Zero card? This particular card is indeed very cool – you have a mystery code that allows access to cool stuff on the website but you can only see it by putting the card in the freezer. After a while in sub-zero temperatures, all is revealed. This has led to a rampant market at online auction sites for cards with unused codes, which earn a hefty premium. I started to bid for an unused Sub-Zero card on eBay, but my wife blocked me after the highest bid passed £100. In the end, it went for £180. I could have had that. Sorry, I meant my son!

As mentioned, there is a corresponding *Top Gear Turbo* magazine of which I am, naturally, a subscriber ... on my son's behalf. This includes interesting features on cars aimed at the younger viewer, with cartoons of the presenters at the back, showing them going on crazy, fictitious adventures. The information in the magazine also helps you to play the trading card game and also provides tips on setting up your own online garage of supercars. It's really cool ... and stuff!

Some anti-*Top Gear* killjoys point out that the cost of collecting the entire card series is around £1,000 and that's indeed a lot of money, but with computer consoles costing hundreds and individual games £40 or more, the idea of a few cards for a couple of quid appeals to me ... as a parent, of course.